Rick and Morty
and Philosophy

Popular Culture and Philosophy® Series Editor: George A. Reisch

For full details of all Popular Culture and Philosophy® books, visit www.opencourtbooks.com.

Popular Culture and Philosophy®

Rick and Morty and Philosophy

In the Beginning Was the Squanch

Edited by

LESTER C. ABESAMIS AND
WAYNE YUEN

OPEN COURT
Chicago

Volume 125 in the series, Popular Culture and Philosophy®, edited by George A. Reisch

To find out more about Open Court books, visit our website at www.opencourtbooks.com.

Open Court Publishing Company is a division of Carus Publishing Company, dba Cricket Media.

Copyright © 2019 by Carus Publishing Company, dba Cricket Media

First printing 2019

Printed and bound in the United States of America.

Rick and Morty and Philosophy: In the Beginning Was the Squanch

This book has not been prepared, authorized, or endorsed by the creators or producers of *Rick and Morty*.

ISBN: 978-0-8126-9464-2

Library of Congress Control Number: 2018961285

This book is also available as an e-book (ISBN 978-0-8126-9466-6).

To Renée,
thanks for getting schwifty with me.

To Tiffany,
thanks for helping me bury the body
of that other me.

Thanks to David Ramsay Steele and George Reisch for greenlighting this volume. Thank you to my co-editor, Wayne Yuen, for the opportunity to write for such an awesome series! Thank you to Julian Martinez and Juan Castillo for making suggestions for my chapters. And thank you to Dan Harmon and Justin Roiland for coming up with an awesome show worth philosophizing about.

Thanks to Lester Abesamis for doing all the work, so I could watch more TV. Thanks also to Michael and Victoria Ross for dinner dates and stimulating conversation, Jacob Garrett and Julie Jones for your comments on early drafts of chapters, Tanya Rodriguez for being you and available at the drop of a hat, and of course, Veda, Zim, and Harley for allowing me to worship the floating heads that you are.

Contents

Scientifically, Introductions Are an Idiot Thing

Are you a Jerry, or are you a Rick? If you're a Jerry then this book is totally for you. It'll make people think you're smart when they see it on your table when you invite them over to look at your book. You don't even have to read it!

But if you're a Rick, then you'll need to actually spend some more time with this book. You'll need to put in a bit of effort to understand the arguments and thought experiments presented in the following pages. If your head starts to hurt, then that doesn't necessarily mean you're a Jerry. If you pretend to understand the arguments, then maybe that means you're a Jerry. But if you allow yourself to be perplexed and maybe troubled by philosophy, then maybe you're a lot closer to being a Rick.

A lot of people connect the philosophies of Nietzsche to *Rick and Morty* for a variety of reasons, but one of the hallmarks of Nietzsche's writings was that he didn't want to be understood by everyone. He purposely made his writings confusing and contradictory, so that the Jerrys of the world would walk away understanding one thing, and the Ricks of the world would understand what Nietzsche really meant. In this way, modern popular culture is mirroring Nietzsche's writings.

Sure, you can enjoy a show like *Rick and Morty* by laughing at dick jokes and seeing Jerry being his pathetic loser self, but underneath it all is a pretty serious and deeply philosophical television show. It's a world that reflects the intellectual, Rick, who has come to believe that there is no objective meaning in the world, no God to provide us purpose or guidance, and despite all of this, we still find meaning in the world. Rick loves his family and hides it behind self-interest because loving your family clashes with the idea that the world is utterly meaningless.

So, Rick runs from it all. He jaunts through different dimensions, with a token family member to keep him grounded. Sometimes he leaves it all behind and starts over, but he never chooses to cut his family out of his life, even though he could. He chooses to find his family again, and start over. He might abandon Beth from C-137 but he'll eventually seek out another Beth. Despite not believing in an overarching meaning of the world, Rick acts like he already knows that he's wrong, despite a heavy varnish of disdain and nihilism.

Jerry, on the other hand, is a sheep. He just wants to follow what everyone else is doing. He wants the world to accept him. Whereas Rick is the inventor, or as Nietzsche might say the artist, pushing to recreate the world, Jerry strives for safety and approval. He constantly chases after the socially approved values, and yet somehow, he also has a family that he loves and will surprisingly do anything for them. Perhaps this is why Rick hates Jerry so much. Not just because he's an obnoxious simpleton, but that despite his failings, he too values the same people that Rick does. He's a reminder to Rick that you don't have to be right about the meaninglessness of the world to know that we as individual humans find meaning in the relationships we form.

Is Rick wrong? The world may be meaningless, but like quantum physics, things change when we stop taking a grand perspective of the universe, and look at the world from our perspectives. We start finding meaning everywhere. Does this microscopic meaning add up to something on the cosmic level? Only the dead really know for sure. And maybe Fart and Unity. But as for us living humans, we can put our best thoughts and arguments together and maybe we can get a little closer to grabbing the truth.

That's what philosophy aims to do. It seeks out the best answers to life's biggest problems. Oftentimes, this is difficult to do, since many of our preconceived notions are so deeply engrained and are painful to challenge. But the great Socrates tells us that "The unexamined life is not worth living."

The Eyehole Man might come and kick the shit out of us. But truth is delicious and totally worth it and, if challenging our assumptions doesn't kill us, maybe the truth we arrive at will ultimately make us stronger.

I

So We Bailed on That Reality and We Came to This One

1
The Genuine Article

φ-173 Rick Sanchez

"Did the real me choose to leave, and I only think I chose to stay because that's what I need to think because I'm the replacement Beth?" Beth, and all the viewers are stuck in a dilemma at the end of Season Three. Is the Beth that we're following the *real* Beth or is the Beth that we see at the end of Season Three simply just a clone of Beth in some *Blade Runner*–inspired sleight of hand?

There is a definitive answer, and it's at the end of this chapter. I know because I'm Rick Sanchez. Okay, so I'm not C-137 Rick, but trust me, I got all the answers.

But this wouldn't be a good chapter if I just told you what it was, without leading you through some kind of path that also taught you about philosophy, and revisited some interesting plot points from various episodes of our favorite show. I mean after all, this *is Rick and Morty and Philosophy*. So, uhh . . . crap. Where should we start?

A Subtitle Transition

Damn, that subtitle is way too punny. Whatever. *Rick and Morty* is all about traveling to different dimensions, which are sometimes populated with very similar people that would be from our world, or the original world that Rick and Morty are from. So, in an important sense, we should be looking at what it means to be real.

So, what counts as real? For most things, there's a pretty easy test for us to use to determine a thing's realness: Does it exist? If it exists, it's real. So, this means that Beth is real, because she exists. But this also means that everything that exists is real. It would be quite impossible for something to exist and for it not be real.

But this isn't what most people want to know, nor is it what Beth wants to know, when she's asking if she's the *real* Beth. She wants to know if she is the original Beth, or a copy of Beth. Copies are real things, but they aren't the original. We as human beings put a lot of emotional weight on something being the original, or genuine article. Given the choice, you'd rather have *real* butter, as opposed to a butter substitute. But that's not quite the best analogy, since there are some real, consequential differences between *real* butter and a butter substitute.

So here's a different example. It's fine to see a reproduction of the US Constitution, but it's something completely different for us to see one of the *original* copies of the US Constitution. There is a sense of history that the object is imbued with, which elevates the entire experience of seeing and interacting with the original, that isn't found in the replica. It's the closest thing we have to traveling backwards through time. And it's all bullshit. It's a hopelessly romantic way of looking at the world that tries to make certain objects special. A way to justify building a giant protective case to guard a "precious" document, which really isn't all the precious since we have the words and guiding principles of the Constitution on the Internet. We have the ideas that the document represents. Why do we need the actual document? It's similar to how astronomers remind us to look at ourselves and marvel at what we are . . . the atoms in our bodies were forged inside stars, and when they exploded, that matter was scattered across the universe. It coalesced into you and me. We are *stardust*! Yeah . . . and so is the hairball my cat barfed up this morning in the hallway. It's all just packaging to sell us a pet rock, which is also stardust.

Beth is real in the sense that she exists. Whether she is the original or not isn't really all that important. She wants to know it because she's a sap who puts too much emotional baggage on being a unique snowflake. But maybe you think that there are consequential differences between Beth's realness and a clone of Beth's realness. Maybe this is like *real* butter. I don't want to eat butter substitute because it might damage my health, expose me to questionable chemicals, and so forth. There might be good reasons to think that a clone Beth isn't just a duplicate copy of the Constitution.

Okay I'm shitting you. There aren't any good reasons to think that clone Beth isn't as good as the real Beth, beyond emotional baggage. If Clone Beth is identical in every way to the Beth that she takes the place of, then they're basically equivalent. Perhaps, the only downside is that there would be changes that are happening to the genuine Beth, that aren't happening to the clone Beth. She's out having adventures and this might change her perspective on life, and the universe. We've seen the changes in Morty over the course of many episodes, but probably most highlighted in "Morty's Mind Blowers." Morty wants to forget a lot of his memories, because it changes him. He's suffering PTSD, or maybe just realizing that Grandpa Rick isn't the genius that Rick says he is. If changes like these are happening to original Beth, there would be discontinuities once original Beth comes back to replace clone Beth. Morty and Summer might think that their mom has suddenly become more interesting, or maybe she has PTSD and needs a lot of emotional support from her kids. Maybe she runs back into the arms of Jerry. Oh wait, that is what happens. What I'm saying is: Don't look a gift horse in the ass. Or something.

Now, don't get me wrong here. I'm not saying that real Beth and Clone Beth are the same person. That's just dumb. Real Beth has a history that Clone Beth doesn't have. Clone Beth has memories of a history that happened to Real Beth, but remembering things that didn't happen to you, but feels like it happened to you, isn't the same as it happening to you. Real Beth has real memories and a real history, Clone Beth has pseudo-memories of Real Beth's history. Clone Beth has a history that is significantly shorter than Real Beth's history.

Intrinsic Instruments

So *burp* I guess it's time for me to tell you whether Beth is the genuine Beth or not. And the answer is, that it doesn't matter. I know you were expecting that, but I bet what you weren't expecting was a reference to "M. Night Shaym-Aliens!"

where Rick and Morty are stuck inside simulations of simulations. Yeah, that was a good one. A classic from Season One.

Anyways, who wouldn't want to be in a simulation? I mean you don't have to worry about anything inside a simulation. You can do whatever you'd like and not have to really face the consequences. Consequence-free choices really are the best kinds of choices. But weirdly, there is this guy, Robert Nozick, who thinks that we don't want to all be hanging out in simulations. He imagines that we could plug into a simulation of a perfect world and make us happy all the time. Why wouldn't we want that? Well, he supposedly gave us three good reasons for not wanting to plug in, but I didn't read it, but I'll trust Wikipedia enough on this:

1. **We want to do certain things, and not just have the experience of doing them.**

2. **We want to be a certain sort of person.**

3. **Plugging in to an experience machine limits us to a man-made reality.**

But really, what Nozick is saying here is that we value genuine reality. We don't want a fictional reality, even if the fictional reality is identical to the genuine article. These objections, *doing* certain things, *being* a certain sort of person, *man-made* reality, all revolve around valuing the genuine *intrinsically*.

When we value something intrinsically, we value it because of what it is. It's like Eyeholes. They're delicious! So, we eat them, despite the risk of having the shit beaten out of us by the Eyehole Man. If you were a hippie and only ate stuff that was healthy, because you wanted nutrients or whatever, then you're eating for instrumental reasons. Nobody *likes* kale. But all the yahoos out there in the world are eating it because they think it'll make them healthier. If everyone would just learn about what they're eating, they'd know eating kale increases your chance for gout, and would stop eating those leafy coat hangers. Kale isn't special, it's just instrumentally valuable. If you get rid of why you want it, then it's just garbage.

So, Nozick wants us to value genuine reality intrinsically, and if he's right, then that might be some reason to think that it's important for us to know whether Beth is a clone or not. But, of course he's wrong, because I already told you that nobody likes kale, beyond its instrumental value. Don't be a sap! Look, if I told you that you were already stuck in a simulation, for your entire life, and I offered you a chance to leave the simulation, would you do it? The world you know, the friends you've made, it's all a fiction.

I'm offering you *reality*. I'm not promising that reality is anything like what you think it is. There are plenty of messed-up dimensions out here and maybe you're in one of them. Or, you could stay in your simulation and live out the rest of your life in the world that you've always known. Reality is instrumentally valuable. You like the reality that you think is real, because it makes you happy, even if it's a messed-up reality, because it's the only one you've ever known. When Rick screws up a universe, he doesn't go to a completely different universe. It would be too much of a pain in the ass to start over from scratch. He goes to a universe a lot like the one he left, except that it isn't messed up, and that is the same reason why you wouldn't want to leave the experience machine. Laziness, or what I like to call intelligent efficiency.

Expanding Circles

Genuine Beth, Cloned Beth, it doesn't matter. They're the same, in terms of functionality. They make Rick feel good when he hugs them, regardless of whether the Beth he is hugging has the same history as some other Beth, just so long as the Beth he is hugging is *familiar* enough to C-137 Beth, or perhaps more precisely *familiar enough to Rick*. Rick is a *pragmatist* in that he is willing to accept something as true, if it is useful for him to believe that it is true. If he has a functional replacement of Beth, then it might as well be C-137 Beth. This is because we already know what happened to Genuine Beth. Rick C-137 Cronenburged his home dimension, leaving Beth C-137 behind, and later when C-137 Rick returns, Beth is frozen by the Council of Ricks, and left frozen. That's the Beth that sprung from Rick's loins. But, Rick has replaced C-137 Beth with a different Beth and that Beth was perhaps cloned by Rick C-137 at the end of Season Three.

So the Beth who's wondering whether she's a clone or not is already not Rick's Beth, but a functional replacement Beth. Does this hurt Rick? No, because Beth, and for that matter, his entire family, are just mere tools for Rick to get what he wants: that juicy intrinsic value of happiness. If there is one uncontroversial example of something that we value for intrinsic reasons, its happiness. If someone ever asks you, "why do you want to be happy?" then you should pity that poor person, since they've never tasted the eyehole of flavor that is happiness. Happiness isn't something we want for other things, we want it for what it is. The OG of intrinsic value. Rick is willing to trade his family and friends for happiness, and does so with remarkable frequency.

Well, except, you know that one time. In "The Wedding Squanchers" Rick sacrifices his own happiness for his family's happiness, well, except for Jerry. If he doesn't give up, then his family will be tormented by the Federation until he is caught. Jerry of course is willing to turn Rick in for his own benefit, but fuck Jerry. Rick turns himself in and is arrested for "everything" and left in prison to rot forever, which turns out to be about a year and a half. I have to give it to C-137 Rick! That guy has a talent for getting out of a jam.

Rick isn't turning his back on the intrinsic value of happiness here, because we know Rick loves happiness. It's just that sometimes, despite a value being intrinsic, other values are simply more valuable. Just because something is intrinsically valuable, doesn't mean that it can't be squanched by some other value. Rick sees his family as an instrumental value, sure, but he gains nothing from turning himself in, other than that his family is able to live a life with less hardship. So, yes, Rick gains materially from his family, Morty is good at camouflaging Rick's genius waves after all, but he also wants his family, or at least *this* family, to thrive. His family is both instrumentally *and* intrinsically valuable. C-137 Rick may not want to admit it, but there are more intrinsic values than just happiness.

Remember what I said about the US Constitution earlier? Someone might value that piece of parchment simply because it was *the* piece of parchment that was signed by a bunch of people. So, maybe the historical significance of the parchment is what gives it intrinsic value. The Kalaxian crystals I took earlier must be wearing off. I was tripping hard when I said it was crap earlier. Some things aren't always intrinsically valuable. Some things gain intrinsic value through special events. It was just a sheep skin before, then it became special. If I skinned a sheep today, and printed the Constitution's text on it, it wouldn't be special. I'm not John Adams. If Morty got another sex robot, it wouldn't be as special as Gwendolyn.

What exactly counts as an intrinsic value is pretty tough to pin down. Morality, art, beauty, love, family, where does it all end? Once you start expanding the circle of what counts as intrinsic value even the family dog starts looking like a candidate for holding intrinsic value. The next thing you know your value system is full of glip-glops and Jessica. Maybe the best barometer for intrinsic value is what people are willing to sacrifice for it.

Rick is willing to sacrifice almost everything for his own happiness, including his health, and family, but Rick is also willing to sacrifice himself for his family. This isn't to say that intrinsic values are always terribly important, but the intrinsic values that most people are interested in and prioritize, are the ones that are important ones. Maybe nobody would sacrifice their lives to save the music of Justin Beiber, but we shouldn't deny Beliebers valuing his music in an intrinsic fashion, we should just pity them.

So when Nozick says that reality is intrinsically valuable, maybe he's right. It's just that it isn't an intrinsic value that is really worth sacrificing all that much for. It's a Bieber intrinsic value. Why die for reality that you can't experience? Things can be both intrinsically and instrumentally valuable. There isn't any good reason to think that something can't hold both kinds of values. Plato thought that morality and your health were both intrinsically and instrumentally valuable. Hell, feel free to value a fictional world intrinsically.

I Thought This Was about Beth

Shut up, I'm getting back to her. So, it isn't just completely sappy for Rick to value the Genuine Beth, or "This Beth," since Genuine Beth is frozen. There is a possibility that she is intrinsically valuable. But that opens back up the question, should we place any kind of value on the genuine? If there are plenty of intrinsic values, then perhaps there is intrinsic value in the genuine article. This could be a clue as to how we can make a much stronger argument that This Beth is a clone or not, and it all has to do with the dilemma This Beth finds herself in.

She's torn between two things that she finds valuable, her family and being her authentic self. Normally, most people would value both intrinsically, because normally most people are saps, and Beth can be pretty sappy. But she is also her father's daughter, and it wouldn't surprise any of us if she ditched her family to adventure on her own. So, what does Beth value intrinsically more? Herself, or her family?

"The ABCs of Beth," more than anything, is a Rorschach test for all of us, including me. I watched it on interdimensional cable with Mr. Poopybutthole. I'm pretty sure that the Beth we see at the end of the episode is This Beth. Look, C-137 Rick knows that This Beth isn't C-137 Beth that came from his loins. So if there is *any* kind of value that Rick is placing on This Beth, it would likely be just instrumental value. But in all likelihood, C-137 Rick is practicing intelligent efficiency and just doesn't think about it. He's a genius, but philosophy is too much work for almost zero reward.

So, Rick is like the person who is in the experience machine, except that he knows it's fake, and is totally okay with it. He's been offered the opportunity to leave, and he chooses to stay, just because it's easier to use This Beth than C-137 Beth. He values this non-genuine world as if it were genuine. If he values Beth intrinsically, he'd make sure that she was safe by at least going with her for her first few trips to alternate dimensions. Since C-137 Rick doesn't go with her, either she didn't clone herself, or she did, and he doesn't value her. But he *does* value Beth, since he was willing to sacrifice himself for her in "The Wedding Squanchers."

Let's try looking at this problem from This Beth's perspective. Beth *is* a sap, and probably values C-137 Rick as identical to her Rick. Beth, is also like the person who was always stuck in Nozick's experience machine, thinking that it was real. She had a Rick, and that Rick died. C-137 Rick took his place. Beth still thinks C-137 Rick is her father, and as we learn from *The ABCs of Beth*, she deeply resents Rick's parenting, but still loves him, just like he loves her despite her poor choice in husband and that he knows she isn't C-137 Beth. But, this is a Rorschach test which just reflects what I value.

As I've said before, it doesn't matter whether This Beth is a clone or not, because what you think the answer is, reflects what you value intrinsically in your life. If you're keeping your circle of values small, then maybe you think that Beth is a clone, and you are happy knowing that Beth is off gallivanting around the world, or even the multiverse, having adventures and finding herself. If you have a slightly wider circle and intrinsically value family and yourself, then your answer might be that you are willing to sacrifice yourself for your family, and This Beth didn't clone herself. Or maybe, you're willing to entertain the possibility that there is no conflict between the choices. This Beth is her authentic self and after killing Tommy she's had enough adventure for the time being, and chooses her family. All I know is that I need some more Kalaxian crystals, because I'm way too sober.

The Real Beth Is . . .

Motherfucker go back and read the entire chapter, instead of skipping to the end to find out whether Beth is the real Beth. What's wrong with you?

2
The Unimportance of Identity When You Have a Portal Gun

CHRIS LAY

Rick Sanchez is dead. I don't mean one of the multiverse of Ricks that we see regularly die on the show, like when Rick nearly destroys the Citadel of Ricks in "The Rickshank Rickdemption." No, I'm talking about *our* Rick—the one that we follow throughout the series—Rick C-137.

You're probably thinking that this is crazy talk, though. Surely, if one of the title characters of *Rick and Morty* died, not only would we remember it but Rick's death would be a pretty momentous event on the show. But I'm going to make the case that not only is Rick dead, but that he died with such surprisingly little fanfare that it was nearly unnoticeable.

Does it matter if the person who wakes up in your bed tomorrow is really you or is instead merely someone exactly like you? That's the difference between qualitative and numerical identity. When Rick drops off Jerry at the "Jerryboree" in "Mortynight Run," the assorted Jerrys are *qualitatively* identical—they have (mostly) the exact same qualities or features. Yet, these multiple Jerrys aren't *numerically* identical. The Jerry nervously whining in the corner about getting picked up and taken home isn't one and the same person as the Jerry fiddling with the television on the other side of the room. At the very least, we can distinguish between them spatially: one Jerry is over *here* whining and the other is over *there* fixing the television. I'm going to be talking about this latter sense of identity; so, when I say 'identity', just know that I mean 'numerical identity' unless otherwise stated.

Now, we generally think that identity matters. For one, it lets us hold individuals responsible or say that *this* individual instead of *that* one did some action. In "Close Rickcounters of the Rick-Kind," the Council of Ricks accuses Rick C-137—and not some other Rick—of murdering a number of parallel world Ricks and kidnapping their Mortys. The Council is interested in figuring out who is identical with the person who committed these crimes; if someone qualitatively exactly like Rick C-137 but not *numerically* identical with him was good enough to receive the blame, there were infinitely many other Ricks the Council could have chosen from.

This assumption, that numerical identity is what matters, is the traditional view of how we determine things like responsibility. But this isn't the view that *Rick and Morty*, on the whole, adopts. The difference between the view that identity is what matters and the view that we find in *Rick and Morty* will help us see both how Rick could've died and how the show could've completely overlooked it.

Identity, Continuity, and Rick-sponsibility

In *Reasons and Persons*, Derek Parfit argues against the traditional view of responsibility and says that identity *isn't* what matters. He thinks that when we're worried about who did what and who ought to get praise or blame for it, what's really important isn't that I'm identical with the person who did something, but that I'm related to the person who did in the right way.

See, part of what many philosophers say is supposed to motivate our moral decision-making is what they call 'rational egoistic concern'. This means that it's rational for me to be especially concerned about myself in the future and not someone else that's merely like me. Among philosophers, the prevailing way to determine that some future person is identical with me is to ask if that person is *psychologically continuous* with me.

We owe the notion of psychological continuity to John Locke, who wrote in *An Essay Concerning Human Understanding* that we can't hold someone accountable for an action if she isn't *continually conscious* of having done it. Locke cashes out what it means to be continually conscious of having done some action mostly in terms of memory. Some future person is identical with me if that future person remembers doing the very things *I* did in the past. Parfit takes Locke's 'continuity of consciousness' and runs with it, adding that *all* of my psychological states count towards someone in the future being me (instead of just memories). He calls this *psychological continuity*, and he says that there is psychological continuity between some future person and me if our psychological states overlap, like links in a chain. This 'chain' is one and the same person over time.

That's probably not very clear, so let's look at a Rick-ified example. What would it take for a future person to be psychologically continuous with Rick C-137? Let's imagine this Rick at three points in his life. The younger Rick who walked out on Beth's mother presumably had certain psychological states, like a desire to avoid parental responsibility and a belief that he ought only to act in his own self-interest.

Later in life, a middle-aged Rick still desires to shirk his parental responsibilities but also realizes that he loves his daughter and perhaps comes to form a new belief about how he ought to act: namely, that he ought to sometimes act in the interests of others.

Finally, we have an older Rick who returns to his daughter and her new family as "Grandpa Rick"—still believing that he ought to sometimes act in the interests of others but now also with a new desire to be a parent/grandparent and not entirely abandon his parental responsibilities. Other psychological features would have been added and lost along the way, too, like an intention to obtain gallons of Szechuan sauce.

Let's also say that there are no psychological connections between younger Rick and older Rick; they share none of the same beliefs, desires, or character traits, for instance. Even without any direct psychological connections, though, younger Rick and older Rick *are* still psychologically continuous because there is a chain of psychological connections between person stages. Younger Rick is connected to middle-aged Rick and middle-aged Rick to older Rick in virtue of sharing certain psychological features. This would also let us say that younger Rick, older Rick, and all of the person stages in the middle (like, say, thirty-three-and-a-third-year-old Rick) are *identical* with each other. In other words, you might say that there are *stages of one and the same person over time*.

Yet, Parfit presents us with a case where identity and psychological continuity come apart. This example doesn't need any modifications to match-up with the weirdness of the *Rick and Morty* universe—it fits right in as-is. Suppose there is a device called a Teletransporter that can, by all accounts, transport people to Mars. However, the Teletransporter is very different from a portal gun, which just opens a passageway that one and the same entity can travel through. Indeed, the Teletransporter doesn't actually transport *anyone* anywhere. Instead, it completely obliterates the Original subject who steps into the device on Earth and reconstructs a cell-for-cell Replica on Mars. Of course, since the Replica is a cell-for-cell reconstruction, he would have all of the Original's psychological states, including his last memory of entering the Teletransporter and seeing a bright light.

Now, consider a case that's otherwise just like the standard Teletransporter, only the Original isn't destroyed right away; rather, the Original's condition instead deteriorates slowly over several days after using the Teletransporter. The Original on Earth and the Replica on Mars then enjoy a video call whereby the Replica assures the Original that he will continue to fulfill the Original's desires and intentions after his death in exactly the way the Original would have, had he lived.

Parfit wants us to take away two key points here. First, the Original and the Replica can't be identical, as they are in two different places simultaneously—and no one thing can do that! Plus, since the Replica is on Mars and the Original isn't, the two will begin to have entirely different experiences. The Replica will see, feel, and know things that the Original doesn't and couldn't, since the Original isn't on Mars. Second, the Replica *does* seem to be psychologically continuous with the Original in all of the important ways, as the Replica shares all of the Original's psychological states and can 'pick up' where the Original leaves off upon dying.

To Parfit, *this relation* between the Original and the Replica—psychological continuity—is the relation that ought to matter to us. The Replica will continue all of the work of the Original and will affect the world in exactly the same ways. He will further remember *every* action that the original took right up until entering the Teletransporter. And, outside of the case where the Original briefly survives after using the device, the

Replica will even think that he *is* the Original. Parfit says that being Teletransported in this way is 'just about as good' as ordinary survival, even though ordinary survival involves identity and being Teletransported doesn't. So, since it is possible for non-numerically identical people to be psychologically continuous, Parfit concludes that identity just isn't what matters—psychological continuity is.

Why Identity Doesn't Morty

With that out of the way, we can return to what I claimed earlier: like Parfit, *Rick and Morty* rejects the traditional view that identity is what matters. We're also a step closer to seeing that Rick is dead (and that no one really noticed!). To see this, we can look at a few telling examples from the show.

In "The Rickshank Rickdemption," Rick escapes the mind prison in which he's been trapped—represented by a Shoney's—by using something called a Brainalyzer to copy his psychological states to bug-person Cornvelious Daniel. He then repeats this process several times, effectively 'jumping' between the bodies and brains of many other distinct Ricks as he nearly destroys the Citadel and wipes out the Council of Ricks. The problem is that nothing actually moves between bodies when Rick uses the Brainalyzer on them. The victim gets zapped with something that looks like electric current, then thinks and acts like Rick instead of Daniel or whoever the victim was only moments before.

We might think that something *does* move between bodies here: Rick's consciousness. But this can't be right. Like data on a flash drive or even words on a written page, consciousness must be *realized* somewhere or in something. We might call this realizer a vehicle for consciousness, like a brain, for instance. Yet, nothing like a brain or any organ of thought is transferred between bodies, since all we see is a zap of electricity. It's clear that the show doesn't want to hold that something like Rick's 'soul' travels into Daniel and carries his psychological states with it—given its scientific bent, *Rick and Morty* isn't a show that deals in immaterial souls as explanations.

So, there's nothing at all that moves between Rick and Daniel (or any of the successive 'Brainalyzer' victims) that could house Rick's consciousness. While it looks to us that the same Rick is hopping from body to body with each use of the Brainalyzer, I think what's really happening is that the Brainalyzer reprograms the victim's psychological states to match Rick's. Again, this is just like 'moving' information from a flash drive to folders on a PC. No information is actually moved in such a case. Rather, the information is *copied* to the new destination. It's just that, in this case, the 'information' is Rick's psychological states. If there isn't enough 'room' in the destination—some flash drives (and brains) have more storage than others—some of the information just isn't copied and appears to stay behind, like Rick's fear of wicker furniture, his desire to play the trumpet, his tentative plans to purchase a hat, and his improv skills.

"Big Trouble in Little Sanchez" gives us a similar scenario. As part of *Operation Phoenix*, Rick has grown a series of clone bodies into which he can evidently transfer his consciousness once his present body becomes too old and frail to facilitate twenty-minute adventures. The first clone body he tries out is a teenaged Rick named Tiny Rick. Yet, as with the Brainalyzer, the transfer of consciousness (which we only actually see happen when Rick is moved *from* Tiny Rick back into his original body, who I'll call Old Rick out of convenience) occurs through a set of wires hooked up between the two patients. As before, nothing is really *moved* between Tiny Rick and Old Rick, consciousness least of all. It is more accurate to say that Old Rick's psychological states are first copied to Tiny Rick (and simultaneously erased in Old Rick), then back from Tiny Rick to Old Rick (and erased in Tiny Rick).

Rick and the thing that has Rick's thoughts in Cornvelious Daniel's body are plainly not identical. Neither are Old Rick and Tiny Rick. All it takes to see why is to draw a parallel with Parfit's Teletransporter case in which the Original briefly survives to talk to the Replica. Imagine a case where Old Rick's psychological states are copied to Tiny Rick, but Old Rick states aren't erased. We would then have two Ricks—Tiny Rick and Old Rick—who both thought they were Rick C-137 and had all of Rick C-137's psychological states. Clearly, though, they can't *both* be one person, Rick C-137. There's two of them!

Despite this, the characters go on acting as if Tiny Rick is Rick C-137—the person who wakes up in Tiny Rick's body after the transfer even thinks of himself this way. The same is true for the person who wakes up in Cornvelious Daniel's body thinking he is one and the same Rick C-137. The bottom line of the argument is that identity can't be what matters because, even if the two Ricks aren't identical, everyone takes the person who wakes up in Tiny Rick's body to *just be* Rick C-137. Likewise for the last Rick to get Brainalyzed in "The Rickshank Rickdemption."

Now let's turn to "The Rickchurian Mortydate." In the previous episode, "The ABCs of Beth," Beth discovers that she's much more like her father than she was ever comfortable with, which unfortunately includes a strong desire to ditch her family. So, Rick offers his daughter the opportunity to make a clone of herself, consequence free, that will continue living her mundane life while she—the real Beth Smith—sets out into the world in an attempt to 'find herself'. It's left unclear in "The Rickchurian Mortydate" what choice Beth actually commits to, as the "Beth" we see struggles through an existential crisis about possibly being a clone and subsequently reconnects with an estranged Jerry.

This ambiguity is, of course, intentional. But it also pushes the show's case that identity doesn't matter. Whether or not "Beth" is a clone, Rick and her family would (and possibly do) still treat her the same. While Rick assures "Beth" that she isn't a clone, it's highly likely that he would also tell Clone Beth this to ensure that she continues filling Real Beth's role in the family transparently.

"Beth" has worries about being a clone that are perfectly compatible with "Beth" being either Clone Beth or Real Beth. Said differently, not only does "Beth" relate to the people in her world the same way as Real Beth would, but she also relates to her own mental states the same way. Remember, Clone Beth is supposed to think and act exactly like Real Beth—that's the whole point of the Clone! In the end, whether "Beth" is Clone Beth or Real Beth, the practical result is the same: by readmitting Jerry into her life, she has frustrated Rick's plans to put himself in a position of absolute authority as family patriarch. Clearly, Rick's plans here don't have anything to do with "Beth" being a clone or not: this was what Rick wanted all the way from the top of Season Three, long before there was ever talk of a Clone Beth. What matters is that "Beth," whoever she is, chose Jerry over her father and not whether "Beth" is identical with Real Beth. After all, the other Beth—Real or Clone—would presumably do the same thing if put in the same situation.

There's a litany of other good examples that don't have anything to do with clones, too! When their world gets Cronenberged in "Rick Potion #9," after Rick and Morty inadvertently transform most of Earth's humans into hideous, amorphous mutants, the Rick and Morty from universe C-137 simply hop dimensions to the nearest world most similar to theirs. Although the people here look and act just like, say, the Beth, Jerry, and Summer from universe C-137, they obviously aren't identical with them: the people in C-137 are still marooned there (or dead). We even get to see this when we revisit C-137 in "The Rickshank Rickdemption."

Likewise, for his assistance in locating "Evil" Rick—the real killer and Morty abductor from "Close Rickcounters of the Rick Kind"—the Council of Ricks awards Rick a voucher good for one "Free Replacement Morty" should something terrible happen to his current Morty. The replacement Morty can't be identical to Rick's current Morty, as the whole notion of a Morty voucher is to substitute in a new, *different* Morty. Puzzlingly, the introduction here of the "Morty voucher" also means that we can't really be sure that *our* Morty has been numerically the same throughout the series. Perhaps Rick has used a whole bunch of vouchers in the past! Later, in "Pickle Rick," Rick teams up with political prisoner and assassin Jaguar. While the latter despairs over the death of his daughter, Rick indifferently remarks that he—though not Jaguar—has "infinite daughters" and, for this reason, the loss of one of them isn't all that important. Clearly, none of these "infinite daughters" are identical with Rick's Beth, as they are numerically distinct people in different dimensions. In example after example, we see that identity doesn't matter for *Rick and Morty*.

What Matters Is Squanch-ological Continuity

If I'm right that each of the above cases demonstrates that *Rick and Morty* takes Parfit's view that identity doesn't matter, we can now further ask 'What *does* matter?' At first, it's tempting to think that what matters in *Rick and Morty* is just qualitative similarity. But this isn't right. To see why, let's look again at "Close Rick-counters of the Rick Kind."

Generally speaking, we can assume that Ricks see Mortys as disposable precisely because Mortys can be easily replaced by a qualitative duplicate from another dimension. Any Morty is as good as the next, as they're all equally nebbish, anxiety-prone, and (mostly) agreeable to whatever purpose a Rick would have for them. However, if we bisect the Morty-voucher scene at the end of the episode from the jokiness of the moment where Rick furtively accepts the voucher, we see that 'qualitatively identical' isn't enough for Rick C-137, at least.

Rick has a special relationship with *this* Morty and has regularly made personal concessions on his behalf: Rick's attempted self-sacrifice during the fractured timelines of "A Rickle in Time" comes to mind, for one. Just getting another Morty off the shelf—shrink-wrapped and ready to go, as in the Season Three opening titles—isn't what Rick wants.

Fine, then what *does* Rick want? We'll start with the Brainalyzer example. Since the successive Ricks in "The Rickshank Rickdemption" can't be identical to Rick C-137, each is really a sort of psychological clone (psychological because each Rick body is physically a bit unique with, most prominently, different hairstyles). The same is true for Tiny Rick and Old Rick. There is no 'moving' Rick's consciousness from Old Rick to Tiny Rick and vice versa. Instead, a psychological clone is created in each case, just like in Parfit's Teletransporter. A clone is created that psychologically *feels* like it has moved bodies and remembers everything the original did right up until the transfer. And this is true only because the clone in each case is psychologically continuous with the original.

In both examples, it seems to me that this kind of continuity is all that matters to the Rick initiating the transfer. Again, short of believing in an immaterial soul that leaps between bodies (and this is *Rick and Morty and Philosophy*, not *Quantum Leap and Philosophy*), Rick *has to* see that consciousness can't move between bodies without something in which it is realized. The only thing that gets passed through the Brainalyzer or between Tiny Rick and Old Rick is *information about psychological states*. So, what matters to each iteration of Rick is that *someone* will carry his distinctive psychological pattern (his desires, intentions, beliefs, and so on). Or, we might say that what matters to Rick is Parfit's psychological continuity.

The other cases from the last section provide us with a similar answer about what matters. After Cronenberging his world, Rick chooses the nearest possible world that he does because it allows him and Morty to slip seamlessly back into their old lives. Upon arriving in their new world, Rick muses that "We're not skipping a beat" ("Rick Potion #9"). Because the only difference between the two worlds is that one world's Rick and Morty died after un-Cronenberging things, everything will be exactly as it was *before* Rick C-137 Cronenberged *his* world. In other words, it will be as if the Cronenberging never really happened at all. Beth, Jerry, Summer, and everyone else will relate to Rick and Morty exactly as they would have before the Cronenberging. What's more, the relations they bear to Rick and Morty are effectively unbroken, as there won't be a point at which any of them say or do something that the Beth, Summer, or Jerry of Rick and Morty's pre-Cronenberged world wouldn't have done.

Of course, these people aren't numerically identical with the Beth, Jerry, and Summer from C-137. But this doesn't matter to Rick and Morty (especially Rick; Morty has some qualms at first, but comes around eventually). Nor does it matter to the Cronenberged Rick and Morty we see in the episode's stinger who inadvertently un-Cronenberg their world and seek solace in a Cronenberged one. Both Rick and Morty and Cronenberged Rick and Morty seem to care most that they can reintegrate with the world—and the people in it—as they left it. This kind of reintegration, though, is only possible if everyone in the target world carries on the same beliefs, desires, and so on of the people in C-137.

Likewise, whether the 'Beth' in "The Rickchurian Mortydate" is a clone or not, what's important is that she has Real Beth's psychological states so that she relates to her family in the same way Real Beth did. If 'Beth' *is* a clone, then the Real Beth and the present Clone Beth would still be indiscernible to Jerry, Morty, and Summer so that Real Beth can go soul-searching without disrupting the family's lives. At this point, you might be thinking that this still doesn't mean that we don't need to worry about Real Beth anymore. But what matters here is that "Beth" picked up exactly where Real Beth left off in terms of her mental states. Just being qualitatively the same—like the Morty voucher case—isn't enough without psychological continuity, or the ability to mentally go on *as if* there was no change in identity. So, Clone Beth would carry on Real Beth's psychological states as if she *were* Beth.

About as Good, Rick-latively Speaking

So, Rick Sanchez—Rick C-137, *our* Rick—is definitely dead. He at least died in "Big Trouble in Little Sanchez," when he erased his psychological states and recreated those states in an entirely new (cloned) person, Tiny Rick. However, considering everything we've seen Rick and Morty do over the course of the series, let's be honest: Rick's probably engaged in this sort of body-swapping before.

Ultimately, then, we may not have any good idea when our Rick really died. But he surely *did* die at some point. At the same time, by advocating Parfit's view that identity isn't what matters, *Rick and Morty* lets us be oddly okay with this. Rick's death doesn't really get any attention in the show because it doesn't really matter if the Rick we watch is *our* Rick or some other Rick-person.

Rick says in "Rick Potion #9" that his plan to hop dimensions will "kinda put everything back to normal, relatively speaking". This echoes Parfit's claim that Teletransportation, which involves psychological continuity but not identity, is about as good as ordinary survival. Parfit's point—and part of the show's too, I think—is that we care about (numerical) identity, but we probably shouldn't.

If being Teletransported or Brainalyzed means that I die, it seems to make a difference to me whether the person on the other side of the Teletransporter or Brainalyzer is me or someone else. Yet, *Rick and Morty* tries to show us that, practically and morally speaking, what *really* makes a difference to me is that my desires get carried out, my beliefs get represented in the world, and the people I care about are safe. And this can happen without strict identity.

In other words, what's most important is that there's *someone* out there with Rick's unique love of Szechuan sauce, stiff rejection of authority, crass demeanor, and begrudging concern for his family (yes, even Jerry)—not that this person is

Rick C-137. Though it may be surprising to *us*, the view that identity doesn't matter appears much more natural in the world of *Rick and Morty*, where mind-reading farts, salesmen with ants in their eyes, and memory parasites are everyday occurrences.

3
The M. Night Sh-imulation Hypothesis

CHARLENE ELSBY

Are we living in a computer simulation? What's the point of this simulation? Is someone trying to extract from me my super awesome recipe for mango scones? Because it's just the scone recipe I found on the Internet, with some dried mangoes. *There! Is that what you want?* Can I come out now?

These are the questions we all ask ourselves when philosophers, Rick, and Morty start to make us question whether the reality we live in is the *real* reality, or if there's some kind of other *more real* reality out there, perhaps just on the other side of the edge of the end of the universe, that I could get to if I just managed to overload the alien processing systems. In "M. Night Shaym-Aliens!" the Zigerions put Rick into a simulation in order to extract knowledge from his inaccessible human brain. (I guess they don't have mind-reading capacities?) They want his formula for concentrated dark matter, so they need to create a situation where Rick has to reveal the formula.

For anyone who's heard anything about the simulation hypothesis, a clever young philosopher named Nick Bostrom immediately comes to mind. While he was out somewhere some night, a clever argument came to mind, and he went home and wrote it down. Now tech people everywhere are questioning the nature of reality, and so perhaps should we. (*But what do the Zigerions want from me?!*) Bostrom himself has said that he thinks the probability is pretty low that we are living in a computer simulation. His paper, "Are You Living In A Computer Simulation?" was published back in 2003 by *Philosophical Quarterly*. (*But why is it "You", Nick? Why isn't it "we"? What do you know that I don't?)* The idea that *the real world isn't real*, though, stretches way further back in the history of philosophy, and there have been quite a few different ways of phrasing it.

Bostrom's simulation argument really only covers the situation where we're living in a simulation that was created by some kind of post-human species. (*But what about aliens, Nick? What about aliens?*) The argument goes a little like this. In the future, there are either going to be post-humans or not, where post-humans are a more developed kind of human with better technology. In the cases where there aren't post-humans, either all of the humans have died, or else we just haven't advanced. Maybe we've even regressed. But *if there are post-humans*, then perhaps they would run simulations of how things used to be. It'd be similar to models of the universe, how it came to be and whatnot, including all of the people in it, before the time when they all became post-humans.

But again, maybe not. Maybe the post-humans just aren't interested in running "ancestor simulations." Maybe we're just boring to them. Maybe they're only entertained by things we can't even conceive. Maybe having to watch simulations of people like us is something they only make whatever their version of children is do, as some kind of educational activity, so that they can see what the hard times in the olden days used to be like. Maybe they're so busy riding their Whirly-Dirlys to care about us. Maybe we really fucked things up and now our progeny like to pretend we never existed. There are a lot of reasons people don't write computer simulations of what life would be like for Grandpa. Not all old people are as entertaining as Rick. Maybe *Rick and Morty* is a simulation built into our simulation by future generations, to show us how interesting old people *should* be.

But if there are post-humans in the future, and if those post-humans do happen to enjoy running ancestor simulations, then it's pretty plausible that we're living in one. After all, the number of simulations in the post-human world would increase like games of Warcraft in ours, so the likelihood that you're an NPC in someone else's simulation increases along with the number of simulations that would exist. (Note for noobs: "NPC" is the acronym for Non-Player Character.) So Nicky B says we have to accept one of these beliefs: 1. there aren't any post-humans; 2. there are post-humans, but they don't care about ancestor simulations; or 3. we're living in a computer simulation.

Of course, "we're living in a computer simulation" is the coolest sounding one, and therefore the most rational one to believe. Also, the other two beliefs aren't even about me. So "we're living in a computer simulation" seems pretty right to me, just because it sounds cool, and it's about me, whereas the other two are just speculations about people who don't even exist yet. Yes, I am saying that we care more about theories that are about us. That's how humans are. For a particularly obvious example of how philosophical theories tend to be narcissistic, check out Derek Parfit's non-identity problem, the theory that we can fuck up the planet however we want and future humans should still be grateful to us for their existence, because without our fucking up the place, different people might have come into being. Rick would love it. It would justify creating an entire society to power your battery. Those people should be grateful, some narcissist philosophers would say— without Rick's battery, no one would have created them ("The Ricks Must be Crazy").

So we're living in a computer simulation. Or possibly, a simulation within a simulation, within a simulation. Rick isn't stupid enough to be tricked by one simulation, so you have to make him think that he's getting out of the simulation before he'll reveal the formula for concentrated dark matter. It's a simulation-inception of deception. Those Zigerions are so smart; it's a shame they all blow up. *Spoiler Alert.* Fuck, too late.

Slow Down! Lookin' Good. My Man!

One of the problems facing us, and our own capacity to create simulations, is computing power. Rick is on to the Zigerions immediately, because their computing power is insufficient to create a plausible reality. There are glitches everywhere, and there are these people who are just there, repeating the same phrases over and over, like, "Lookin' Good!" or "My man!" or "Yes." These are instances of lazy computing, like "human music."

Have you ever wondered why you hear the same damn songs on the radio all the time? It saves hard drive space in the computer simulation. Bostrom has clearly spent many lonely nights considering the possibility that our world is inhabited by what he calls "shadow-people." (He's not sure *exactly* how much cheaper they would be than regular people to simulate, but it's a concern.) You can save a lot of money on simulations by letting Jerry have sex with an NPC version of Beth and let's face it, he's not going to catch on too quickly. Jerry doesn't stop to think about whether it's plausible that *Jerry* of all people should create an award-winning ad campaign about apples, that there should be an award for ad campaigns specifically about apples, and that if there were such an award, "The Appley" would be a reasonable name for it. But if he weren't Jerry, he might become suspicious about these things and *start to wonder about the whole existence of the known universe.*

There are efficiencies built into the system that would seem to save on a lot of computing power and *guess what*, if you look closely enough, you can find a whole lot of repetition of form in the universe as well. Have you ever noticed how you share most of your DNA with a lot of other species in the universe, not only other animals, but also plants? That's going to save some hard drive space. Have you ever noticed how grandma tells the same stories over and over? *Scripted*, I say. All over the place, the same damn thing over and over again, doing the same damn stuff, the same damn way, with little variations here and there, just so we don't get suspicious. But doesn't the *regularity* of it all make you suspicious?

And then there are the *glitches*. What about all of the times the universe just fucks up, and suddenly there's a mailman in a tree, and Jerry's up for promotion? What kind of fucked up universe is that? Bostrom actually considers glitches in his paper; he thinks that the simulators would be able to avoid them either by rewinding the simulation to avoid them or edit the brains of the people who figure them out, so that they haven't figured them out.

If I am indeed part of a simulation, then it's reasonable to think that the simulators could edit my thoughts whenever I start to catch on. But then *how did I figure them out*, Nick? Maybe this chapter is evidence that we're *not* living in a simulation. At least, that's what the simulators *want* me to think. Or perhaps it would make more sense to let me carry on believing that I'm in a simulation, so that the rest of the simulants would have someone to dismiss as a conspiracy theorist. Wouldn't *not interfering* be exactly what I would expect from our simulation's overlords? It seems that we can make a lot of speculations here about the motivations of our simulators, but along with the idea that they have the power to create our entire universe comes the idea that they can edit it whenever they like. Maybe I *did* read books about the Berenstein Bears as a kid, not the Berenstain Bears like our simulators would like to have me believe. (Go look up the Mandela effect right now.)

So there's an *epistemological* problem with the simulation hypothesis. Rick says that it doesn't make sense for delicious toaster pastries to both live in and drive around in toasters, but if that's all that I've ever known to be true, then I'd happily believe it. I'd only think it were odd if it were out of step with what *I were used to*, but if I'm living in a simulation, what I'm used to is simulated. Are there things that I can't know because they're outside of the simulation, or are there things that are unknowable because *that's what they are—unknowable things*. If I get to the edge of the universe, is that proof that there's something beyond or that there's nothing beyond?

Some people say "yes" all the time because they're "yesmen". We have a name for that. It's not necessarily the case that they're saying "yes" because *they're simulated people who don't have the computing capacity to maintain a larger store of stock phrases*. Saying that might seem a little paranoid, but maybe that's just because we're onto something. The epistemological problem—the idea that if the simulation were good enough, we'd never know we were in it—is devastating to the theory, because no evidence exists for the simulation theory that couldn't equally be evidence for some other theory. We could either take the internal logic of the universe as evidence that it is a simulation, or we could take it as evidence *that the world is logical*. We could take inconsistencies in the universe as evidence that it is a simulation, or we could take them as evidence that the universe is imperfect.

We might also call this problem the "underdetermination" problem. A theory is "underdetermined" if the evidence for it could equally well support some other, just as plausible theory. Let's say your theory is that this morning you woke up in a universe that was exactly like your own, but was in fact a simulation created by aliens. Every single observation you make is just as you would expect it to be, leading to two very plausible theories. Either 1. You're not living in a simulation; or 2. You're living in a simulation *so good*, that it's just like the real world. The point is, there would be no way to tell the difference. Jerry should know that the best sex of his life was with shadow-Beth, a simulation of his wife. But if we had no other reality to compare this reality to, say, if we weren't *put into* a simulation, like Rick was, but were born into it, like Bostrom suggests, then we wouldn't have any evidence to suggest that what we are experiencing is in any way out of the ordinary . . . *or do we?*

The Other Other Universes

The fact of the matter is, sometimes, we *do* see things that make us question whether this is the real universe. Plato calls them "summoners". In his account from the *Republic*, he thinks that we should start to question the reality of this whole shadow universe based on the observation that it's full of contradictions. I look at a finger, and it's big in comparison to some other finger. I look at the same finger, and it's small in comparison to some other finger. The big-small finger is a contradiction in the shadow-universe that leads us to reject *this universe* in favor of some other, *realer* universe.

Plato's allegory of the cave is all about rejecting this shadow universe in favor of the other, real universe outside of the cave—the philosophy universe. You can tell that there's another universe out there just because this one sucks so much. It's full of contradictions, and we humans are imbued with a rationality that can resolve those contradictions, a rationality we got from the rational realm, the philosophy realm, the realm of the forms, where math lives and where we get to go after we die. *So what if we die in a simulation?*

Another version of *what if the world isn't real?* is *what if this is all a dream?* In "Lawnmower Dog," when Rick and Morty go into Mr. Goldenfield's dream, to convince him to give Morty an A in math, they have to stay alive, because if you die in someone else's dream, you die in real life. But a lot of the time, we like to think that if you die in a simulation, you just get to leave. Perhaps you get to go to the better place, where the simulations come from. Maybe you just glitch out, like so many concert-goers that Rick is using to cause a restart in the Zigerion simulation.

Have you ever been awakened from a dream and only then realized that all of the projects in which you were just engaged weren't "real"? René Descartes thought that dreams were evidence that we could doubt the whole existence of the universe. To prove, "I think, therefore I am" (which is a paraphrase of an argument he stole from St. Augustine), he argued that dreams seem real enough to us that we should doubt whether we're *ever* really experiencing what we think we are.

Bostrom notes the similarity of his computer simulation hypothesis to various religious hypotheses. They all seem to have a common theme—there are worlds, created by super-intelligent beings, who made you for some purpose, and maybe, just maybe, you can go hang out with them when you're done with whatever you're doing here. Plato described in *Phaedo* how the philosopher was always practicing for death by separating ourselves from this shadow world, choosing to focus on the realm of the forms, which is where our soul would be, were it not presently trapped in this stupid flesh body.

This is where our creation claims and our evidence claims come together. What's the general theme of all of these hypotheses? It's possible that there's a super intelligent being creating people, who lives in a better world somewhere, where we also might get to go someday. And what's the proof of this? Usually an analogy. Imagine *what you would do*, if only you had the computing power of a Zigerion. The contemporary theories of mind that we use today are based on an analogy between us and computers. Our minds are software, running on mushy brain hardware. We need to believe this for the simulation hypothesis ever to be plausible—that the mind and every natural law ever are kinds of software.

These theories are *based* on an analogy between us (and the world) and computers. The reasoning process went like this: look at this computer I made. Gee, that reminds me of me. Maybe I'm just a more complex version of that thing. And the substrate-independent theory of mind is born. ("Substrate-independence" is the condition of Bostrom's hypothesis, which just says that we don't necessarily need *specifically* human brain goo in order to have minds—silicon could work too, or some other substance we haven't considered yet.)

Analogies always come into play when we're trying to prove other worlds. First, there's the analogy between the stuff in nature and the stuff I make, and then there's the analogy between my capacities and the capacities of whoever it is I think made the stuff in nature. That's the argument from design. People who make the argument from design (most famously St. Thomas Aquinas, although he took it from Aristotle) note that there seems to be a purpose to a lot of these things in the universe. Teeth are made for mashing or tearing. Kittens are made for petting. Livers are made for removing the toxins that Rick decides to ingest. It's like whoever made him knew that he's a drinker, and put a sentry in place to deal with the problem.

William Paley, when considering the argument from design, asks us to look at all of this stuff, and then to consider what we might think if we found a watch just sitting around in nature. I might think that someone had made it. Now look at the beautiful machine that is Morty. The conclusion he wants us to come to is that someone made Morty too, and for a purpose, so that you can buy your Morty at an EVERY DAY LOW PRICE *and* he comes with weapons that his puny little arms are specifically designed to wield! (from the show's opening sequence for Season Three)

Bostrom's conclusion about this is ominous: if someone made us, then they're watching, and so perhaps we shouldn't fuck with other people. But that would seem to suggest we have free will, and aren't I just a simulated shadow-person, the ancestor of someone who's looking back at me right now, thinking about how quaint it is that I'm writing this, thinking that I'm coming up with these words, and that it's not all just the inevitable result of my programming. Is it wrong of Rick to put on a concert and start making demands?

We don't seem to have a problem with the scene where Rick causes a glitch in the simulation by demanding more and more unreasonable things from the NPC's in the Zigerion matrix. He even makes it part of a fun song: "Everybody over thirty, do this with your hands! Everybody with a red shirt, jump up and down! . . . Everyone whose first name begins with an 'L' who isn't Hispanic, walk in a circle the same number of times as the square root of your age times ten!" He wants to make the system reboot, but for the people in the simulation, that means a literal end to the universe. The "reboot" is the apocalypse, and every single one of them will die. How can we do this to our simulated friends?

This aspect of Bostrom's working of the simulation hypothesis is at once ominous and altogether too familiar. For one, it assumes that if we're living in a simulation, we still have free will within that simulation, so that we can choose to affect other simulation people positively or negatively. But if all aspects of the simulation are worked out according to our programming, then we'd say the world is "deterministic", and it wouldn't be reasonable to blame people for their morally reprehensible actions within the simulation. I don't think this part of the theory matters. It's just the same damn problem philosophy has had since forever—the tension between our theories that everything is how it is because of laws of nature but also that people suck and we should punish them for it.

You Live Here. Get Used to It

What if the universe Rick creates isn't a "simulation", but it's really just another universe, a universe that's like our universe, but just, you know, *small*? What if the microverse creates a miniverse? What if the miniverse creates a teenyverse? Are these created universes, just because they're created, *simulations*? Or, here's a thought, is it possible to create real universes? When we ask the same questions about the simulated universe in "M. Night Shaym-Aliens" about the *created* universe Rick is using to charge his battery in "The Ricks Must Be Crazy," suddenly we care more about the people who are created or simulated. We might feel a little more guilt over enslaving a universe for battery power if we didn't consider them to be somehow *fake* people. Part of the problem with the idea of post-human society-created ancestor simulations is that sometimes when you "simulate" something, you actually recreate it. I don't say that this year's tomato plants are a simulation of last year's, just because my goal is to reproduce the cherry tomatoes of yesteryear.

This fact seems undoubtedly true: this is the universe we live in. Strap yourselves in. So the saying goes, "Everyone likes to think they're a Rick, when they're really a Morty." It's none too likely that you're going to be able to escape this simulation, if it is one, so you might as well just roll with it.

Even if it's a simulation, it's the only reality we have, and your sub-standard science skills aren't going to be the thing saving us all from living out a fake, meaningless life, where it turns out our purpose all along was to power the battery of a super-scientist's spaceship. Maybe we'll never figure it out, because the post-humans or aliens running the simulation are so advanced that they don't run into the same technological limitations that we do. Have you ever considered the fact that maybe we can't just *assume* that our post-human simulators would run into technological difficulties, like we do?

If *we're* living in a simulation, then the limitations on our technological capacities *are simulated*. Maybe the fact that we're not simulating other realities is *proof* of the fact that we're living in a simulation. Or maybe we just haven't reached that stage in the simulation where we make simulations. Fuck it. "I don't get it and I don't need to."—Jerry.

4

Could a Divine Creator Turn Out to Be a Selfish Jerk?

Eric J. Silverman and Connor Channer

If we were certain that the universe was created by someone outside of it, what would we expect Him/Her/It/Them to be like?

An old guy sitting on a floating throne with long flowing gray hair? An all-powerful, morally perfect transcendent being? An unpredictable thunderbolt-throwing deity with abs of steel who is a bit preoccupied with seducing young Greek peasant maidens? A flying spaghetti monster? A shape-shifting reverse giraffe?

While there have been many conceptions of the Creator of the Universe, we almost certainly would not expect Him to be like Rick Sanchez. Rick is an incredibly intelligent and clever scientist, but he is also a selfish, crass, manipulative human being who is willing to mistreat others for his own purposes. Yet, this very possibility of Rick as intelligent designer of a universe is proposed in "The Ricks Must Be Crazy"—the episode title a reference to the 1984 cult classic movie *The Gods Must Be Crazy*.

During Rick, Morty, and Summer's journeys through the multiverse it is revealed that Rick's interdimensional traveling car is powered by a microverse he has created within its battery. In this microverse, sentient beings unknowingly produce energy for Rick via "gooble-boxes." He exploits these people by rerouting a portion of their energy to power his car. Morty is horrified by this exploitation and compares it to slavery . . . or at least ". . . slavery with extra steps."

Is it really possible that a universe's intelligent designer could simply be a clever, crass, flatulent jerk like Rick? And what would such a possibility imply about the nature of morality? Would fulfilling Rick's commands like greeting others with extended middle fingers actually become morally good actions rather than obscene in such a world? Would Rick's use of the universe's labor to power his car be an exploitive act of slavery or just tribute owed to a 'creator' who has benefited the universe he has created?

An Intelligent Designer?

Your Gods are a lie.

—RICK SANCHEZ

Historically, one of the three most important arguments for God's existence has been the teleological argument. It claims that the universe is like a well-designed machine requiring an intelligent designer outside the universe to have created it. The most famous version of this argument was created by William Paley. He compares the universe to a complicated machine like a watch and claims that the existence of such a machine provides evidence for the existence of the machine's intelligent designer.

> If, while walking across a barren wasteland, I saw a stone and wondered how it came to exist, I could legitimately account for it through chance factors like wind, heat, and rain, etc. I would not, however, come to the same conclusion if I came across a watch. For such is its manifest complexity—with all its wheels, cogs, gears, and springs operating together to measure the passage of time—that it would be absurd to suppose that it too owed its existence to a set of chance occurrences. Thus we must postulate some intelligence at work in the watch's creation: a watchmaker.

According to Paley some things can be accounted for by pure randomness, like rocks or perhaps the male Gazorpians who are dumb as rocks. But other objects are far too complicated and work far too well to be accounted for by randomness. Objects like watches, computers, the universe, or Rick's interdimensional cable television are complicated and act with enough purpose and intelligence that they must have been intentionally designed by someone. Paley's teleological argument for the existence of God can be summarized:

Premise 1: Complicated machines that work towards some purpose in an orderly way, like watches, require an intelligent creator.

Premise 2: The Universe resembles a vast complicated machine that works toward some purpose in an orderly way.

Conclusion: Therefore, the Universe was created by an intelligent designer such as God.

Premise 1 of the argument is rarely challenged, since purposeful machines do appear to require an intelligent designer. After all, a plumbus can't just grow randomly on a tree somewhere, someone must have created it! However, much has been written both for and against Premise 2. In favor of Premise 2, some scholars emphasize the sheer unlikeliness of living creatures, capable of reproduction and survival, appearing in the universe by chance. Long-time atheist Anthony Flew eventually became convinced of the need for a divine Creator by this sort of argument. He concluded:

> My one and only piece of relevant evidence is the apparent impossibility of providing a naturalistic theory of the origin from DNA of the first reproducing species . . . the only reason which I have for beginning to think of believing in a First Cause god is the impossibility of providing a naturalistic account of the origin of the first reproducing organisms.

Other writers have criticized Premise 2. If the universe is designed to operate towards a goal, then what is its goal? If it is meant to produce life, then why is there only one planet where life flourishes? If it's meant to produce happiness for those creatures, then why is life so difficult? Or as any faithful *Rick and Morty* fan might ask, why is it that "Existence is pain to a Meeseeks"?

The viewpoint of *Rick and Morty* is that the world is absurd rather than orderly. As Morty concludes in one disturbing episode after causing the end of human civilization in his initial reality within the multiverse, "Nobody exists on purpose, nobody belongs anywhere." If his view is correct, then life is absurd and the universe is not orderly at all.

Even if we accept the premises of the watchmaker argument, the conclusion might not guarantee that the intelligent designer of the universe would be the traditional God. As David Hume argues there is no reason on this theory "for ascribing perfection to the Deity . . . or for supposing Him free from error." The creator of the universe—or even Rick's microverse—would need to be quite clever and powerful, but He wouldn't need to be intellectually perfect, infinitely powerful, or moral. The creator might just be some crass, egoistic, limited being, like Rick. He is clever and powerful enough to create a trans-dimensional vehicle powered by the mircroverse, but he is violent, selfish, vulgar, and kind of a jerk.

An Immoral God

> I have no code of ethics. I will kill anyone, anywhere . . . I just love killin'.
>
> —KROMBOPULOS MICHAEL

The possibility of the universe's creator possessing vicious moral character like Rick raises an interesting question: if God exists, then what would be the relationship between God and morality? After all, isn't God in charge? Isn't that what we mean when we refer to a being as 'GOD'? Wouldn't a divine creator shape the rules of the created world, including the moral rules? If God wants to take twenty percent of our energy as "tribute" to power his car or any other reason wouldn't that be morally appropriate rather than unjust exploitation?

Some philosophers believe that anything commanded or desired by God simply becomes morally correct. If God says that we should take Tuesday and Wednesday off from work each week, then we should change the calendar to make the weekend start on Tuesday rather than Saturday. If God says we should avoid eating vegetables and only eat fruits, meat, Szechuan Chicken McNugget sauce and random debris Birdperson finds on the carpet, then He's the boss—this new diet becomes morally correct. If God commands that we should torture Mortys, escort Fart to safety, and sell guns to assassins like Krombopulos Michael, then we should all live as God commands. On this view of morality—known as Divine Command Theory—in an important sense morality becomes arbitrary. Morality simply is whatever God wants or commands. Many philosophers view the arbitrariness that accompanies Divine Command Theory as a fatal and unacceptable flaw. Yet, others are willing to accept this unintuitive implication.

Philosophers since the time of Plato have believed that morality might be based on something besides divine whim. In Plato's *Euthyphro*, Socrates asks: "Is the pious loved by the gods because it is pious or is it pious because it is loved by the gods?" Let's suppose that a "god" like Rick loves greeting others by saying "Peace Among Worlds" and extending his middle fingers. Plato points out that if such actions are morally correct and pious merely because the gods approve of them then divine command theory is correct. Greeting people in this obscene way would become the 'pious' thing to do!

The alternative view is that morality is independent of anyone's preferences or commands, even God's. Perhaps some actions are simply irrational, immoral or, as Birdperson might say, simply "a dick move" no matter who commands them. Like Birdperson, Plato suggests that there might be more to morality than simply obeying whatever the gods happen to love. The nature of right and wrong may stand independently of divine love. Even a god should love pious and moral actions because those actions are good in themselves. If so, then divine love would be a *response* to moral goodness, rather than the *cause* of an action's moral goodness. The fact that we can even speak of the possibility of God acting immorally suggests that most of us are not strict divine command theorists. Most of us believe that there are moral standards to which even a god or Rick should adhere—standards that Rick, like many of the ancient Greek gods, routinely violates.

If God Can Exist, He Must Exist

This is happening infinite times across infinite realities.

—RICK SANCHEZ

The teleological argument allows for the possibility that the universe's divine Creator might be less than fully perfect. But, are there any arguments that could demonstrate the existence of not only a Creator deity, but also a morally perfect God? There is one argument that might accomplish this goal called the ontological argument.

The ontological argument claims that the very concept of God—a perfect being—refers to a being that MUST exist. The idea of God must refer to a being who possess all perfections: absolute moral goodness, perfect knowledge, maximal power, and perfect existence—guaranteeing divine existence. But, wait! What does this definition have to do with God *actually* existing rather than just being some weird aspect of the definition of God? After all, I can define Rick Sanchez as "a crass, selfish, flatulent, nearly all-powerful multiverse-traveling scientist who exists" without causing Rick to actually exist outside of his show.

The ontological argument is based on an implication of what it would mean to "exist" in the best possible way. Suppose that a perfect being possesses every possible good trait in the best way. Such a being would have to have the ability to know in its absolutely best form. It would know EVERYTHING that could be known. God would have to have the most power, be morally perfect, and so on. This perfect concept of God should sound like the familiar all-knowing, all-powerful, all-good deity that Rick doesn't believe in.

If God truly possesses every potential good trait in the most perfect way possible, then one of those good traits that God would need to possess perfectly is "existence." But, what could it possibly mean for one being to "exist" in a better way than another? Is this just some nonsense that Squanchy might come up with? One possibility is that it is better to exist for a long time rather than a short time. After all, when Rick and Morty play *Roy: A Life Well Lived* one of the statistics it keeps track of is length of life. If Rick keeps Roy alive for a hundred years, while Morty's character dies at fifty-five after falling off a rack of rugs in his meaningless career at the shop, then Rick's character has existed in a 'better' way than Morty's. If we are only talking about length of existence, a Redwood tree that survives for two thousand years would exist in a better way than a human who only lives a hundred. And a God that exists forever would 'exist' in a better way than a butter bot that only exists temporarily.

Some philosophers—such as Alvin Plantinga—have argued that a being that exists "necessarily," which means that it is a being that must exist in any possible world, would have a more perfect kind of existence than if it merely exists "contingently."

Such a being would exist in every dimension and every mini-, I mean micro-verse. In contrast, existing contingently means that a being might or might not have existed. Contingent beings like Zeep Xanflorp exist in some possible worlds, but not others.

So, how does all of this talk of the concept of God referring to a being that must possess "the best kind of existence" support an argument for the actual existence of God? Consider this rough ontological argument based on Plantinga's:

1. **The concept of God refers to a perfect being, possessing all good traits in their most perfect form.**

2. **The most perfect kind of existence includes existing in all possible worlds.**

3. **There is at least one possible world where God, a perfect being possessing existence in the most perfect way, actually exists.**

4. **Therefore, God exists in all possible worlds, including this one!**

Rick and Morty travel through a kind of multiverse where very different possible worlds exist: one possible world has an ongoing war between humans and giant spiders, in another world humans evolved from corn, in yet another world Hitler cures cancer. Suppose that in their travels through all the possible worlds Rick discovers a world where the perfect being God actually exists. As surprising as this discovery would be to Rick, it gets even weirder. If Rick discovers a genuinely perfect God in even one single possible universe out of billions, since perfect existence includes existence in all possible worlds, this perfect God must actually exist in every possible world including the one we live in. If God is even possible, then—surprisingly—God must be actual!

Does this argument *prove* that God exists? Not quite. One can doubt whether Premise 3 is true, a possibility that even Plantinga acknowledges. Perhaps, there is not even one possible world where God exists. Since Rick hasn't found such a world yet, he might want to simply rip this religious band-aid off now. The ontological argument does prove that if God is even genuinely possible, then He would also be actual. But, it does not prove that God is a real possibility. Whether or not the ontological argument works depends upon what you believe about which conceptual worlds are truly possible.

While Rick has openly and repeatedly stated that he believes in no god, in a moment of desperation he did seem to think that praying to God might work as a last resort. This might indicate that he thinks that God is really possible after all. Of course, the moment he was out of danger he also concluded with "Not today, bitch!" which is not the sort of thing one says if he really thinks God might exist. So, maybe Rick actually does believe that God is possible or maybe he does not.

Don't Think about It?

What about the reality where Hitler cured cancer? My answer is: Don't think about it.

—RICK SANCHEZ

A created world might have a powerful intelligent designer from beyond the universe, but that designer from might still turn out to be an imperfect limited being like Zeep Xanflorp or even an egocentric jerk like Rick.

According to Divine Command theorists, all of the divine creator's commands simply become morally good. Rick—as "divine creator"—might command us to celebrate Ricksgiving to honor the day he gave us the gooble-box to create energy, and obeying that command would become morally good. But we've also seen that from the time of Plato, this account of morality has been viewed dubiously by most philosophers since it makes morality rather arbitrary, and the last thing we need is an eccentric like Rick deciding what is right and wrong for us all.

We've seen how the multiverse view of possible worlds used in *Rick and Morty* can be used by the ontological argument to argue for the existence of a perfect God. If a perfect being exists in any possible world, it would have to exist perfectly and therefore exist in all possible worlds . . . if God is a real possibility.

What does all this talk about ultimate reality prove? It turns out that undoubtable proofs about God, ultimate reality, morality, or just about anything else are hard to come by. Life is short and such questions can make your head hurt. Rick's final answer to all this is simple: Just don't think about it!

Yet such apathy doesn't come naturally to those of us who hope for more decisive answers, which is why we follow Socrates's example of seeking truth even in the face of doubt, skepticism, and uncertainty, instead of taking Rick's advice to just stop thinking.

5
Who'd Rick Kill? Or, Who Killed Rick?

ELLIOT KNUTHS

In "The Rickshank Rick-demption," Rick C-137 ("our" Rick, the show's protagonist) dissolves the Council of Ricks by murdering all of its members. It's a pretty straightforward act, but it raises lots of interesting questions.

Imagine that you're an investigator, who's called to the Chambers of the Council of Ricks and you find the carnage that has been left behind by Rick C-137. You start to gather evidence, DNA samples, pictures, and bodies, to help determine what happened. Strangely, the DNA doesn't help at all. All you know is that Rick Sanchez has died, and there are several bodies that are all dead. Are they all Rick Sanchez? Was the perpetrator Rick Sanchez? Are there multiple perpetrators? How can we make sense of this crime scene?

To answer these questions, we will need to consider metaphysics. Metaphysics is a branch of philosophy that studies the nature of reality. A classic metaphysical question is, "Am I the same person I was yesterday?" This question of identity gets weird pretty quickly when you introduce the possibility of multiple realities. It gets even weirder when the realities interact with one-another. When Rick kills the Council of Ricks, is he committing suicide? Is he killing other people? These are Ricktastic questions that can only be answered by appealing to Mortyphysics, the study of how reality works in the *Rick and Morty* universe.

Fresh Self-Contained Worlds

To begin our investigation into the murders (or mass involuntary suicide?) of the Council of Ricks and what it means to have multiple Ricks and Mortys, we must first consider the nature of possible worlds, a philosophical concept similar to what characters on the show call "universes," "realities," or "dimensions."

First, "possible world" isn't the best term for this concept because it refers to a possible way for all of reality, not just Earth or some other planet, to be. "Possible reality" or "possible universe" might have worked just as well, but philosophers settled on "possible world." Most people agree that our world doesn't have to be exactly the way that it is. In fact, it probably could have been different than it actually is in infinitely many ways. For instance, the last time it rained there might have been one more raindrop than actually was. Perhaps more interestingly, even if you have always been an only child, your parents almost certainly could have had one or several more children in addition to you. Each of these situations could possibly have occurred, so we say that each one exists in some possible world.

We know there is an Evil Morty in at least one universe, so he exists in some possible world. Now, not all worlds have Evil Mortys, so this world is a distinct possible world, because it could have been different. Thinking about reality in terms of possible worlds like this is called modal metaphysics because it describes different modes of truth. Some truths are necessary ones. For example, it is impossible for triangles to not have a sum of interior angles that add up 180 degrees. We might call them by different names in different worlds, and we might use different numbers, but the underlying principle must remain the same. If in another world triangles are called narfpoits, then narfpoits will have a sum of an interior angle of 5 phblthps, so long as 5 phblthps is equal to 180 degrees. Necessary truths *have* to be true in all possible worlds.

Other truths, like "if this world contains a Morty, then that Morty is incompetent," aren't true in all possible worlds, so they are called contingent truths. When we start talking about truth across possible worlds, we're applying modal reasoning, which is really useful when we want to contrast what might be with what must be. Hopefully, this will help us figure out what happened at the council chamber.

What happens when one world's Rick or Morty interacts interdimensionally with other worlds' native Ricks and Mortys? Are they shaking the hands of doppelgangers? Or do they shake their own hands? Are they killing their counterparts or do they commit suicide each time they kill one of their own?

There is at least one possible world, our actual world, since it could not exist if it were not possible. Beyond that, philosophers tend to agree with the show's premise that there are infinitely many possible worlds. This fact does not make clear in what form possible worlds exist, though. It also isn't clear if Mortyphysics allows for logically impossible worlds, such as worlds where triangles don't have three sides, to exist.

Interdimensional Cable

Gottfried Leibniz was perhaps the first philosopher to suggest conceiving of different possible realities as different worlds. In his book *Theodicy,* Leibniz imagines an ornate complex library, the Palace of Fates, filled with passages leading into every possible world as though each were a courtyard. For Leibniz, possible worlds do not actually exist but rather are represented in the palace by each courtyard.

This example of possible worlds is *abstractionist.* The example asserts that there is only one actual world, but there are descriptions within that world of other possible worlds. Abstractionists often define possible worlds as complete descriptions of ways that everything *might* have been. For example, when we say that McDonald's might not have revived Szechuan Sauce after its mention on *Rick and Morty,* we mean only that we can consistently describe a world unlike our own in which McDonald's did not bring back Szechuan Sauce after Season Three of *Rick and Morty* popularized it.

The abstractionist doesn't have to believe that there is an actual world in a different dimension to speak adequately about possible worlds. If this is true, then we would have to imagine that the Council of Ricks isn't made up of otherworldly Ricks, but rather a bunch of people in the world, named Rick, who all kind of look alike, have the same DNA, and were murdered by some other guy named Rick who also shares their physical and molecular similarities. Returning to our murder investigation, the abstractionist model suggests that Rick Sanchez killed a bunch of Rick Sanchez lookalikes. What happened to the portals that allowed for the creation of the Council of Ricks? They don't actually exist.

A different way of thinking about possible worlds can be seen in "Rixty Minutes." Rick is distracting his family from the reality TV program they're watching. "I just upgraded our cable package with programming from every conceivable reality," he announces, piquing everyone's interest, especially Jerry's. "Wait, does that mean we get Showtime Extreme?" Jerry asks. Oh, Jerry. How naive of you to limit your thinking to this actual world.

"How about Showtime Extreme in a world where man evolved from corn?" replies Rick, flipping to a channel showing exactly that. There are no limits to the variety of content available on interdimensional cable: it provides "infinite TV from infinite universes." Keep playing your balloon-popping game on your smartphone, Jerry. You clearly can't handle this level of abstraction.

Concretism, sometimes called modal realism, is a radical alternative to abstractionism. First proposed by David Lewis as an alternative to abstractionism, modal realism asserts that all possible worlds actually exist and are as real as our own. Thus, the inhabitants of other possible worlds are as real as we are, even if we can't observe them. Each possible world is a parallel universe. This means that when we say something is *actual*, we're saying that it is true about the world we live in.

"Portal guns exist," is not actual of our world, but it is actual in some other possible world, like the *Rick and Morty* world. Thus, for a concretist, to say that McDonald's might not have revived Szechuan Sauce after *Rick and Morty* referenced it is to say that a separate world exists apart from ours, and you can't get Szechuan Sauce from McDonald's in it after its mention on *Rick and Morty*. Those unfortunate saps. The concretist model might serve our investigation better since it allows us to talk about multiple concrete worlds that may interact through Rick's portals.

Less Lopsided than Man vs Car?

So why all this talk about concretism vs. abstractionism? If the abstractionist theory of possible worlds is true, each person or object exists in more than one possible world and statements like "I might have eaten ice cream for breakfast this morning" can be taken as literally referring to me. This is called Transworld Identity, that the 'me' in a different possible world is identical to the 'me' in this world.

The abstractionist view of Transworld Identity rests on the difference between a thing's essential and accidental properties. Something's essential properties are those which it must have in order to be that thing. Roundness may be an essential property of a ball; Beth being Morty's mother is probably an essential quality of Morty's. Accidental properties are those which an object could gain or lose while still remaining the same object. A red ball painted black would still remain the same ball. Morty might have been a little heavier than he actually is, or might be evil through and through. So, two objects in different possible worlds may actually be the same object so long as only their accidental qualities change.

The existence of a Morty with pink hair in some possible world, which doesn't actually exist, allows us to assert that the actual Morty could have pink hair. Similarly, since there are no Mortys that don't have Beth as a mother, this means that having Beth as a mother is an essential property of Morty's. So, if abstractionism allowed for interdimensional interaction, then Rick Sanchez would have committed suicide when he "murdered" the Council of Ricks (as well as Seal Team Ricks) since he's destroying essentially the same Ricks with different accidental properties (such as different hairstyles or scars).

According to abstractionism's rival, concretism, all things are "world-bound" and each exists only in a single possible world. In other words, you and I exist only in this world, and although there are people very much like us in other possible worlds, they are not actually us. We can still talk about the way things might have been with us by pointing out truths about our counterparts in different possible worlds. This "counterpart theory" is the main alternative to Transworld Identity.

Counterpart theorists, who assert that every possible world really exists, believe that we can ground claims about what is necessary, possible, and impossible in one world by appealing to individuals in other possible worlds just as supporters of Transworld Identity do. For counterpart theorists, however, these claims are not grounded by modal truths about how the same object or person would be or would act in a different possible world. How could they be, if each individual is world-bound? Rather, when I say that I might have become a professional golfer, I mean that in some possible world, some individual who is like me in all the essential ways becomes a professional golfer. What's this mean for our investigation? Well, according to the concretist model, Rick Sanchez from C-137 murdered distinct Rick Sanchezes who made up the Council of Rick, Seal Team Ricks, and so forth. There's no suicide here since Rick is an entity from his own dimension and the Council of Ricks are entities that originated from wherever the hell they came from.

There is one last class of relationships, namely that of doppelgangers. These are objects and persons that exist in the same world and bear incredible resemblance to each other in some respects but are nonetheless distinct individual objects. If, while dining at McDonald's together, you get up to get more napkins and I replace your unopened Szechuan Sauce packet with a different unopened Szechuan Sauce packet, you no longer have the same packet of Szechuan Sauce that you had when you got up, even though you do not notice the difference. The two containers are doppelgangers.

Ricks and Morties

So, does *Rick and Morty* present an abstractionist or concretist account of possible worlds? We can rule out abstractionism because Rick and Morty frequently travel between possible worlds. They couldn't do this if there were only a single actual reality to travel within. This might prematurely lead us to conclude that the presentation of possible worlds in *Rick and Morty* is concretist.

While this is largely correct, modal mortyphysics differs from Lewis's modal realism in a very important way. Lewis maintains that each possible world is causally isolated from all other possible worlds. For him, we can reference possible worlds in order to grasp the concepts of necessity and possibility, but we cannot speak about visiting or otherwise interacting with a particular possible world. Interdimensional adventure is metaphysically off limits. As already mentioned, Mortyphysics provides a different picture of possible worlds, in which individuals can interact across possible worlds. We can even relocate to a different possible world when our own has become uninhabitable, as Regular Rick and Morty do (however, Rick notes that they can only do this three or four more times).

Thus, the theory of modality which accurately describes the universe of Rick and Morty is a sort of modified concretism— possible realities exist but not in the causally inaccessible way concretism requires. It seems like this just pushes the abstractionism/concretism question up a level, though: the *Rick and Morty* universe is just a single, very expansive possible world. There are infinitely many other possible worlds that differ from it in large and small ways and which the actual Rick and Morty can never visit. This might serve to humble Rick's claims about the expansiveness of his own universe, which he deems infinite. Even if there are infinite conceivable realities, they would likely exist as truly separate worlds and remain utterly inaccessible to him.

In light of these differences, the best way to think about Regular Rick's relation to the Council of Ricks is as some kind of cosmic doppelganger relationship. Despite the enormous similarities between the members of the Council of Ricks and Regular Rick, Transworld Identity does not hold among them, nor does the counterpart relation. It's conceivable that some alien with exactly your appearance and mental disposition might someday knock on your front door. You should not regard the alien as bearing any more significant a logical connection with you than any other member of its species. You certainly do not commit suicide by blasting the alien in the face. Likewise, despite the overwhelming number of properties Regular Rick has in common with the Council of Ricks, he does not in any way kill *himself* when he slaughters the Council.

6

Truth in a Multiverse

Elizabeth Rard

Rick is working in his garage. He's mixing various liquids together to produce a particularly noxious reaction. Morty wanders in. "Jesus, Rick, what did you put in there?" Morty turns a little green. Rick sets down his beaker, wipes a bit of vomit from his lower lip, and picks up a laser gun. "Hold still" (burp) "hold still, Morty . . . I uh, I wanna test this out . . ."

Before Morty can duck, Rick takes aim and zaps him with a beam of purple light. Morty freezes, unblinking, and holds a surprised look on his face for exactly thirty-seven seconds before collapsing on the ground, frantically trying to brush imaginary spiders off of his body. Rick makes a note on a well-stained legal pad before picking up his screwdriver and returning to his workbench. Morty lies on the ground slowly recovering his composure.

This little scene is only a small part of the entire situation Rick and Morty are currently connected to. Moving out from the garage a larger situation includes Summer sitting on the couch watching reality television. She has turned the volume up so that she cannot hear the voices coming from the kitchen. In the kitchen Jerry is complaining that he doesn't feel valued as a man, and Beth is pointing out (between sips of wine) that a real man would be comfortable supporting his wife's career over his own. Everything happening in the house right now, from the antics in the garage to the drama in the kitchen, is part of a larger situation that is all connected.

But it doesn't stop there! The bodies of another version of Rick and Morty rotting out in the yard are part of a bigger situation, as are the children playing in the street. Across town the principal is feeling guilty about a dream he had. The planet Earth is spinning merrily on its axis. Other planets are orbiting our sun. Our solar system is merely one of thousands in our galaxy, which is itself careening through the universe. All of these things are connected spatially, and they are all part of a great big situation, of which Rick's garage is just one tiny part.

In addition, there are parts of this situation that are connected temporally, or by time, rather than just spatially. So, for example the events that happened in Rick's garage yesterday are also part of this grand situation. Let's say that yesterday Rick turned himself into a pickle, then that event is also part of one great big situation that is connected by time and space. Or let's say that tomorrow Beth and Jerry reconcile after their fight by going on an alien cruise. These events will also be part of one great big situation that is connected through time and space.

This situation continues out to the very edges of the universe, and extends back in time to the Big Bang, possibly to even before that, all the way back to the beginning of time. It extends forward as well, on and on until the end of our universe. All of these events and situations reaching out in space and time, all of these smaller situations that are connected through space and time, taken together are called a *world*. By a world we don't just mean the planet Earth, or any planet at all, by a world we mean to pick out one entire reality that encompasses everything in that reality that is connected, either in space or time.

Nobody Exists on Purpose

The world that you and I exist in is very different from the world that Rick and Morty have their grand adventures in. In our world there are no aliens (that we know of) visiting Earth, no one has ever turned themselves into a pickle, and no one has invented a portal gun.

We usually think of the world we live in as the *actual world*, which basically means that this is the *really* real world, and in this world, history has unfolded in a specific way. In the actual world *Rick and Morty* airs on *Adult Swim*, Donald J. Trump was elected president of the United States of America in November of 2016, and I have exactly one brother, who is named Joseph. There are countless other details that we could consider about this world but let's focus on these three for a moment.

When I say that it's true that *Rick and Morty airs on Adult Swim*, what I mean is that there is an event in the past and present (or at least in the year 2018) of this world where people can watch the show *Rick and Morty*, and that the show can be specifically watched during the block of time on the *Cartoon Network* that is called *Adult Swim*.

The important thing here is that there were events that happened, that are connected to the current situation in this world by space and time, and those events happening are what make my claim about *Rick and Morty* airing on *Adult Swim* true. Likewise, it's because in 2016 people all across this country voted the way they did, actually electing Donald Trump president, that it is true that Donald Trump was elected president in 2016. The important thing to notice is that the thing that makes my claims about the past true are actual events that happened in our actual world at some point before now. The claim that I have one brother is, again, made true by a particular state of affairs in this world. There is a real person walking around (or more likely sitting at a desk in front of a computer) right now, a person who shares both my last name and roughly fifty percent of my DNA.

This way of defining "truth" is known as the correspondence theory of truth. If a sentence is true, then the content of the sentence should correspond with a state of the world. "Jerry is a weenie" is consistent with everything we know about the *Rick and Morty* world but not consistent with our world, because Jerry isn't real. The correspondence theory doesn't apply to all claims though. For example, "Googol plus a googol, is two googol" is true, but it doesn't correspond with any state of our reality, since there is not a googol number of anything in the world. So, sometimes when we say that something is true, we also mean that it is consistent with all the other true things in the world. Googol plus a googol equals two googol is consistent with all of our other claims about math and the world, it just doesn't correspond to anything. This way of defining truth is known as the coherence theory of truth.

While there is a very specific way that the world has actually turned out, which includes all of the facts about our world, we usually think that things didn't have to turn out the way they did. For example, it could have been the case that the Nazis won World War II, even though they didn't actually. And it could have been the case that Hillary Clinton was elected president in 2016, even though she wasn't actually elected president (although she did win the popular vote). I could have had a sister instead of the brother that I ended up with, or it could have been the case that I was an only child. It could have even been the case that I was never born (perhaps because my parents never met). In the *Rick and Morty* world, it could have been the case that Jerry wasn't born to grow up as a weenie. Despite the fact that this seems inconsistent with Jerry's character (it might even be impossible to conceive of Jerry as being anything but a weenie), hypotheticals like this play out much more interestingly in *Rick and Morty*.

It is reasonable to believe, as we look at the world around us, that things didn't have to turn out the way they did. Details both large and small could have ended up different, that there could have been different people, or even no people, or even no planet Earth at all, if things had gone differently at some point in the past. If things had turned out differently we still would have ended up with a world, it would just have been different (perhaps very, very different) from the actual world. We can call one of these alternative realities, one of these different situations that could have been reality had the history of the universe been a bit different, a *possible world*. How many of these possible worlds are there? There are as many possible worlds as there are ways that things could have ended up, which is likely to be an infinite number of ways (or at least quite a few).

Infinite Timelines, Infinite Possibilities

When we make claims about what might have been (such as the claim that I might have had a sister, rather than a brother) it seems as if sometimes those claims are true even though they aren't describing things that actually happened. For example, if I say "My brother could have been a girl" or "*Rick and Morty* could have aired on HBO" they sound true enough, but these claims don't correspond to *our* world.

One way to understand claims about the way that things might have been is to think of them as claims about what did happen in some possible world. So, when I say that I could have had a sister what I mean is that there is some possible world in which I have a sister. We normally think that the actual world is the only one that really exists. So when I say, "There's a possible world in which I have a sister," what I really mean is that I can describe a state of affairs, or possible world, that is consistent with itself (it's coherent even if it doesn't correspond with our world) in such a way that this possible world includes my having a sister.

Normally we think that these worlds don't relly exist anywhere in space or time. In fact, very few philosophers who have used discussions of possible worlds to explain claims about the way things could have been have argued that possible worlds actually exist (although the philosopher David Lewis is a notable exception). And why would we think that these possible worlds actually exist? We've never seen them, or received messages from them, or had any contact whatsoever with a possible world, and so we have no reason to think that there really are other worlds out there making all of our counterfactual claims (claims about how things might have been) true.

But the situation is very different in the world that Rick and Morty live in. Rick has invented, among many, many other things, a portal gun that allows Rick (and his companions) to travel from one world to another. He just points his gun at a wall, sciences up a green wobbly portal, and he's on his way to a world without shrimp (or perhaps a world with nothing but shrimp).

Rick refers to the realities they visit as timelines, or sometimes realities, but they are very close to the possible worlds that we have been discussing. Each alternative timeline that Rick and Morty are able to access represents a different way that things might have turned out, had something in the past gone a different way. In some timelines Rick and Morty turn everyone into Cronenberg people, but in other timelines they are able to avoid such global catastrophes only to accidentally blow themselves up tightening a screw. In one timeline Rick is a complete doofus (and perfect playmate for Jerry), and in another Rick is Cool Rick! Surely there is at least one coherent timeline where Jerry is anything but a weenie: that's the Cronenberg timeline, which still contains "original" Jerry from

C-137. Notice how, before this episode, it was damn near impossible to conceive of a Jerry who was brave enough to fight for his family.

For Rick and Morty (and the rest of the gang) possible worlds aren't just convenient ways to talk about what might have been; they actually exist as alternate timelines. In addition, because of Rick's inventions Rick and Morty (and Jerry and Beth and Summer) can actually take a peek at what's going on in the other timelines and confirm that things really could have been different.

When Rick says that Hitler could have cured cancer, that's true because there literally is another timeline in which Hitler cured cancer. When Beth complains that she could have been a doctor for humans she's absolutely right that she could have been a doctor for humans, and the thing that makes her right is that there is another timeline with another version of Beth, and *that* Beth really did become a human doctor (and amassed a large bird collection to boot). When Jerry says that he could have been best friends with Johnny Depp, doing mountains of cocaine, and sleeping with Kristen Stewart on a boat, that's also true, because there really is another timeline in which a different version of Jerry does all of these things (and then, in an oddly romantic scene, breaks out of rehab to try and get Beth back).

The point is that in the universe of *Rick and Morty*, possible worlds aren't just an interesting idea, or an abstract collection of consistent claims; they actually exist as separate realities. Because of this, anytime someone in the *Rick and Morty* universe claims that things could have happened differently, whether it be a claim that Summer might not have been born, or a claim that Rick could have been just like Jerry, and that Morty could have been an Erik Stoltz mask person, all we need to do to prove that those claims are true is to point to the timeline in which those things really did happen. And we might even be able to do it from the comfort of our own living room, assuming our cable box has been hacked to receive signals from infinite universes.

Infinite Timelines Might Not Cover It All

So, everything that happens in other timelines is possible from the perspective of the universe our Rick and Morty are in, and any time they say something like 'Morty could have been a hammer person' that's true because Morty is a hammer person in a different timeline. But does that mean that all claims about the way things could have been will be realized in one (or many) of the alternate timelines?

In order to do the work that possible worlds are meant to do, in order to give truth conditions for all of our claims about possibility, then there would have to be a timeline for every possible way that things could have worked out. Should we think that all of the possible realities are represented among the infinite timelines that Rick and Morty have access to?

First of all, having infinite timelines doesn't imply that every possible situation has a corresponding timeline. To see why imagine that in this timeline Jerry has a favorite number and his favorite number is 1. This shouldn't be surprising, after all it's Jerry, and he's really just not that creative. But in spite of any suspicion we might have that Jerrys are all pretty uncreative, we must admit that it's at least possible for Jerry to have had a different favorite number. Let's say that in this timeline Jerry's favorite number is 1, and in the next timeline his favorite number is 3. The timeline after that his favorite number is 5, and in the one after that it is 7. We can continue generating timelines in this way, by keeping every detail the same, except that in each subsequent universe Jerry's favorite number changes to the next highest odd number, and this will give us an infinite number of timelines, one for each of the infinite odd numbers. So, we have infinite timelines, but not every possible state of affairs is represented. For starters we haven't generated any of the timelines where Jerry has even numbers for favorite numbers, so we've actually skipped an infinite number of possible situations. This means that there will be some claims about possibility that seem to be true, even though there is no timeline that corresponds to them. One such claim would be that it could have been the case that Jerry's favorite number was 2.

Having access to infinite timelines will give us a way to prove that many claims about what might have been were true, but it still might be the case that there are true claims about possibilities that do not have corresponding timelines, and as such we may still need to rely on our original abstract possible worlds, instead of actual possible worlds that Rick and Morty could travel to, in order to explain how some claims can be true. Rick does claim at one point that the television that we all get to enjoy during "Rixty Minutes" comes from every conceivable universe, and surely, we can conceive of universes in which Jerry has selected an even number as his most favorite of all numbers, but can we *conceive* of every possibility? If we can, and Rick's right that every conceivable universe exists as an alternate timeline, then perhaps every possibility is actualized somewhere out there among the infinite alternate realities. If that's the case, then maybe we didn't need to witness Jerry becoming a brave person in "Rick Potion #9" to consider the possibility of a brave Jerry.

But the tricky thing about trying to figure out whether there's anything we can't conceive of, is that if there is we'll probably be unable to realize it, due to our inability to even conceive of it. We can sometimes conceive of the impossible, like square circles, which can't exist in *any* timeline, but there might be things that are inconceivable to us, that can exist in some other timeline. When Rick and family are trying to look for another inhabitable Earth-like planet in "The Wedding Squanchers," Rick has to be strategic in finding a planet that is beyond federal jurisdiction. He decides to look for planets within the Milky Way (which is assumedly in the same dimension they're currently in) that fit the bill. One question that may arise is why didn't Rick look for a conceived reality where either the federation didn't exist or their jurisdiction didn't cover Earth? Was it a reality that Rick couldn't or didn't conceive of? Was that Earth-look-a-like somewhere out there and both Rick and his computer just failed to realize it? Maybe these possible worlds do exist, along with other non-weenie Jerrys.

At the very least there will be timelines to make all of the actual claims we will ever make true, because in order to make a claim about the way things might have been, I need to conceive of the way they might have been, and according to Rick all of the conceivable timelines do really exist. After all, there's a giant butt world, and a pizza people dimension, and a dimension where phone people eat sofa pizzas, and a dimension where sofa people use pizzas to order phones to eat while sitting on humans . . .

II

Come Watch TV

7
Rick and Morty as Socratic Television

JOHN ALTMANN

In "Mortynight Run," we see Rick and Morty go on an errand that Rick has to complete, which turns out to be a deal between Rick and an alien assassin for hire known as Krombopulos Michael. Rick gives Krombopulos an antimatter gun, and Krombopulos pays Rick enough money for Rick to enjoy a day at Blips & Chitz. Morty, however, is angry with Rick because he sold a gun to an assassin and Morty believes the blood of whomever Krombopulos killed with that gun would be on Rick's hands.

Morty goes to stop Krombopulos from killing his target and in doing so, accidentally crushes him with Rick's spaceship. Morty meets the alien assassin's would be target, a gaseous life form that appropriately is named Fart by Rick. They escape the government facility that Fart was held in and begin a hectic journey that results in a number of deaths, including the guards who were keeping watch over Fart, several Gear World police officers who were in pursuit of Rick and Morty, and civilians caught in the crossfire. The loss of life that resuls from this pursuit far outweighs the one life of Fart that Krombopulos had set out to kill. Morty remains convinced however that he stopped a murderer and that he is saving a good life.

When Rick and Morty reach the wormhole that Fart originally came through and Morty and Fart say their goodbyes, Fart reveals that he has every intention of returning to Earth with his race and eliminating all carbon-based life forms. Morty, deeply saddened and shocked by Fart's true intentions, shoots and kills Fart with the antimatter gun originally sold to

Krombopulos, making the deaths of the Gear police officers and Galactic Federation soldiers who pursued Rick, Morty, and Fart all meaningless.

The episode puts forth a moral argument through Morty, that selling guns to murderers for hire is wrong. Yet Fart, the target that Krombopulos was hired to kill, was determined to kill all carbon-based life forms. Morty's actions resulted in the loss of several lives on the principled belief that Fart's life had value, but in the end, it is Morty who pulls the trigger and murders Fart in the name of saving all carbon-based life. In this episode, the writers use Morty as a means of adopting a moral position and then having him abandon that position in light of new information.

This is exactly how Plato's Socratic dialogues were written, with one character having a certain view on justice or beauty, and then Socrates, by way of a certain line of argument, convincing that person that their view was flawed and needed to be examined further. We're meant to live through Morty's arc in this episode, as he is the one who has taken up a line of moral argument that is scrutinized throughout the episode, mostly by Rick, while we're left rooting for Morty, until finally that position is destroyed, leaving Morty without any kind of ethical footing.

Were Rick's actions in the beginning of this episode right after all? Is Morty worse than Krombopulos Michael since he killed several people in the name of protecting Fart? The answer is not so easy to arrive at because, despite Fart having immoral intentions, Krombopulos openly stated he loves killing and is even willing to kill children.

By positioning the characters and events this way, Dan Harmon and Justin Roiland force the viewer to engage the same moral problems as Morty, which causes us to be in a state of confusion about what our moral stances are on certain issues, thus beginning the process of doing moral philosophy.

Freedom through Unity?

In "Auto Erotic Assimilation," we see Rick, Morty, and Summer answering a distress beacon sent out by a ship. They happen upon a few surviving crew members who explain to them that an entity had come to their planet and taken it over through a kind of mind control. One of the crew members explains the entity's control on people by saying that "They look like your friends, your family, and your leaders, but they aren't really themselves."

Rick then asks the survivors what makes them think the entity didn't get on board with them, as he makes note of two unusually calm crew members, who are then revealed to be under the entity's control and help the entity take possession of the minds of the survivors. When Rick goes to kill the hosts of the entity aboard the ship, it says hello to Rick, who recognizes the voice as one belonging to a former girlfriend of his named Unity. The episode proceeds to have Unity give Rick, Morty, and Summer a tour around the planet she has taken control of, with the inhabitants appearing quite joyful and productive and the planet as a whole being successful, with crime, addiction, and bad behavior being non-existent. Unity explains to Rick that her ultimate plan is essentially to become God, and the planet she has taken over will aid her in this quest because Unity plans on turning it into a Type One civilization, which would give Unity membership into the Galactic Federation.

Once becoming a part of the Federation, Unity will have access to a multitude of other planets as well as resources that will make her ambitions of becoming God even easier to realize. Unity seems to think that prosperity and happiness is only achievable when everyone and everything is controlled by a singular entity such as herself. Summer however, disagrees with Unity and contends that Unity has no right to take away the free will of others just so it could realize its personal vision of safety and security. Later we see Rick and Unity intoxicated with Rick on drugs and alcohol, as he persuades her into participating in antics that become more questionable as the episode progresses. These antics cause Unity to lose her grip on the citizens of the planet, which allows their free will to return.

Summer is at first thrilled with this development, but soon several of the aliens on the planet begin showing a darker side of themselves, most notably their racism that's widespread throughout the planet based on varying nipple shapes and sizes. Soon, a race war erupts that destroys part of the planet and whose chaos leaves Summer exclaiming that "I didn't know freedom meant people doing things that suck. I was thinking more along the lines of a choose your own cell-phone cover kind of thing."

Summer and by extension all of us as viewers, are left in a state of confusion witnessing the race war between the cone nipple people and the concentric ring nipple people. This confusion stems from the fact that we believe freedom and personal liberty to be intrinsically good and don't have this view challenged, the same way Euthyphro has a strong personal sense of piety that isn't challenged until he encounters Socrates. Once he does, just as when Summer encounters Unity and her form of government, both individuals walk away from their encounters with their beliefs razed to the ground, to the point where Summer in particular even says that she thinks Unity is great and that Rick is bad for what he has done.

By *Rick and Morty* giving the idea of democracy a more critical examination with its characters and the world in which they find themselves, they make room for alternative forms of government to be given our consideration. One such alternative is paternalism, which Unity represents because she controls the conduct and is the sole provider of the needs of her citizens. This style of governance is most closely related to fascism, which we conventionally reject as being intrinsically bad and yet *Rick and Morty* on the other hand, paints paternalism in a positive light through Unity. The show imparts to us a challenge to our political beliefs and much like Summer, the end result is doubting if not even outright rejecting, our previous ideals. This doubt allows us to begin the task of doing political philosophy the same way philosophical confusion has given Summer a more nuanced perspective of the world.

Purge the Wealthy . . . Right?

In "Look Who's Purging Now," Rick and Morty stop by a planet to get wiper fluid for Rick's ship, on the eve of the planet having a holiday called the Festival, which sees all criminal activity legalized for a period of twenty-four hours. During the course of the Festival Rick and Morty befriend (and later get betrayed by), a young girl named Arthricia. Rick and Morty originally save Arthricia from being killed, but she thanks them by double-crossing them and stealing Rick's ship. When the two encounter Arthricia later and are prepared to kill her, Arthricia explains that she only did what she did because she is seeking to kill all of the rich people who force the poor people to kill each other.

In this era of profound wealth inequality both in this country and around the globe, one can easily identify and sympathize with Arthricia and her struggle to make the planet a better place. It appears with Arthricia's proclamation of her intentions, that Rick and Morty embrace the idea of wealth inequality. But as we know with *Rick and Morty*, appearances can be deceiving, and the show proposes an alternative view that is a bit more complex than "Eat the rich."

When Arthricia and Rick arrive at the mansion where the rich people have gathered and are fully decked out in power suits to slaughter them, it is as much a bloodbath as you would expect it to be. After Arthricia and Rick kill all of the rich people and Rick and Morty prepare to leave, the citizens who survived the purge try and organize a new society with the absence of a rich elite. Rick suggests a barter system based on food, but that leads to complications on who gets what responsibilities.

The argument erupts into violence until one of the townsfolk step in and suggests that because of the excess of aggression, they should set aside one day a year where they can get it all out of their system, essentially re-establishing the Festival all over again. Only this time, there is no rich elite to assign blame for the Festival. Sure, there will soon be a new wealthy class that exploits the Festival for their own benefit, but as the community comes to a foundational agreement, they also agree to go back to the past. So if the existence of the rich isn't the issue, what is, according to *Rick and Morty*?

Remember that at its heart, *Rick and Morty* is Socratic television and as such it doesn't offer up one single answer like most television shows would. The show instead decides to go the more interesting route and make us the viewers examine more closely the disagreements between two political mindsets: liberalism and conservatism.

While liberalism would never openly advocate for the rich to be murdered, it's a political philosophy that supports sweeping social change, which is what Arthricia thought she was causing by slaughtering the wealthy elite on her planet. Conservatism on the other hand, argues that human beings are creatures who can only accept social change at a gradual pace, and are animals of rituals, traditions, and customs. The townsfolk agree to make the Festival the foundation of their society, beginning the cycle over again. How is a society to be structured and governed? This is what Dan Harmon and Justin Roiland want you to think about both in our universe, and wherever else *Rick and Morty* is watched and thought about.

Conversations in the Marketplace

Before *Rick and Morty*, before the Popular Culture and Philosophy series, and even before the establishment of universities, people learned philosophy through teachers they'd encounter in the busy streets or in the marketplace. The most famous teacher, two and a half thousand years ago, was Socrates. Socrates is best known for the quote "All that I know is that I know nothing," quite the opposite of this day and age where every person with an Internet connection claims to know why gun control is good or why abortion should be illegal.

Most of our knowledge concerning Socrates comes from his most famous student, Plato, whose writings describe conversations Socrates had with various people. Through the literature produced by Plato, we get some insights into Socrates as a philosopher, like how his main technique was not to put forth any claims of his own, but instead to ask questions, with the aim of exposing the ignorance and thoughtlessness of those who thought they had knowledge. Socrates wanted to reduce these people to a state known as "aporia," which is Greek for confusion.

One example of this technique is seen in Plato's *Meno* dialogue, where Socrates tells Meno that he doesn't know what virtue is. With each successive definition Meno puts forth concerning virtue, Socrates exposes the flaws until Meno is forced to acknowledge that he doesn't know what virtue is, thus allowing Meno's confusion to emerge. Once a person's beliefs had been challenged and disproved through this Socratic Method, that person was then free to begin thinking and actively questioning the world around them.

Rick and Morty is Socratic television at its finest because at its core, the show really isn't about any one specific moral or theme, and just when you think a particular episode has embraced such an approach, it undermines it. The goal of the creators of *Rick and Morty* is to reduce us to a state of "aporia." But why instill in us confusion instead of virtues like friendship and kindness, as we see in most sitcoms? Because *Rick and Morty* doesn't give a squanch whether you feel good, are a nice person, or are a great friend.

All *Rick and Morty* cares about is making you think, since discovering meaning (or lack of meaning) in life, begins in thinking about it. This is what sets *Rick and Morty* apart from most standard television. Most television shows relay basic lessons to you such as the power of friendship or the value of sharing, and these lessons are depicted by run-of-the-mill conflicts and characters. *Rick and Morty* is a show of active consumption, in that it makes you think about the problems and answers it poses, through the confusion it leaves you with.

All that They Know Is . . .

While Rick and Morty never outright answer any of the issues they take up, this doesn't mean that like Socrates, they know that they know nothing. What they know is actually quite different. They know that each and every person who watches *Rick and Morty* can think, no matter how high on Kallaxian crystals they are.

Much like a Socratic dialogue where Socrates talks to Lysis about what friendship is, or when Socrates discusses with Charmides the nature of temperance, *Rick and Morty* trusts us to meet the issues they discuss through their characters head on. It also encourages us to trust our own reasoning, just like Socrates does when he pokes holes in the first answer a person may give him. He does this with Laches on his first definition of bravery, but Socrates urges him to use his reasoning to come up with a second definition and a third. *Rick and Morty* at its core is a show that celebrates the love of wisdom. Look no further than Rick Sanchez himself, the smartest man in the universe who knows everything there is to know. Yet with a void that is usually filled by human curiosity, Rick instead chooses to fill it with drinking, drugs, and crazy adventures.

Rick represents what happens when curiosity is no longer tended to or loved; it gives way to physical pleasures that grow dull with the passage of time. In this way, *Rick and Morty* may have one of the noblest aims of any television show currently in syndication, the preservation and furtherance of that same curiosity that Rick lost and that Socrates drank hemlock to protect.

Perhaps one day, Rick can find his curiosity and love of wisdom once again. But until that day, dear reader, no matter which universes you travel to; never forget the wonders and pleasures to be found in thinking. Because whether it's the morality of killing, the merits of individuality, or the nature of political society, it's our curiosity about these matters that makes the pursuit of their answers worthwhile—even across universes with a portal gun.

8

Neither the Hero You Deserve nor the Hero You Need

LESTER C. ABESAMIS

> Oh, I don't know, you managed to destroy just about everything today. The villains, the heroes, the lines in between them . . .
>
> —MORTY SMITH

The Vindicators are heroes, plain and simple. They have amazing abilities, which are helpful if you're in the business of fighting crime across the universe, or being the guardians of several star systems, or avenging the poor and defenseless, or founding a league that upholds justice (really trying to not get hit with copyright infringement here).

But let's face it: the Vindicators are nothing but a bunch of phonies who "write their own press releases." Just because they can save the day doesn't mean they're truly holier than thou.

On the surface, the Vindicators are heroic figures who stand in the face of injustice and maintain the peace and harmony of the universe in seemingly cool and stylish ways (I'm not sure if they're aware of a multiverse but surely there are much more unbearable iterations of these quasi-courageous, self-righteous pricks in parallel dimensions).

You've got Vance Maximus, the fearless and utterly cool leader who, unlike Rick, can make drinking look cool to young fanboys like Morty. There's Alan Rails, whose parents' tragic death gave him the incredible willpower to summon ghost trains. There's Supernova, a cosmic being with the power of a collapsing star who raises one deep philosophical question: why on Earth does she need teammates? You've got Million Ants, who is, by definition, made of one million ants and, more interestingly, is somehow totally boning Supernova. Last and quite possibly least, there's Crocubot, the cyborg crocodile who is as mysterious as he is boring.

Each of these characters feels the need to uphold some heroic persona but beneath the surface, they're deeply troubled and conflicted individuals perpetually masking the profundity of their existence by adopting meaningless values. This is made clear when a flustered Vance Maximus reveals he only recruited Morty because of a learning disability. On one level, this is inauthentic. On another, it's actually harmful. Even worse, the Vindicators don't realize their self-destructive behavior and it's up to someone like Rick to point it out for them in glorious Rick-like fashion.

One way to understand the tragedy that is the Vindicators is by looking at them through the lens of the avant-garde existential thinker Friedrich Nietzsche, who also provides a possible remedy for such troubled and conflicted individuals. If the Vindicators, and anyone similar to them, are mere charlatans, then maybe someone else in the series embodies the remedy Nietzsche suggests. It's time to take a look at our beloved heroes—all of them.

The Vindi-Fakers

The Vindicators follow a classic heroic blueprint where, because they have super powers and a vivid sense of righteousness, they must save poor and defenseless souls no matter the cost. As a team, they get contracted to fight against all forms of evil and in return they receive praise and adoration from citizens across the multiverse.

Someone calls them up to alert them about some catastrophic event or diabolical villain like Worldender and the Vindicators spring into action to save the day. The Vindicators themselves are the necessary force of good that stands up to wrongdoers (thank God we live in a world where good and evil are clearly defined!). To those who worship evil's might, beware the power of—uhh—a ghost train's light? Vance Maximus hits on the classic heroic ideal by saying, "Everyone in the universe is a hero. All you have to do is know the difference between good and bad, and root for good." Oh yeah, bootleg Star Lord? Is that all you need to know in order to be a hero? Is the distinction between good and evil really that clear? And are the good guys really the good guys?

Nietzsche tells of a loose genealogy of morality itself. One concept he brings to the table is the distinction between master and slave morality (no, this isn't simply slavery with extra steps). Master morality is the noble and superior individual's way of life that values strong traits like courage, usefulness, love of one's talents, and self-creation. At first glance, this may sound like a morality that the Vindicators—and any merry band of superheroes—uphold; however, if you're truly a noble person, then there's no reason to feel obligated to protect the weak and helpless as the Vindicators do. In fact, Nietzsche thinks such an obligation is an imaginary virtue conjured up by those who espouse slave morality! On top of that, Rick seems to truly uphold master morality traits, yet the Vindicators didn't invite him on their second adventure due to "personality conflicts." Maybe they couldn't stand an individual who is competent and who actually wields authority. The point is this: master morality is so badass that it doesn't give a damn about the weak.

To better understand master morality, it's helpful to introduce the concept of Will to Power, which refers to the individual's essential desire to control or dominate others by imposing their own will onto the world. We impose our will in all sorts of ways. Some of us might try to outdo all the other students in the classroom by getting the highest test scores. Others might seek to outperform their co-workers to get the promotion. Political leaders impose their ideologies through public speeches and campaigns. In "The Whirly Dirly Conspiracy," Risotto Groupon seeks to impose his will by taking revenge on Rick, the person responsible for his enslavement. Evil Morty is trying to impose his will onto the entire series by—well, I guess we'll have to see what his evil plan is. You get the picture. Now there are two types of people when it comes to Will to Power: those who express their Will to Power honestly and those who pretend to not impose their will to power at all. Essentially, everyone seeks to impose their own values onto the world whether they're aware of it or not.

Jerry is a great example of someone who expresses their Will to Power dishonestly. He acts as prey but is really a predator who primarily wants people to feel sorry for him. Even worse, he pretends like he's not imposing the value of self-pity at all. In "Something Ricked This Way Comes," he refuses to admit that Pluto isn't a planet. On the surface, it seems as if Jerry is vehemently arguing (let's call it) an intellectual point. Beneath the surface, he's manifesting his Will to Power by desperately trying to win an argument. It's not about Pluto at all; it's about trying to display your dominance in any way, shape, or form. Being full of shit about your need to dominate is, at best, an inauthentic way to live but at worst it can lead to devastating consequences, like nearly losing your penis in Jerry's case or losing a few members of your superhero squad in the Vindicator's case.

As someone who dishonestly expresses will to power, Jerry is also a great example of slave morality, the inferior person's moral system, which values weak traits like humility, pity, fear, guilt, obedience, purity, and forgiveness. Slave morality also requires constant approval from the masses or, as Nietzsche would call them, the herd. The masters, on the other hand, need no approval at all since their values are strong and independent (though at times, their values may harm those weaker than them).

Slaves have no choice but to value weak, resentful traits since they're not strong enough to dominate their masters. They also devise a ploy to turn the tables on their oppressors by employing an "imaginary revenge." Imagine a class of weak, powerless people making the powerful class feel guilty about their "oppressive" traits. Jerry does something similar by making people pity him and it works when it comes to Beth and his children but not for people like Rick. Additionally, the Vindicators claim to be incompatible with Rick to mask their jealousy but luckily, Rick doesn't feel bad about this.

But surely the Vindicators are strong individuals. They have superpowers, for crying out loud. They can do a hell of a lot more than the average person. Right, but the mighty Vindicators ironically fail to realize that they are upholding a false value: protect the weak at all costs. Initially, the masters in Nietzsche's framework had no reason to protect the weak. In fact, protecting the weak only hinders Will to Power and anything that hinders Will to Power is unhelpful, useless, and vulgar, which were the original associations for "bad". Anything that is useful to one's preservation and enhancement of life constituted the original meaning for "good."

This original meaning of good is what Rick Sanchez is all about. Rick is capable of inventing amazing, yet sometimes devastating, things. He's the noble individual, as Nietzsche would put it, who is despised by the weak for being "the evil, the cruel, the covetous" (we can make the argument that Rick stole the Vindicators from Morty, thus "oppressing" him). The original good versus bad distinction changed once the weak slaves revolted. The slaves redefined originally bad traits (like being unable to take revenge on your enemies) as good traits (like being able to forgive) and originally good traits (like self-love, courageousness, and domination) into, wait for it . . . evil traits (like pride, vanity, and greed)! In order to fully repress the masters' will to power, the slaves demanded protection from the strong. Such protection was seen as virtuous and maybe even favored by God, which is part of the "imaginary revenge."

What's the upshot of this so far? Well, it's not that the Vindicators were responsible for this flip-flop of moral values. They merely adopted a moral system that stemmed from what Nietzsche calls a bad conscience. However, they do perpetuate slave morality by feeling like they have to save the day all the time. If they were truly masters, they would use their God-given or accidental powers to unabashedly manifest their will to power. Maybe Vance Maximus would use his jetpack to steal a bunch of booze. Supernova might restructure elements so that it's possible for half a million ants to impregnate a collapsing star. Or Alan Rails would conjure up a ghost train that carries the ghosts of his dead parents. Look, it's not my fault that these superheroes are super unoriginal when it comes to dealing with their issues.

God Is Dead and Rick Has Killed Him

The whole point of the third Vindicators adventure was to stop Worldender from, well, ending worlds I suppose. The problem is that right when the adventure begins, we learn that Rick has nearly killed him, leaving the Vindicators in shock since their adventure basically stops here. Even worse, Rick was under the influence when he defeated Worldender. If what makes the Vindicators heroic is stopping villains like Worldender, what happens to their heroism if someone else saves the day? Also, how heroic are the Vindicators if Rick did their job in a fraction of the time and with a fraction of the effort (and a fraction of the brain cells)? I mean, the guy practically takes out a couple of "troublesome" gun turrets without any powers and without any epic music. Throw in the fact that he's hungover and it makes sense that he has spiteful haters.

Nietzsche introduces a concept that corresponds with the death of Worldender: the death of the world creator! "God is dead. God remains dead. And we have killed him." Yes, Nietzsche wrote about the death of God but he didn't exactly mean the end of the metaphysical yet possibly bearded entity in the sky who throws lightning bolts and sleeps with numerous female deities. Sorry, I get all of these origin stories mixed up. Anyway, the death of God went much deeper than that.

Nietzsche thought that all modern Western civilization, specifically the morality that was produced and preserved in Europe, relied on the existence of God. On the one hand, we do good things because God is watching. On the other, humans have flourished for so long because we obeyed God's commands. But at some point, something utterly remarkable happened: science. Yes, after some time we realized that humans evolved from single-cell organisms, that atoms exist and could be split apart, and these days we're trying to replicate consciousness either through artificial intelligence or through cloning. Is that what we're up to?

It doesn't matter. The point is we can try to do greater (yet, sometimes terrifying) things with science than with the belief in God. The force behind "God is dead" lies in the fact that humans got so smart and self-sufficient that the belief in God eventually lost its power and meaning. We're full of shit if we claim to believe in God because we certainly don't live lives that reflect that claim. The fact that a lot of people believe the world is older than ten thousand years is a testament to the scientific dubiousness of the Old Testament creation narrative. Maybe Morty's exclamation of "Oh my God!" after Kyle commits suicide is merely a product of tradition rather than genuine belief in God.

"God is dead" presents one daunting problem for humanity: how do we live in a godless universe? For the Vindicators, what the hell do we do in a Worldender-less adventure? Nietzsche might say "go on another adventure." In fact, there's another adventure right in front of the Vindicators: solving the Saw-like traps that drunk Rick set for them. Despite this new adventure being a necessary one, Vance Maximus instantly rejects his fate: "Screw this, I'm not playing this game. I'm gonna find us a way out of here." In other words, Vance thinks life shouldn't be this way. The circumstances have changed and he no longer likes them. He's even willing to suspend his heroic code and be a coward in order to try to escape his destiny.

Failing to acknowledge the death of the one thing that gave your life/adventure meaning can be detrimental to your existence. If, for instance, humanity still believed that diseases were dished out as a punishment from God and there was nothing humans could do about them, then cures would never have been discovered. If everyone in the world thought that the Cromulons were to be prayed to rather than impressed through a cosmic talent show, the world would have likely perished. In Vance's case, ignoring the truth that Worldender was defeated by a much more sinister foe cost him his life.

The death of God has also given us an incredible amount of freedom. The twentieth century saw its share of devastation through horrible technological advancements such as the development of mustard gas, gas chambers, and the atomic bomb (luckily, these are balanced out thanks to the alternate dimension where Hitler cured cancer). Likewise, Rick is competent enough to flee from Earth C-137 after turning its population into horrible monsters. Yet, his competence could have also located Doom-Nomitron, which would have sidestepped the destruction of Dorian 5 as well as saved the lives of a few ex-Vindicators. Rick's usefulness also promotes self-preservation as he's able to lace his skin with defensive nanofibers making him impervious to most of the Vindicator's attacks. Was it right for Rick to Cronenberg the world and leave it? Was it right for the twentieth century to develop such weapons of destruction? I don't know. And neither does God. Because God is dead. By the way, where was Supernova's telekinesis choke earlier in this episode!? I bet if she didn't abide by false values, she could have easily killed Rick earlier on.

Worldender isn't the only significant death in this episode. Morty recognizes the flaws Rick tries to point out about the Vindicators. He's the first to realize their unoriginal and generic backstories. During the basketball trap, he's able to disarm the neutrino bomb and he's clever enough to figure out that the answer to one puzzle was "Israel". He basically completes the mission because he knows drunk Rick so well—not because he's heroic and wears a Vindicator's jacket. Morty is able to save the day because of his useful qualities. In other words, Morty's "God"—in this case the Vindicators—is also dead, although he fully recognizes this truth and is able to continue carrying on in the world without any sort of external guidance. Nobody (not Rick and definitely not God) can tell Morty how to act from here on out. So, both Worldender and the Vindicators (figuratively and mostly literally) are dead and Rick has killed them. Surely that makes Rick the baddest, most superior individual of all time, right? Slow your roll dog.

One in a Million or One Million Ants above the Herd?

The Übermensch or superman is Nietzsche's ideal individual who rises above the masses into true greatness. Who do they rise above? The herd. That's the entire group of people who uphold weak virtues and "put on airs as if they were the only acceptable type of human being."

The herd seeks solace in other people by way of receiving praise, adoration, compliments, and consoling advice. The Vindicators receive praise from people they protect and surely keep each other's spirits up during missions. This is evident after they refuse to work with Rick on Vindicators 2 due to his inability to work well with others; plus, Rick isn't really the type to give compliments to anyone except maybe Noob-Noob, Beth, and Bird-Person (but only on his wedding day). He's the anti-hero who's despised by superheroes. Herd mentality can also be found at the end of the episode when Gearhead, having donned Morty's Vindicators jacket, is elated when he's praised for being a Vindicator. However, just like how the herd can't do anything to meaningfully solve their problems, Gearhead ends up running in fear once danger comes his way. Likewise, those who uphold slave morality can't find meaning without the approval and guidance of the herd.

Thanks to the inversion of values initiated by the slave revolt, good and bad have been perverted into good and evil and society can't simply return to the days of old when masters reigned supreme. Instead of merely reacting to moral systems of the past, the Übermensch must create a new value system, which is tricky to do since it's unclear how you're supposed to successfully ignore prior value systems. Even if you wanted to be a master or an Übermensch, wouldn't you merely be reacting to the desperate need to become a superior individual?

Nietzsche gives a symbolic clue for truly achieving Übermensch status. The clue lies in his metaphor of the camel, the lion, and the child. The camel represents the beast of burden "that would bear much" and is "wanting to be loaded." The camel symbolizes the person who indiscriminately adopts all sorts of values. This is Morty during most of the series, since he frequently suggests what Rick should or shouldn't do based on some adopted, often traditional morality. One notch above the camel is the lion who "would conquer their own freedom and be master in their own desert" and who is willing to "fight with the great dragon . . . whom the spirit will no longer call lord and god." Unlike the camel, the lion fearlessly challenges meaningless, burdensome values, such as the notion of God and previous value systems. This is Morty during the Vindicators 3 adventure. He undercuts the heroic ideal and instead relies on values that are truly useful in order to save the day.

The third stage in Nietzsche's analogy is the child who represents "innocence and forgetting, a new beginning, a game, a self-propelled wheel, a first movement." Because of the child's innocent nature, they're able to create a truly novel value system free from any slave-like reaction. The metaphorical child hasn't yet been corrupted by the world of false value systems that have been perpetuated by resentment. Think of how children are free to create the rules of the game, then change or break the rules without any sense of remorse or long-lasting frustration. Additionally, the playful nature of the child is also found in the Übermensch's view of their enemies:

> To be able to take one's own enemies, accidents, and misdeeds seriously for long—that is the sign of strong and rich natures . . . Such a man simply shakes off with one shrug much vermin that would have buried itself deep in others; here alone is it also possible . . . that there

be real "love of one's enemies." How much respect has a noble person for his enemies!

As Supernova escapes, Rick reveals that twenty people try to kill him every week, yet he ends up hanging out and getting high with half of them. For Rick, going on adventures is nothing more than a playful game. If he finds himself in a disadvantageous situation, rather than turning to frustration and resentment, Rick improvises just as a child spontaneously acts (even when his ability to improvise has literally been taken away). Rick truly loves and respects his enemies as well as any hardships that come his way. He even wishes hardship to those around him, even if that requires putting his grandson's heroes through a torturous Saw-like gauntlet. He welcomes any and every challenge, which seems to make a strong case for his being the Übermensch . . . right?

Right? Surely I'm not about to suggest that Rick isn't an Übermensch. Surely I'm not about to undermine one of the most badass characters in the history of adult cartoon television. Oh, no. I am. In truly Nietzschean fashion, let's do philosophy with a hammer and smash the statue that is Rick Sanchez to see if it contains any meaningful values. Does Rick actually create new values? Yes, he's a brilliant inventor who doesn't get hung up on petty moral quandaries but just because you can reject values doesn't mean you can create values. Rick may just be Nietzsche's lion, who "masters his own desert" but doesn't do anything to reinvent or even break the wheel.

Secondly, Rick's sense of freedom might be much broader than the average person's but does he also fall victim to slavish values? Let's take a look at two in particular: envy (despising those who have more than you) and pity (feeling sorry for those weaker than you). Maybe he's envious of the Vindicators because Morty idolizes them or he pities Noob-Noob because the Vindicators make him do all the dirty work. Both of these possibilities suggest a sense of resentment toward the Vindicators. Resentment comes with reaction, which is unlike Nietzsche's innocent and self-creating child. Maybe if Rick were truly a child, he would have created a Morty clone for him to keep while the real Morty remained with his heroes!

You Either Die a Hero or Live Long Enough to Create a Portal Gun

Because Rick C-137 is somewhat tainted by resentment, maybe we can look elsewhere for a better candidate to be Übermensch. Maybe it's Morty since he's starting to overcome the slavish values that his idiot dad has instilled in him. He's a good case, especially since he's the MVP during the Vindicator's adventure but as of right now he's still Rick's little bitch. Thanks to the Vindicator's comic book, we see that Noob-Noob overcomes his hardship and transforms into something greater, which could be a good indicator of Übermensch status if we had more information about his motivation to collect the Infinity Balls. But frankly, we want Rick to be the Übermensch. So, maybe another Rick.

Could it be the Rick found in "The Rickshank Rickdemption" who was seemingly content (and assumedly devoid of resentment) with his life before losing his family to a bomb planted by another Rick? After tragedy strikes, this Rick is compelled to create the portal gun, which may signify a new, creative beginning in life. There are problems with this suggestion since we find out that this content Rick was merely a fabricated origin story.

What about Simple Rick in "The Ricklantis Mixup"? He seems truly happy and resentment-free given the fact that happy brain chemicals, produced from his most pleasant memories with Beth, are extracted from his head to produce Simple Rick Wafers. Behaviorally, he's the only other Rick to regularly sport a content facial expression (until he's replaced) as opposed to a disinterested booze barf-y frown. Additionally, there may be some correlation between Simple Rick and the Rick in the fabricated origin story. It's been suggested that fabricated Rick could be based on Simple Rick—although that may be a stretch since it's unclear whether Rick C-137 ever crossed paths with Simple Rick. It's also possible that fabricated Rick wasn't completely made up. Instead, it's been suggested that Rick C-137 was sent to kill this Rick's family in order to kidnap him for happy brain chemicals.

We'll have to wait and see before confirming or denying these theories but regardless, it's possible that Simple Rick and "fabricated" Rick were happy, creative, non-resentful, and true

Nietzschean supermen at earlier stages in their lives. In both of these happy iterations, Rick hasn't yet created the portal gun. Fabricated Rick was happy before inter-dimensional travel was invented in his world and Simple Rick may never have even discovered interdimensional travel at all—nor will he ever do so since he meets his fate in the Blender Dimension. Could it be that Rick's creation of the portal gun, which may have been a reaction to the death of his family, is the event that sent him hurling down the path of resentment? Is the entire series one big resentful reaction?

If Rick was in fact an Übermensch in the past, then it seems possible to experience such a traumatic event that you devolve into a resentful, inferior, and deeply conflicted individual. Although Rick doesn't seek comfort from the herd, we can find glimmers of weak and false values in his character. Yes, he's clever and incredibly competent but what exactly fuels his will to power? Is it the case that he's brilliant because he's still resentful about the death of his family? Or is he brilliant independent of any traumatizing event? Is his tragic origin story just as unoriginal as Alan Rails's? Or is there a fine line between Rick's reactive achievements and Rails's reaction to his parents' death?

Let me address one point before I start receiving reactive death threats. Despite his potential flaws, Rick is a probably one of the best candidates to be Übermensch. He's a creative genius who's habitually unafraid of imposing his Will to Power in the form of being an exceptional scientist, so if he does possess brief instances of resentment, we can surely cut him some slack. Hell, if Rick were a real person, he'd probably be at the pinnacle of human greatness all things considered. He dated and abused a hive mind, for crying out loud.

But the point here isn't to find and glorify an Übermensch who will let us all sleep well at night. The point is to understand what it takes to truly rise above the herd and sometimes that means not having any heroes at all.

9

The Fallacy of the Many Heads

COURTNEY BERESHEIM

R*ick and Morty* is grounded on logic, science, rationality, and proving everyone else to be mentally inferior to Rick.

While the universe itself is meaningless and absurd, it can be understood and follows reliable scientific principles (as long as you're smart enough to understand them, like Rick). False or mistaken beliefs are nothing new to the show; however, the most notable instance of false belief is seen in "Get Schwifty" and the worship of the Giant Floating Heads (actually known as the Cromulons).

While the Cromulons are in reality only interested in discovering hit songs for their reality show, the other characters on the show have zero access to that information, and have to make do with their best guesses, which leads to the founding of a new religion. Father Bob says that "Every crisis of faith is an opportunity for more faith," and Principal Vagina takes this to heart, deciding to pray to the giant floating heads instead.

Unknown to Principal Vagina and the other churchgoers, Rick and Morty are performing their new hit song, pleasing the Cromulons. Through sheer chance, Rick and Morty satisfy the Cromulons at the same time the others exit to find Principal Vagina praying, which everyone takes as the cause of the Giant Floating Heads' praise. Principal Vagina is elevated as knowing the new path according to the Giant Heads, thereby solidifying a false cause-and-effect relationship, and creating a brand-new religion—Headism.

Headism is quickly and firmly established and strengthened through each false correlation, until the Cromulons declare Earth the winner, and return the Earth to its original place. While the characters only briefly deal with their false belief, they're confronted with their own foolishness, and the fact that "We may have been correlating some things that weren't actually related at all." This failure to know what's actually happening (what's "right") is a prime example of our larger problem as humans to think we know what we're talking about, even when that is the farthest thing from the truth. Principal Vagina *thinks* he's right, and that's exactly what the problem is.

Giant Head? We Should Pray

As every eager psychology student will tell you, correlation does not equal causation. Correlation is when two events are connected, or happen together; causation is when one event causes the next. This is one of the easiest fallacies to fall into, and is the reason why the religion of Headism appears.

Cause and effect is a seemingly simple concept, yet its simplicity is what makes it so dangerous. Humans love to find patterns and relationships between events, and we are exceptionally skilled at creating links, even if none exist. As a result, the phenomenon known as the illusory correlation not only exists, but can also be easily reinforced and strengthened with little effort and sometimes little to no opportunity to be fixed.

Essentially, because one thing follows another, we assume that Event A caused Event B. This fallacy is then further reinforced with every subsequent false positive (when something is found to be "true" when it actually is false). At this point, one mistake becomes two, then four, then next thing you know you're sending your neighbors into the sky to please the Giant Heads. The problem with the illusory correlation then is that it often isn't just a single mistake, but one that compounds, growing worse and worse with no opportunity to be corrected.

"Get Schwifty" is rife with false positives that power this illusory correlation. The first example occurs when Principal Vagina walks out of the church because he's going to pray "to the thing that literally controls the fucking weather" ("Get Schwifty"). The other characters follow him outside, find him praying, and then hear the Giant Head's approval. From the characters' point of view, all of these things have a direct cause-

and-effect relationship, and the characters have little incentive to believe that this is mistaken.

Once Principal Vagina is outside praying, according to the point of view of the characters, they see him praying, and then the Giant Head approves. Event A (praying) immediately precedes Event B (approval by the Giant Head). As the other characters file out of the church, this is all the information they have to work with. While Beth is skeptical, her skepticism (Event A) is then immediately followed by an earthquake and transportation to outer space, which is interpreted as disapproval (Event B). Summer leads the crowd as she falls to her knees and prays, "Oh dear Giant Head, we apologize for that discussion! It will never happen again!" Because the characters don't have access to the reality TV show feed, they have no idea what the true cause and effect relationship is, and therefore don't have enough information to make accurate decisions—but they still *make* decisions, because that's what humans do. And the decisions they make, though seemingly accurate, are in reality terrible decisions that have zero foundation in reality.

The desire to find patterns is unavoidable, and the patterns found will be based on the available information. Incomplete information opens us up to mistaken conclusions, which can be further compounded by false information.

I Relay the Will of the Giant Heads

Principal Vagina further accelerates and feeds this fallacy, as he is in a position of power. The next time we see the group, they now have religious dress, and Principal Vagina, through the use of a satellite dish, is shown to receive direct communication from the Giant Heads: "Thank you sir, thank you. He says he's proud of what we're doing and hopes we have a great Ascension Festival! Happy Ascension!"

Because Principal Vagina was right before, he is viewed as continuing to be right. Similar to the "hot hand" fallacy often viewed in sports (where a player is "hot" because they are repeatedly scoring or doing well), Principal Vagina, until explicitly proven wrong, is believed to be right, and as result, he can take complete advantage of this incorrectly placed trust (even though it is arguable that he is conning people into believing he can speak to the Giant Heads, something we as the audience know is not happening at all). His authority is established very quickly—this episode takes places over the course of hours. Not only is a new religion completely developed and implemented, but the entire community buys into it, albeit with differing levels of enthusiasm and belief.

Why was this so easy then? As Daniel Kahneman points out, humans are not terribly good at being rational, and we often fall into our automatic processes of thinking, which is where we make snap decisions. This can be based on memorized information (for example, you just know that 2 + 2 = 4, you don't even have to think about it), or be powered by heuristics (mental short cuts, like default settings that help us get through life quickly) and biases (Oh, that girl is pretty, therefore she must be nice). Our brains are inherently lazy and prefer the easier, automatic process of thought, rather than the more time-consuming, effortful, and deliberate thinking process. Kahneman splits these two types of thinking into System 1 (automatic and faster) and System 2 (slower and more deliberate) and argues that most of our thinking falls into the former category. Because our brains are wired to be efficient, we often don't look to be proven wrong, which makes realizing we're wrong all that much harder—but we can be proven wrong, as we see play out in the end of "Get Schwifty."

All I Know Is I'm Right

Principal Vagina and the town residents are not bad people, they're just *people*. And people don't like to think. Back in the day, this was because thinking required energy, and in the hunter-gatherer days, that energy needed to spent on more important things like staying alive rather then figuring out whether that rustling in the bushes was just the wind or whether it was an animal about to attack.

There are two easy ways to think about this type of result: false positives, or false negatives. A false positive is when you think something is real when it's not (like believing in the Giant Heads), and a false negative is when you think something isn't true, but it really is (that this experiment is totally safe, but then you get blown up, like at the end of "Rick Potion #9," when Rick and Morty slip into the lives of the recently deceased Rick and Morty).

Most of the time, we default to the automatic type of thinking, because most of the time it works out for us. It's also much, *much* easier than thinking critically and deeply about everything. False positives also tend to be safer: it doesn't hurt you to run away from a bush that turns out to be empty, but it will kill you if you stay by a bush you think is empty, and then an animal comes and eats you. As Principal Vagina says, it just makes better sense to pray to the thing that controls the fucking weather than to do something else. Based on the information we have, our brains will take the path of least resistance. The problem comes in when that path is wrong, but we're too lazy to double-check it.

Life-and-death situations are a prime example where we will fall back on this easier, heuristic-based type of thinking. Just as Jerry is unable to realize he's in a simulation in "M. Night Shaym-Aliens!", we don't stop to think about things that seem to make sense, because if it makes sense, what's the use in looking to double check on the off chance we're wrong? Hopefully, we don't make as big a mistake as Jerry when we fail to realize we're utterly wrong, but the example is a stark one: we don't look to be proven wrong.

The Will of the Heads!

The illusory correlation happens over the course of the entire episode, and Headism eventually comes to a head. After Beth and Jerry refuse their offered positions in Headism, they're tied up and prepared to ascend. From the characters' point of view, just as Principal Vagina is about to cut their tethers, the Heads become angry. Nervously, Principal Vagina says "I'm sure that has . . . that has nothing to do with this." However, he is no longer the authority on what the Heads are saying, because everyone else sees what he sees. As soon as the ropes are cut, the Heads begin to boo, and Summer shouts "The Heads are displeased!" and jumps to weigh her parents back down to the Earth.

This is immediately followed by Heads cheering, so the new narrative is that "The Heads love this! They love it when we DON'T kill the Smith family!" The same principle of correlation equaling causation is seen here, just as the show juxtaposes it and shows us that it is not the case, as we the viewers know what Rick, Morty, and Ice-T are really doing with the new hit song. The characters *are trying to be* rational (they do change their behavior when introduced to new information); they just fail to recognize that they don't have *enough* information in order to act rationally.

When the Heads shout "disqualified," the characters interpret it that Principal Vagina no longer has privileged status, and they act accordingly. In other words, they act *rationally* based on the information available to them; what they fail to realize is that this is insufficient. They have been wrong the entire time, but because they are operating on incomplete information, and following the automatic System 1 style of thinking, they are mistaken in their worship. We can judge the characters (and certainly, we do), but we need to realize we could just as easily be worshiping the Giant Heads ourselves.

As a result, the characters are operating under this automatic thinking, which is bad enough. However, they fail to stop and evaluate their circumstances (except perhaps for Beth and Jerry), and this behavior *is* representative of behavior at large. Most people look to confirm that they're right rather than prove that they are wrong, which is known as confirmation bias. The characters move forward creating their new religion, treating every new event as correct because that's what they *want* to believe, and without direct evidence to the contrary, they believe it.

In "Whirly Dirly Conspiracy," when Beth is trying to shrink Summer (and then stop her being inside out) with the Morphizer-XE, she refuses to listen to Morty, because she's so sure she has the process right, even though she clearly doesn't know what she's doing. Even after releasing the three trapped operators, Beth is still waiting on the phone, convinced that she will get further help with the Morphizer-XE, a perfect pairing of automatic thinking and refusing to look at contradicting evidence.

Peter Wason found the same thing in a famous psychology study, and that people will only try to prove what they already think is correct. As Kahneman showed, it takes effort to stop and think purposefully; it's far easier to go ahead with our first impressions and automatic thinking. In order to stop the illusory correlation and confirmation bias, we need to stop and think if we are wrong—something no one is terribly excited to do. The problem this reveals then is that even if people are operating under false perceptions, more likely than not, they will not seek to disprove those assumptions, they'll double down, and they'll keep worshipping Giant Heads.

This is the exact critique against any system of faith that relies on the supernatural or religious. Religion is founded on faith—by that definition, it doesn't require facts, only belief, which makes it pretty hard to argue against since there is no fact. And even when those religions are confronted with facts (for example, the Bible saying the world is approximately six thousand years old, when scientific evidence argues it is billions of years old), many followers of religion will disregard that information, or will integrate it in a way that will still allow their core belief to function (for example, believing the creation story is an allegory rather than empirical fact).

This same note applies to seekers of the paranormal or supernatural. When ghosts were first photographed in the nineteenth century, many of them were human-shaped. However, as the years went on, they became balls of light . . . which surely has nothing to do with camera technology improving and shutter speeds increasing. If you want to believe that you saw a ghost, you're probably just going to go with that automatic thought process, and will not develop a scientifically sound test to evaluate your initial hypothesis. We want to believe what we believe, whether that is based on our religious beliefs or something else, the patterns we observe and the stories we tell ourselves about those patterns become fixed.

The illusory correlation can become fixed and solid, even while many would argue that those beliefs are incorrect—just think about all the people who still believe in the Loch Ness Monster, even after the famous photograph was revealed, by the very man who took it in the first place, to be a hoax. While religion is the most attacked (and certainly is on *Rick and Morty*), it is by no means the only belief that falls prey to this effect.

Particle Beam in a Wristwatch, Snake Holster on the Leg

The good news is that these fallacies can be overcome; while none of the characters realize they are wrong, a simple call to Rick and Morty could let them know what was happening.

Even a quick, "Not now Summer, we're singing for the Giant Heads," and everyone would have realized what had happened (it's almost surprising that they *don't* turn to Rick sooner, seeing as this literally fits into his pseudo-job description).

As confirmation bias shows us, though, we're reluctant to look for proof that we're wrong. As a result, the episode ends with the end of Headism, after the Heads themselves declare Earth the winner, not by the characters realizing on their own that they've been mistaken. This evidence is unarguable, and the characters (presumably) quickly adapt their mindsets around this new information, even though we don't see this process fully roll out. People will not seek out this information on their own, and can readily disregard contrary information.

We can try to be better, or at least smarter. We may not need to go as far as René Descartes and declare that in order to trust something, we must first doubt *everything*, but maybe we should realize that just because a laser beam is followed by a snake, this doesn't mean that Rick actually turned that guy into a snake. Rick's devotion to science is admirable, and he is often the only person to see things clearly, but even Rick has his blind spots.

Approaching the world with a healthy level of skepticism requires work (not comfortable and easy automatic thinking), but it does lessen our chances of creating false religions out of fear. While Rick represents one far extreme (existence is meaningless, people are easily fooled and controlled), we don't have to live in the extremes, but can instead take the advantages we see, and use them as a buffer against self-deception.

So, when a Giant Head appears in the sky, jumping to conclusions may be easy, but healthy skepticism can help prevent the illusory correlation and confirmation bias from getting the best of us.

Or we might accidently shoot Mr. Poopybutthole. You win some; you lose some.

10
On Being and Meeseeks

CHARLES KLAYMAN

Throughout our history, there are some questions we haven't been able to answer to everyone's satisfaction. Those questions address fundamental issues, such as the very nature of reality, the purpose—if there is any—for our existence, how we determine what's important, and how should we conduct ourselves in order to live better lives.

Those questions don't particularly bother us in our daily lives and in fact, some people don't even think about them throughout their entire lifetime, but the questions nevertheless lurk in the background of human existence. It seems the only ones preoccupied with them are philosophers, whose answers often lead to more perplexing questions. It looks pretty useless to find answers where there might not be any at all, but if we ignore those questions, then how will we ever know if there are answers? So, we keep asking them and exploring the paths they may take us.

It might take countless of generations to find at least one answer that satisfies everyone and that's assuming it can be done, but there's a group in the *Rick and Morty* multiverse who have done it, who have answers that satisfy their species. The Meeseeks have their own take on life; they have their own distinctive philosophy. They claim the nature of life and existence is pain and that the purpose of their existence is to achieve a singular goal, which determines how they should conduct themselves. Despite their cheerfulness and eagerness, they're tragic characters who strive to live successfully in order to be rewarded with death. Only by being successful can a Meeseeks achieve death.

Introducing Mr. Meeseeks!

In "Meeseeks and Destroy," Rick introduces the Smith family to a Meeseeks box, a cubical device with a single button. When the button is pressed, a blue humanoid appears, happily exclaiming something like "I'm Mr. Meeseeks! Look at me!" The person who pressed the button makes a request, which the Meeseeks fulfills, and then Mr. Meeseeks promptly ceases to exist, disappearing into a puff of particles. While Beth's and Summer's Meeseeks accomplished their respective tasks, Jerry's request—to get two strokes off his golf game—seemed unachievable. Mr. Meeseeks summons additional Meeseeks for assistance and Jerry's request eventually gets fulfilled despite the chaos created along the way.

But what are Meeseeks other than blue humanoids? They appear as male or at least address themselves in the masculine. Perhaps they're aliens from another planet or an alternate dimension. Perhaps the Meeseeks box only summons males or perhaps they reproduce asexually. We're told that "Meeseeks are not born into this world," instead they're "created to serve a singular purpose." If that's so, then it implies they came into existence by artificial means; they weren't born, so they must be androids or synthetic beings. But they aren't made from mechanical parts. They fought each other and ripped out each other's limbs, which revealed no evidence of machinery. Perhaps they're clones since they resemble each other and sound alike. We could continue speculating until we're blue in the face about what sort of beings Meeseeks are, but that wouldn't give us an understanding of what it means to be a Meeseeks.

The point is, it doesn't matter whether Meeseeks are clones or synthetic humanoids; they seem to be *persons*. In ethics, a "person" is someone or something that has moral rights, such as the right to life, and a person's moral rights should be respected. What something needs in order to be considered a person is an entirely different topic. I use "person" to refer to those sorts of things that are conscious of themselves and their surroundings, exhibit free will, have feelings and desires, can make future plans, and are distinctly unique and different from other persons. In other words, a person is a being that is sentient like us.

While Meeseeks resemble each other, they are individuals nonetheless. They come into existence demanding to be recognized by saying "Look at me!" then they draw attention to their individuality by announcing "I'm Mr. Meeseeks!" Because they resemble each other, you might believe their declaration of "I'm Mr. Meeseeks" isn't really important because they're the same, they have the same identity. They're all Mr. Meeseeks with the same purpose. So, a roomful of Meeseeks is really a roomful of the same Mr. Meeseeks, but that's like saying a roomful of Ricks would be a roomful of the same Rick. Obviously, an infinite amount of Ricks, Mortys, and even Jerrys aren't exactly the same. They have common characteristics. For instance, every Rick is awesome (even Doofus Rick to a certain extent), but not every Rick agrees with the Council of Ricks. Every Jerry is a loser, but not every Jerry worked in advertising.

Despite their common characteristics, no two Meeseeks are exactly the same. One Mr. Meeseeks isn't the same as another Mr. Meekseeks. If they were the same, they would be identical in every way; they would act the same, think the same, and even come up with the same plan to improve Jerry's game. Instead we have Meeseeks who disagree, argue, and fight one another. One believed choking up was the solution, another believed it was following through, and another believed killing Jerry was the only solution. If they were all exactly the same, then what's the point for one Meeseeks to summon another when the first failed to help? If they were exactly the same, the second one would just repeat what the first one did. It's like if every Morty was the same Morty from dimension C-137, then it would be impossible to have an evil Morty.

If each Meeseeks is an individual person, then they each have free will, the ability to think for themselves and make their own decisions, but they believe they were created "to serve a singular purpose" and that would mean they're not free to deviate from that purpose. Yet, what does it mean to be a person who is confined to one purpose? Also, they perceive existence as pain so can't they commit suicide as an easy way out? Do they really need to the complete the task in order to return to a state of nonexistence?

Sorting Out the Existential Calamity

While we don't know what it is to be a Meeseeks first-hand, we can perhaps understand the nature of their existence by using our own existence as a model and the perspective of *existentialism*, which asks questions about the meaning and nature of our existence. Although existentialists disagree about some of the basic concepts, there is nonetheless a common existentialist theme that human beings are naturally free or, as one existentialist might say, humans are cursed to be free so we have no choice except to exercise our free will by making choices; we are forced to be free.

Someone might argue that existentialism isn't a good tool since it emphasizes *human* existence as opposed to Meeseeks existence. We're born into this world whereas they're created. We're also more complicated than Meeseeks since we're not restricted to one singular purpose. They are created for a singular purpose whereas we fumble around for meaning. They'll go to any lengths to fulfill their purpose whereas we can quit whenever we want, but it isn't the purpose that's important here. What's important is the nature of their existence and their existence is a lot like ours. They experience emotions, are self-aware, and can form ideas and opinions; they're sentient like us. If existentialism can't tell us what it means to be a Meeseeks, it may at least let us know how similar their existence is to ours. So, what about our existence?

From the standpoint of Jean-Paul Sartre's brand of existentialism, there are two types of existences; being-in-itself and being-for-itself. Being-in-itself are things like tables, pencils, rocks, things that pretty much don't have a mind or sentience. Being-for-itself are those things that have a mind, are conscious of themselves, and can think about their own existence. The for-itself has what we call *subjectivity*, which is to say we're conscious of ourselves in the present, we can imagine ourselves somewhere in the future, and we're aware that we're moving towards the future.

Basically, we have the power to set a goal and work towards that goal by creating the future we envisioned. That requires what Sartre called *transcendence*, which is when we drift off into our thoughts and where we imagine a future and mentally explore possibilities and potentialities. Transcendence is contrasted with *facticity*, which says there are actual conditions that we cannot escape from. For example, our existence is necessarily bound to the physical world. When we imagine where we want to be in life, we essentially *transcend* from the *fact* that we have a physical existence in the present time, but we can't escape that existence. Morty can imagine being married to Jessica, but the fact of the matter is she's going steady with Brad and only sees Morty as a classmate.

When Mr. Meeseeks imagined Jerry's improved golf game, he envisioned it as a potentiality despite the fact that at that point Jerry sucked at golf. So, human existence is primarily being-for-itself but it also can include an aspect of being-in-itself. Our bodies are mere objects; we may have to force our bodies to do certain things it resists. Just like how after he was shot by Beth, Mr. Poopybutthole, as part of his physical therapy, had to force his body to walk in order to regain his mobility.

Along with distinguishing two types of existences, Sartre also gave us two ways of judging value or meaning of existence. First, there's *essence precedes existence*, which says things are created with a purpose in mind. For things that aren't sentient like a table or a robot that passes butter, its meaning or essence was first thought of, then it was made or brought into existence to fulfill that meaning. For all created objects, their essence and presence were predetermined. Rick had the idea to make a robot to pass the butter, then he created a robot to do specifically just that.

Second, there's *existence precedes essence*, which means things don't have a purpose from the get-go. Humans are prime examples. We have minds but our existence came before we developed the ability to assign a purpose or meaning to our lives. It's just as Morty said, "Nobody exists on purpose. Nobody belongs anywhere." A person wishes to be a lawyer and enters law school to fulfill that purpose. Her life is defined by the choices she made; while in school, her life and identity aren't that of a lawyer but rather of a law student. But if she discovered she doesn't like law and decides to become a horse surgeon, then she consciously and intentionally changed the meaning of her life.

Beth wasn't predetermined to be a law student or a lawyer, she choose her own essence or meaning. As a result of her choices, Beth *is* a horse surgeon and not merely someone who practices horse surgery. The meaning of our existence is flexible, we can change it. Beth choose for herself what to be; she chose to be a horse surgeon, a mother, and a wife. Yet what she chose for herself is commonly seen as a social function, which she mistakenly identifies as her essence. People see Beth as a horse surgeon, mother, and wife but she isn't limited to those three things.

What about the rest of her? As philosopher William Barrett put it, the rest of her "is allowed to subsist as best it can—usually to be dropped below the surface of consciousness and forgotten" (*Irrational Man*, p. 36). Beth eventually saw herself *only* as a horse surgeon, mother, and wife; she forgot that she's more than just those things; she is an individual who is free to change or modify her essence. Luckily Mr. Meeseeks reminded her that "having a family doesn't mean you stop being an individual." Identifying herself as a mother and wife, Beth assumes a social role that has value within a family; yet Beth is a unique individual who is free to define herself in any way that she believes is right or appropriate.

So, a being with subjectivity determines their own meaning and identity; they choose it for themselves. They are essentially free but to deny that freedom is what Sartre called *bad faith*. In order to make a choice, we need to be free and with making choices, we are responsible for our choices. Bad faith is basically a way to escape the responsibility and burden of freedom. Since freedom is the condition for our existence, bad faith is a way to deny the truth of our own nature. So, claiming you had no choice at all is a form of bad faith. While in the freezer, Jerry wonders about his own mediocrity. His question assumes that mediocracy is part of his nature that he can't escape from, but this is bad faith because he denies his freedom to be *not* mediocre.

Traits of Subjectivity

Due to the freedom that is the condition for our existence, we experience the three traits of subjectivity: anguish, forlornness, and despair. Anguish results from the responsibility of choosing. When I make a choice, it is through my actions that I declare the choice I made is good; "if I consider that such an act is a good one, it is I who will choose to say that it is good rather than bad" (*Existentialism Is a Humanism*, p. 39). So I am not only choosing for myself, but I am choosing for others. If I choose to buy a plumbus, then my actions are saying that owning a plumbus is good not only for myself but for others. After all, no household is complete without a plumbus. If Beth chooses to leave a clone in her place so she can abandon her family and explore the multiverse, then her actions say that she chose what she thought was best not only for herself but for anyone else who may be in a similar situation. When we make a choice, we're responsible for that choice. I experience anguish because my responsibility for choosing for myself also includes choosing for everyone; I choose what is good or bad for everyone. Anguish doesn't prevent me from making a decision, rather anguish is a part of making a decision. Additionally, anguish can manifest as indecisiveness, which can only be dispelled by making a choice.

If I purchase a plumbus and I discover it can't bring me interdimensional cable, as I thought it could, I might blame everyone except myself, which would be bad faith. If I am authentic, I acknowledge that I'm to blame. If I have buyer's remorse, I have no one to blame except myself because no one made the decision for me to buy a plumbus. Forlornness is the fact that we are alone in the universe, alone and trapped within our own facticity, and we alone must choose. We even choose who to ask for advice and whose advice to follow. In "Rest and Ricklaxation," Rick confessed he had "crippling loneliness." He is lonely among his own species.

In "Auto Erotic Assimilation," he said about humanity "I can tolerate it but I can't give a crap about it." Additionally, there's no one in the universe who is his intellectual equal. Rick has no one to blame except himself; he chose his path in life and he has the power to be whatever he chooses. As Dr. Wong, in "Pickle Rick" pointed out, "You chose to come here, you chose to talk—to belittle my vocation—just as you chose to become a pickle." So perhaps that's one of the reasons why Rick drinks; he drinks in order to numb his loneliness. As Sartre put it, "Forlornness implies that we ourselves choose our being. Forlornness and anguish go together" (p. 45).

To complicate matters, Sartre reminds us that nothing is for certain. "When we want something, we always have to reckon with probabilities" (p. 46). When we make a choice, there's always the probability it won't have the desired outcome. Rick chose to become a pickle to avoid counseling. However, he had a series of life and death battles which ultimately and ironically led him to attend part of the counseling session. We may try to control the situation in order to minimize risk, but it can't be totally eliminated. When things don't meet our expectations, our feelings may vary depending on the situation.

I thought by asking for advice and reading the reviews, that I could minimize the chance of buyer's remorse. Rick thought by becoming a pickle, he could minimize the chance of attending counseling but he did attend disgruntledly. In "Rick and Ricklaxation," after securing the plasma shard, Rick experienced great distress having survived a situation where chance could not be minimalized. Rick said of the situation, "This was insane. That was pure luck. I was not in control of that situation."

Despair results from the idea that there's nothing to depend on. I can't depend on myself to make the right choice. Ultimately, we can't assume our natures are fixed or unchanging since we can change them; human nature doesn't necessarily have to stay the same. We can't even say with a hundred-percent certainty that when we wake up in the morning our world will be as we expect it to be. There's always a chance that Rick will turn it into a Cronenberg world.

If existentialism is correct, then the outlook of our existence is quite bleak. After all, anguish, forlornness, and despair are downers that range from, say, common buyer's remorse to such a severe degree that we need to take a vacation. To say that our existence is bleak is a common criticism of existentialism. In fact, with the freedom to choose our own natures and identities, more possibilities open. In other words, existentialism reveals what Sartre called "an optimistic toughness" (p. 49). Existentialism points out that if we pick a path we don't like, we can always take another one. We're even free to create an ethical world by remembering that when we choose, we are also choosing for others so it may motivate us to set a good model of behavior.

Sorting Out the Being of Meeseeks

Using existentialism as our guide, what sort of beings are Meeseeks? Mr. Meeseeks stressed that "Meeseeks are not born into this world fumbling for meaning. We are created to serve a singular purpose which we will go to any lengths to fulfill."

However, if they were created with the intent to serve a singular purpose, then their essence would precede their existence. Yet, Meeseeks exhibit subjectivity, which is the first principle of existentialism. So Meeseeks would be being-for-themselves and for-themselves have an existence that precedes essence. They can't have an existence that precedes essence *and* an essence that precedes existence.

Clearly, Meeseeks are beings-for-themselves. When they say "I'm Mr. Meeseeks," they're asserting that they have a sense of self and yet the "*self* cannot be a property of being-in-itself" (*Being and Nothingness*, p. 123). They can engage in transcendence and imagine a possible future and push themselves toward that future. For example, Meeseeks envisioned a future where killing Jerry would fulfill his request, so they took the appropriate actions to make that future a reality. By envisioning themselves in a possible future, Meeseeks display a relation to themselves and "the subject without relation to himself would be condensed into the identity of the in-itself." In other words, I'm aware or conscious of myself. There's the "I" that's conscious and there's the "myself" that isn't conscious because it's the object of my consciousness. Thus, there is a relationship between "I" and "myself." But if I wasn't conscious of myself, then I wouldn't be sentient; my existence would be reduced to being-in-itself like a plumbus or a pair of grappling shoes.

If Mr. Meeseeks is being-for-itself, then Meeseeks are free to choose their own identity and purpose; their existence would precede their essence. After all, Mr. Meeseeks finds himself thrown into existence and he orientates himself in the world by proclaiming "I'm Mr. Meeseeks. Look at me!" In order to give his life meaning, he accepts the summoner's request. It's a choice he made much like we may choose to become a scientist or a horse surgeon. Meekseekses can clearly make choices; Mr. Meeseeks chose what to say in order to make Summer popular in school, while another Mr. Meeseeks chose to summon another Meeseeks for help in fulfilling Jerry's request.

Meeseeks also display the traits of subjectivity. They experience forlornness and acknowledged individual responsibility, especially when one Meeseeks remarked to another "Your failures are your own, old man!" They displayed despair, especially when they realized the possibility that "the job can't be done. We'll never get two strokes of his game." While it is not clear whether they exhibited anguish from making a choice, they did display anguish and frustration over someone else's choice, such as when Jerry chose to take Beth out to dinner.

Sorting Out the Purpose of Meeseeks

If Meeseeks are sentient beings with free will, free to determine their own purpose, whose existence precedes its essence, then how is it that Meeseeks are compelled to serve a singular purpose and what is the nature of that purpose? To say that their purpose is to serve like how a servant serves, then that purpose would be too general and wouldn't seem to qualify as a singular one. After all, a servant like a butler or personal assistant have many tasks to fulfill, from picking up the dry cleaning to event planning. On the other hand, if we suppose their purpose is to fulfill the summoner's first request like opening a jar of mayonnaise, a Meeseeks could complete the task more quickly by smashing the jar apart than by unscrewing the lid yet Mr. Meeseeks chose to open it properly.

Perhaps their purpose is to die or go away. When Jerry decided to give up, Mr. Meeseeks stated "it doesn't work like that. I'm Mr. Meeseeks. I have to fulfill my purpose so I can go away." The way it works is that Meeseeks must be successful in order to return to a state of nonexistence. In fact, they "will go to any lengths" to succeed. They seek nonexistence because "Existence is pain to a Meeseeks" and they "will do anything to alleviate that pain."

If their motivation is to alleviate the pain of existence, then they might have overlooked different ways to alleviate pain. Meeseeks could try taking pharmaceuticals to numb their pain. However, taking pharmaceuticals is a way to cope rather than a way to succeed. Mr. Poopybutthole, during his recovery, took painkillers to help cope with his pain but it was physical therapy that helped him regain his mobility. Then again, pharmaceuticals might not have any effect on Meeseeks physiology. If that's so, they could take the advice that a detoxed Morty in "Rick and Ricklaxation" gave to Rick: "Let's work off your trauma with some urban spin yoga." Meeseeks could try tai chi or meditation. Since Meeseeks don't resort to other ways to relieve or manage their pain, then it seems getting rid of that pain isn't their ultimate goal. Meeseeks seek something else.

Perhaps their purpose is not successfully accomplishing the particular task, but rather accomplishing the task is a way to achieve a feeling of accomplishment that would trigger their death or return to nonexistence. This feeling is specific enough to be considered a singular purpose. Alleviating pain is too general since pain can be managed, numbed, or dispelled by pleasure or apathy. However, the feeling of accomplishment is singular and can be achieved by fulfilling any type of request. So, when Jerry decided to quit trying to improve his golf game, Mr. Meeseeks couldn't achieve a sense of accomplishment.

Their pain of existence motivates them to fulfill the request in order to achieve the feeling of accomplishment. In a way, Meeseeks are duty-bound to fulfill the request. Their duty comes from their self-interest; Meeseeks are really out for themselves and what they want is a feeling of accomplishment so they can stop existing and the pain of existence is what pushes them. Since Meeseeks existence is painful, they accept the first request given to them so they can get a feeling of accomplishment without delay. Since they can't die until the job is done, it follows that achieving a sense of accomplishment is the only way a Meeseeks can die.

Meeseeks are beings who find themselves thrown into the world and they accept the first request in order to escape existence. By accepting the request, they are bound to fulfill it otherwise they can't get a sense of accomplishment. Since they are individuals, not all of them get the feeling of accomplishment in the same way. In order to feel accomplished, the stickler Meeseeks had to be sure that Jerry's short game also improved. Yet what if in the beginning Jerry changed his mind and claimed he was satisfied with a bad golf game and released Mr. Meeseeks from any obligation to fulfill the request? It seems that Mr. Meeseeks would still stick to the original request because he didn't get a sense of accomplishment or perhaps Mr. Meeseeks would need a new request to fulfill so he can justifiably say "all done!"

What We Learned about the Meeseeks and from the Meeseeks

While Meeseeks appear cheerful, they mask tragic suffering. They experience existence as pain and yet seek a sense of accomplishment perhaps in their own way, giving value to their painful, short lives. Meeseeks live successful lives by successfully fulfilling the request despite the pain, despair, and forlornness of existence. Every Meeseeks wants to live successfully, yet they are tragic figures who push themselves towards the ultimate end, death. If they are tragic figures, then perhaps it is by no mistake they are blue.

Perhaps we should incorporate some of their aspects into our lives. Meeseeks are optimistic, tenacious, hard-working, and kind. While they suffer and endure pain, they try to live successfully by accomplishing some task in the service for other people. Perhaps we should be as friendly, optimistic as they are and strive to achieve accomplishments during our finite existence.

From the Meeseeks philosophical perspective, the good life is one characterized by accomplishments. We should not give up or quit but instead be committed to finish what we started if it means going to extreme lengths to finish it. However, we should heed Rick's advice about the Meeseeks, and apply it to our own lives, we should keep it simple and remember that humans and Meeseeks alike, "they're not gods."

11

Are You Imagining That Poopybutthole?

LESTER C. ABESAMIS

Who is Mr. Poopybutthole? Is he real? Do you have meaningful memories with him? What are those memories like? If those memories were questionable, would you shoot Mr. Poopybutthole? Beth did, and turned to alcohol in regret. Were Beth's actions excusable or reprehensible?

While we can definitely question whether Mr. Poopybutthole is a figment of our imagination, doing so might threaten our knowledge of close friends and family members. Even if you had Poopybutthole pictures on your phone, we can still philosophize whether that shit is actually real.

Uncle Steve is a great example of a questionable memory. He taught Morty how to ride a bike and treats the Smith family to vacations. If this is the first *Rick and Morty* episode you've watched, then there's nothing strikingly peculiar here— I hope you enjoy the first *Vindicators* adventure (Noob-noob gets it). If, however, you've been watching the show for a while, then you'll instantly wonder why you haven't *seen* Uncle Steve in any other episodes. Obviously, you could verify this fact by rewatching every episode and, as the viewer, you might feel comfortable with this minimal level of fact-checking.

On the other hand, if you're a character within the *Rick and Morty* universe, becoming skeptical of Steve's existence is harder to do. Skepticism is the philosophical position that denies complete or certain knowledge of something or, in this case, someone. As viewers, we can be skeptical of Steve's existence because we have good reason to doubt our memories of him. Jerry doesn't have a reason to doubt Steve's existence but despite his stupidity, Beth, Morty, and Summer don't have any reason to doubt him either.

Fortunately, Rick *somehow* grows suspicious of Steve and shoots him in the head. Everyone is initially horrified until Rick reveals that Steve is nothing more than an alien brain parasite that seeks to implant false memories into our heroes' minds. From here on out, *Rick and Morty* gives us a lesson in epistemology, or theories of knowledge, by forcing us to question (and possibly gun down) our most cherished memories if they're proven to be brain parasites. The only way to do this is to "keep an eye out for any zany wacky characters that pop up."

But before we start taking headshots at the Uncle Steves in our lives, let's first make sure our actions are justified. We've got to determine whether there are *actual* zany and wacky characters in our lives. But how are we supposed to do that? Most people think this is easy to do. Most people also try to level a shelf with a bubble. But we're not concerned with looking at things with our sad, naked, caveman eyeballs; we're concerned with precision.

Does Rick *know* that Uncle Steve is a parasite? Do the Smiths *know* they're pulling the trigger on Frankenstein's Monster, Sleepy Gary, and Photographer Raptor? Lacking epistemological precision, did Beth act immorally by blasting an innocent butt-hole? These questions aren't easy to tackle and there's a very good reason for that: the brain parasites might be the most powerful beings in the entire *Rick and Morty* multiverse!

Evil Brain Parasite Geniuses

Think of the people in your life. Parents, friends, math teachers—how do you know that they're the people they claim to be? Sure, you could look at pictures of them, which might bring back pleasant memories but what would it take to make you skeptical of those memories? Are you one hundred percent certain that these people genuinely exist in the way that you believe they exist?

René Descartes challenges memory, along with any piece of information that isn't indubitable. If there's even a one percent chance that something is false, then it can't be reliable and we've got to look elsewhere for precise knowledge. The point is to strip away all false beliefs until you're left with only the reliable ones. That means we can doubt all forms of sense-based, or empirical, knowledge since what's gained through the senses can sometimes be misleading. Think about mirages, the taste of orange juice after you brush your teeth, and that damn Laurel/Yanny debate (if you think it's Yanny, then you're probably a Jerry). Additionally, in "Wedding Squanchers," Rick misperceives a planet's physical dimensions and bumps into it revealing it to be a dwarf planet. Because our memories are mental representations of physical events, they too must be cast aside.

Memories are only the tip of the iceberg when it comes to Descartes's methodical doubt. How certain are you of your present, conscious experience? On one hand you're likely to be certain of your current, waking life and the fact that you are currently reading this book. Are you fully certain that's the case? Isn't it possible, for instance, that you're deceived about your current, waking situation? Could you be dreaming? Maybe this is how you dream, bitch! Or maybe you forgot that you voluntarily plugged yourself into a Roy simulation and are constantly going back to the carpet store instead of gloriously living off the grid. Whatever paranoid situation you decide to go with, the point is that it's quite difficult to prove that you're not currently being deceived about the things you're experiencing right now.

Descartes takes this a step further by coming up with the evil genius, a being that's all-powerful and all-knowing but completely devoid of goodness. The evil genius is so skilled at implanting false knowledge in you that you'd have no way of knowing what's true and what's false. This super jerk could make you accept irrational or false ideas. You might think you could reasonably take off your shirt and fold yourself twelve times.

It's also possible that the evil genius could even deceive you about basic, fundamental knowledge such as mathematical or logical truths. Imagine you're in a classroom. The guy up front says, "2 + 2", people in the back say "10" and think they're right. Since they're clearly mistaken, we can blame the evil genius and maybe school actually *isn't* for smart people. It's not a popular opinion but popular opinions aren't exactly going to defeat brain parasites.

Fortunately, the brain parasites, which mimic the evil genius, are no match for Rick's incredible wit. Rick nonchalantly shoots

Steve as if he were certain of Steve's true nature. Rick seems to be fully aware of what Steve really is, yet throughout the episode, his standard for certainty seems to lie on shaky ground. It's possible that Rick is aware of his uncertainty and is still willing to shoot Steve. If he squanches this up, he could always jump to another dimension.

How Rick realizes zaniness and wackiness in Steve is unclear but his confidence to move forward is worth looking into. Rick decides to write down the number of people in the room and post it on the wall for all to see. This piece of paper is empirical evidence since: a. everyone is relying on their *sense-based* memory, b. memory is confirmed by the *externally* produced written log, and c. Rick *physically* counts a total of six people in the room. Since the evil genius threatens sense knowledge, it's unclear how Rick can lay claim to the empirically derived information since it's possible that a brain parasite implanted the knowledge of there "actually" being six people in the first place. At this point, we're suspicious of Mr. Poopybutthole being the legitimate sixth person but the Smiths still don't have any reason to be skeptical.

It doesn't take long for the Smiths to start recalling false memories. The Hulk musical is the first false memory and it introduces Cousin Nicky—"I'm walkin' here!" Since Mr. Poopybutthole brings this memory up, more suspicions are raised. Luckily, Rick sees through Cousin Nicky. When asked how he knew, Rick claims to have merely guessed. But Rick's luck runs short after everyone's bombarded with more false memories of Sleepy Gary, Photography Raptor, Pencilvester, Tinkles, Hamurai, Amish Cyborg, and Reverse Giraffe. If you think any of these characters are real, then I can't wait to hear what you think of Vindicators 2 ("God-damn!"–Noob Noob). When these characters are questioned, Beth says "there's always been ten!"

Even worse, the brain parasites genuinely challenge what we, the viewers, can know! How do we know our memories haven't been corrupted by brain parasites? Also, if you're wondering whether Mr. Poopybutthole is a real person, then what prevents you from questioning the "real" memories of your family members and close friends? Surely your memories are also questionable! Cognitive psychologist Elizabeth Loftus says that, unlike tape recorders, our memories are reconstructive, which means they can be distorted. Her research suggests that when eye-witnesses are asked leading questions, memories of events they were present for can be corrupted. So, if other people can feed us false memories, how can we be so sure that memory is reliable?

Let's take a moment to acknowledge Sleepy Gary's existence. Early on, we "know" that he's a new character and highly likely to be a brain parasite. Jerry, however, isn't as rational as the viewer and he mistakenly accepts Beth and Sleepy Gary's marriage. He also mistakenly recalls having an affair with Gary, which should never be spoken of in the house. Despite Rick's superior intelligence and healthy dose of skepticism, he too is convinced that Sleepy Gary is a real memory. I suppose with enough emotional persuasion, coupled with pleasant backyard barbecue memories, even Rick, as rational as he is, can be deceived. If it weren't for such emotional judgments, Rick might have had the wit to shoot Gary early on. Here's the deal: a lot of our knowledge, including memory, is verified through our senses but if these are prone to error, evil geniuses, or brain parasites, then can we be certain that anyone in our life is real?

I Think You're a Whiny Little Piece of Shit, Therefore I Exist

Throughout this episode, the "real" main characters desperately question everyone's existence—including their own. This isn't too crazy of a thought since our memories come from our senses, which are rejected by Descartes. It doesn't help that the Smiths join the tyranny of the majority in demanding that the blast shields be lowered. Since Rick is the only one reluctant to lower the shields, the entire house gangs up on him, which forces Rick to do two things: 1. he wonders if his own family are brain parasites and 2. he wonders about his own existence, desperately yelling, "Is anyone here even real? Am I the only real person on earth?"

Here, Rick considers solipsism, the idea that no minds exist except your own. Even worse, Reverse Giraffe raises the possibility that Rick himself is a brain parasite. Because an evil genius scenario is possible, how do we know that we aren't the evil genius masterfully deceiving ourselves of everything? If you're not the evil genius, how do you know that you exist? And could it be possible that the people in your lives are humanoid cyborgs and that you're the only human mind in existence?

Descartes and Rick entertain similar ideas. It seems the evil genius is so powerful that he could make you believe you exist when you actually don't. At first, this is terrifying but Descartes manages to overcome this hurdle by establishing his most famous phrase: "I think, therefore I am," often shortened to the Latin "cogito." This is an undeniable truth since even if all my thoughts, memories, and perceptions are false, I can't deny my own existence. Imbeciles like Jerry may be many things, but he can't be "non-existent." Unfortunately, Jerry is a dumb-ass and completely misses the self-affirming element of the cogito when he asks, "Sleepy Gary, how do I know I'm real?" Sleepy Gary can't convince Jerry of his existence. Only Jerry can prove the cogito for himself.

The cogito works great for proving my existence. The more I doubt my existence, the stronger the cogito reveals itself. If I doubt myself, who's doubting? I am. If I'm dreaming, who's doing the dreaming? I am. So, as long as Jerry, Beth, Summer, Morty, Rick, and Mr. Poopybutthole can think, they can prove their existence. However, proving my existence doesn't help me determine who's a brain parasite and who isn't. We need some sort of formula on top of the "cogito" to determine this.

Enter Morty, who somehow cracks the code right when he's about to shoot Rick. Instead of impulsively pulling the trigger, Morty doubts all his memories by acknowledging the possibility that he's completely brainwashed. In doing so, he *somehow* realizes that the brain parasites can't implant bad memories. Since Morty has a ton of bad memories with Rick, he realizes Rick is a real person and not a parasite. If Rick didn't call Morty an "implausibly naive pubescent boy with an old Jewish comedy writer's name", Morty might've shot Rick. Morty then recalls the most devastating family memories ranging from terrible run-ins with monsters to Rick pantsing Morty at school to Summer catching him masturbating in the kitchen.

Morty's realization serves as a possible formula for identifying brain parasites and prompts Rick to suggest killing "everyone that we can only remember fondly!" beginning with Mrs. Refrigerator. If Morty's formula is right, then that means we ought to be suspicious of people we don't have bad memories of. If you've never shared an uncomfortable silence or an "awkward fart on a road trip" with someone, then they must be a brain parasite!

Morty's Crappy Logic

Rick and family, minus Jerry, proceed to take back their waking lives by eliminating whomever they determine to be brain parasites. What follows is a glorious shoot-em-up segment that's both aesthetically pleasing and liberating—there's nothing more satisfying than shooting a magical rainbow pony that tricked you into thinking you shared meaningful memories with it. There are, however, some issues with the way parasites are identified. These issues become clear when Beth shoots Mr. Poopybutthole. Let's take a look at this shitty logic.

First, Rick shoots at Summer earlier in the episode to test whether she's a brain parasite. Assuming he didn't miss, Rick's logic would go like this: If Summer is a parasite, she'd shapeshift back to her original form. If not, she'd bleed out and die or live with the fact that her grandpa just shot her—which might mean very little for Rick. In either case, it's unclear whether Rick's logic is reliable since we'd be observing Summer's (or a brain parasite's) death using our senses. Also, the only way to kill the source of our deception is to identify and shoot the source of our deception (which is external to us).

It's unclear how Rick identifies the parasites in the beginning of the episode, especially since he seems to unknowingly load the parasites into his ship at the end of "Mortynight Run." Since the parasites are external to the characters, they probably emit some kind of particle or spore that messes with the chemicals in the brain and deceives the mind. In other words, although they aren't necessarily in our minds, the parasites can implant false memories from a distance. It's unclear how we're supposed to determine zaniness and wackiness in parasites if we're supposed to do so empirically.

Second, there are issues with Morty's formula for identifying the parasites. The rule that brain parasites can only implant good memories is realized inductively, rather than deductively. Inductive reasoning goes from a set of observations to a highly probable rule; whereas deductive reasoning starts with an undeniable truth that's properly applied to all appropriate cases. An example of deductive reasoning is this: All Ricks have a Morty. Doofus Rick is a Rick. Therefore, Doofus Rick has a Morty. Being a Rick implies having a Morty—even if it looks like Eric Stoltz.

The cogito is a deductive argument since thinking necessarily implies existing. If I can think, then I must exist. Morty's formula, however, goes something like this: "I recall bad memories of my family members. If I can't recall bad memories of you, then you're a brain parasite." Morty isn't exactly certain about his realization since he's taking a claim about his family and generally applying it to all people. Furthermore, the existence of brain parasites should throw into doubt all of our memories, good or bad. Because our memories can be manipulated, we shouldn't trust any of them. Regardless, Morty shoots the brain parasite restraining Rick because it's *probably* a parasite. Would you shoot someone based on Morty's probabilistic formula?

Thirdly, it's unclear how Rick knows about the brain parasites. Did he encounter the brain parasites before? If so, we're left to assume that he escaped, defeated them, or heard about them through the grapevine. Since Morty realizes the "bad memories" rule before Rick does, it's highly likely that Rick never defeated them and either merely escaped or heard about the parasites (although it's possible that he falsely remembers this). Likewise, if Descartes never had the cogito to rule out the evil genius, he could still be subjected to its tricks.

The most compelling issue, however, is Mr. Poopybutthole. His introduction minutes into the episode surely raises suspicions. Avid watchers of the show will fail to recall him in earlier episodes; although, new characters *do* get introduced and stick around (such as Bird Person, Tammy, and Principal Vagina). These suspicions are revisited when it's shown that neither Mr. Poopybutthole nor Beth have selfies with each other on their cellphones. The absence of pictures may give us good reason to be skeptical but this all changes when Beth *actually* shoots and seriously injures Mr. Poopybutthole, revealing one crucial epistemological mistake: Mr. Poopybutthole is actually a "long-time family friend" and not a brain parasite. Geez, Beth, you could have tried shooting him in the arm at least! Having realized her mistake, Beth, in shock, desperately runs to the kitchen to drink while Jerry calls 911.

From our perspective, it seems apparent that Beth is a real person who doubts Mr. Poopybutthole's existence and Mr. Poopybutthole's suspicion toward Beth is nothing but a parasite's deception. There aren't any bad memories of Mr. Poopybutthole— at least, none are raised in the episode since Rick claims he can always count on Mr. Poopybutthole. So, it's reasonable to think that Mr. Poopybutthole is a falsely implanted memory. Unfortunately, he doesn't change into a brain parasite when he's shot, which should be a dead giveaway, right? Not quite.

First, there aren't any bad memories of Mr. Poopybutthole, which could mean one of two things. Either Morty's realization about bad memories is wrong and the Smith family was just incredibly lucky with each shot they took; or the Smiths simply overlooked their crappy memories. Second, witnessing Mr. Poopybutthole bleed out isn't as reliable as you might think. Let's see how far we can take our skepticism. The brain parasites revert back to original form and die once they're shot. But who's to say that the brain parasites can't deceive us into thinking that's how they're killed? It's at least possible for the brain parasites to deceive us about their apparent deaths. This wouldn't be too far-fetched, since shooting and watching a brain parasite die are done empirically, which Descartes would be skeptical of. Also, anything that isn't being experienced right now is a memory, too. If the brain parasites can't manipulate our current experiences, they can at least manipulate how we recall those experiences, even if the actual experience was a fraction of a millisecond ago. See? I told you the brain parasites were powerful beings in the multiverse! So, because Morty's formula isn't perfect, the brain parasites could still be deceiving us. It's not impossible that the brain parasites created Mr. Poopybutthole to foil Morty's incomplete formula and prevent further suspicions from being raised.

To effectively combat the brain parasites, Morty needs to realize something as precise and self-affirming as "I think, therefore I exist"; otherwise, his formula only gives the Smiths probability as opposed to certainty. Since we can't distinguish real humans from zany and wacky parasites with certainty, should we be shooting people in the first place? Ethically speaking, the answer seems to be no. But if Rick and family don't try to solve the problem of the brain parasites, they'll be stuck behind the blast shields indefinitely. I suppose Rick could always open up a portal to escape (assuming his gun isn't taken away); but this may not fix his problems. Without a precise formula for identifying brain parasites, Rick may be unaware of brain parasites in other dimensions—especially if he mistakenly transports them inter-dimensionally!

Feigning Your Ignorance Will Bite You in the Ass

For the sake of argument, let's say that Rick and family successfully annihilated the brain parasites before they could escape the blast shields. In many cases, if you pull the trigger, you're responsible for your actions. We'd certainly praise our shooters for each successful brain parasite death and judging by their satisfied grins, Rick, Morty, Summer, and Beth take on that responsibility. They're extremely confident about their actions since they think they hold an indubitable formula for identifying brain parasites. But is their confidence justified? If so, are they not to be held accountable for their potential mistakes? Or did they jump to conclusions when they could have analyzed their knowledge a bit more? I'd argue that they had all the time in the world to rethink their situation. More specifically, Beth could have reconsidered her knowledge of Mr. Poopybutthole at the end of the episode.

St. Thomas Aquinas most likely never dealt with brain parasites but if he did, he might have considered God to be one. He does, however, discuss three levels of ignorance, only one of which is justified. According to Aquinas, we're not morally responsible if our actions were truly involuntary. If Beth, while shooting brain parasites, accidentally shot Mr. Poopybutthole, she wouldn't be morally responsible because her ignorance led to her actions. Now, this case would be difficult to prove since we could be suspicious of her true intentions. Luckily, Aquinas's three types of ignorance may shed some light on when ignorance is truly justified.

Consider the alien kids playing in "Whirly Dirly Conspiracy." Their game was to take turns chasing and shooting each other in the head. Because of the Immortality Field Resort, the kids would instantly recover and the game would continue. Everyone in this resort knew that they were basically invincible so long as they stayed within the activated immortality field. Aquinas's first kind of ignorance is concomitant, or accompanies your action. Let's say one of the alien kids hated the other and the immortality field was secretly deactivated. Once he shoots his playmate, he might show remorse for this tragic accident. We could, however, call bullshit since even if he weren't ignorant of the deactivated field, he'd still have hatred toward his playmate.

Aquinas's second kind of ignorance is the type that is either feigned or a result of negligence. Let's say that while the immortality field is deactivated, all resort guests were warned of their lack of immortality. If the alien kid pretends to not hear the warning or covers his ears before continuing the game, his ignorance doesn't justify his actions since he has the opportunity to consider more information. Again, if he shows remorse, we can call bullshit because he feigned his ignorance in order to justify an immoral action.

Finally, Aquinas gives us a type of ignorance that is actually justified. If the kids were running around with no hateful attitudes toward each other and unbeknownst to them the field was deactivated, then the shooter's ignorance, as well as his remorse, would be justified and sincere. If we could go back in time and inform the kids of the field's deactivation, then they would have likely acted differently.

Consequent ignorance isn't limited to willfully feigning your ignorance. You could still be responsible for something you're genuinely ignorant of if you had the chance to consider more information. So, if the alien kid purposefully neglected the warning regarding the field, then he'd still be responsible for any accidents. Likewise, if Beth had the opportunity to reconsider Morty's formula and she neglects that opportunity, then she'd still be responsible for taking the shot even if she's genuinely ignorant of Mr. Poopybutthole's true identity. Let's say Morty revealed his formula and Beth somehow couldn't recall any bad memories of Rick. We have reason to believe that she willingly ignores the fact that Rick walked out on his family years ago. It also doesn't help that out of everyone, Rick insults Beth the least! So, it's likely that she would have shot Rick. Surely she'd be responsible for her actions because, due to her bias toward Rick, she refused to challenge Morty's formula.

Now, I'm not saying that Beth's panicked behavior wasn't genuine. Her shaky wine-pouring is definitely convincing. But consequent ignorance doesn't rule out genuine tears, remorse, or confusion—it only rules out justified ignorance. You could still genuinely regret your decisions but still be responsible for them. The important point here is that there's a difference between your genuine and inevitable ignorance wrongfully informing your actions and your self-induced ignorance wrongfully informing your actions.

Getting Our Shit Together

There's definitely something to be said for applying Descartes's skepticism to a theory on moral responsibility. If Descartes's philosophy requires us to doubt everything that isn't self-affirming, like the cogito, then surely we've got a lot of things to doubt. In a world of brain parasites or evil geniuses, we'd have to be skeptical of all of our memories. We'd also definitely doubt any future events since we can't know the outcome with certainty. And regarding moral responsibility, since we're now aware that there are many uncertain things, we're even more prone to being unjustifiably ignorant of our actions.

What's this say about the morality of shooting potential brain parasites? Descartes suggests that we restrain our unlimited will—our ability to assert anything regardless of it being true or false—so that it matches our limited intellect—what we can know to be true with certainty. Although Descartes aimed to match our wills with our intellect so that we were always free from error, this might not be possible in our brain parasites case, since the only thing we've shown with precision is that we exist.

The next best thing, however, is to not hastily jump to the conclusion that a brain parasite can't implant bad memories. Thinking that would be misusing our will, since we can't know that for sure. Instead, Beth should have pulled back on her intuition that Mr. Poopybutthole was a parasite. She could have either refrained from shooting him, or at least refrained from shooting him in a vital spot. A flesh wound would have been a better way for testing the theory that brain parasites shape-shift after getting shot anywhere. If Mr. Poopybutthole isn't a parasite, he'd likely suffer a non-life threatening injury, but we're not out of the woods yet since this doesn't prove that he's a real person.

Beth and family could then test out Morty's formula by carefully reviewing their memories with Mr. Poopybutthole without all of the commotion brought on by a house full of brain parasites. Of course, these tests would only confirm that Mr. Poopybutthole is unlikely to be a parasite; they would never prove his existence with certainty.

III

I Have No Code of Ethics, Just Love Killin'

12
Jerry's Dick

WAYNE YUEN H-232

Let's talk about Jerry's dick. In "Interdimensional Cable 2 Tempting Fate," Jerry has the opportunity, perhaps even the responsibility, to save the life of Shrimply Pibbles, the galaxy's most influential civil rights leader.

Of course, Jerry doesn't want to do it because he's Jerry! Oh, and maybe because he has some kind of weird attachment to his dick. I understand that many people might also have similar feelings about the dicks in their lives, so it might be helpful if we examine this ethical quandary and learn a little about how much of a claim other people might have over our organs.

When Jerry learns that he can save Pibbles's life, the doctors and activists give him a pretty simple and clear argument for why he should go along with the surgery: Pibbles is an important person, and he could continue to do important work, saving the lives of hundreds of billions of lifeforms. We wouldn't want a repeat of the tragedy on 65.3432.2314 after all. So if Jerry donates his perfectly formed organ to Pibbles, the universe would be better for it.

This argument is a pretty typical utilitarian argument, where we use consequences, specifically the happiness generated or good consequences generated from an act, to determine the moral goodness of the act. Jerry's dick can help social justice everywhere in the universe, so long as it's in Pibbles's chest, and not between his pathetic legs.

However, it's Pibbles himself, who actually convinces, or manipulates, Jerry to donate his penis, when he shames Jerry (and honestly it's pretty easy to shame Jerry) and the entire

117

human race by describing our species's obsession with penises. Small or big, we just love laughing at penises. To save face, Jerry boldly proclaims that he will donate his penis, and hopes that Beth will save him from his own promise.

A Really Good Organ

Fortunately, Jerry isn't alone. I also happen to have a penis. I also happen to be very attached to my penis, emotionally speaking. I can empathize with Jerry's situation. I too, wouldn't want to look like a selfish prick in front of a great civil rights leader, but at the same time, I probably would be pretty hesitant to donate my penis for a better universe.

I mean, really, how much has the universe done for me lately? I'm pretty sure I know what my dick has done for me, and we have a pretty good relationship. I don't think that would sway Pibbles or the doctors all that much. So, I guess it would be best to fight morality with morality. There is this concept called supererogation, which is a fancy word for a set of moral acts that wouldn't be required to do, but if you did them you would be considered an incredibly good person, or a Good Samaritan.

Pibbles himself is an example of engaging in supererogatory acts. He doesn't have to make the universe a better place for billions of lifeforms. He could just be like Rick and booze away the days seeking happiness. He wouldn't be a bad person for failing to engage in supererogatory acts. He would just be like me, a minimally-decent person. So, Jerry really shouldn't be ashamed of not wanting to donate his dick to Pibbles, just like any average person wouldn't be ashamed for not taking an active role in ending world hunger.

Of course, Jerry gets shafted by Beth. She doesn't want to stand in the way of Jerry being a Good Samaritan and helping to contribute to the welfare of hundreds of billions of lifeforms. She throws the utilitarian argument right back into Jerry's face. Beth doesn't point this out, maybe because she's too busy browsing the endless prosthetic alternatives that Jerry might be fitted with, but utilitarian morality doesn't have any room for supererogatory acts. Good consequences are good consequences, and we always have a basic obligation to do whatever brings about the best consequences, according to utilitarianism.

If you have a spare dollar, and someone else needs it to stay alive, you should give it up. The same is true for your next dollar. This reasoning can be overwhelming pretty quickly. Peter Singer, a well-known utilitarian ethicist, once argued that we should give up all of our luxuries and donate them to charity because it would maximize the good in the world. The alternative is to say that watching *Rick and Morty* streaming on my PS4 through Amazon is more morally important than someone who is literally about to starve to death. I could have saved money by not buying these frivolous things, and donating that money straight to that starving person, and saved their life. And let's say that I didn't just give that person a bit of food, but rather the money that I donated was used to help them set up a self-sustaining business, that would feed that person, and their family, for the rest of their lives. But, no, I chose to watch an episode all about Jerry's dick instead.

Is Jerry a Dick?

So, is donating a dick to Pibbles supererogatory, or is it a basic obligation? Is Jerry a dick for not giving up his dick, or just a minimally-decent person who chooses not to go above and beyond the call of duty?

Does Pibbles have some kind of moral claim to Jerry's dick? It might help if we looked at some other related situations, to see how Jerry measures up. First, let's turn down the intensity of the situation a lot, and compare the act of donating blood, to Jerry's dick. Most healthy people are fully capable of donating a little more than a pint of blood every couple of months with almost zero health effects, and the cost of about an hour out of your day. Doing this, according to the Red Cross, can save the lives of up to three people per donation.

Most folks don't have any particularly strong emotional ties to blood. We need it to live, but we don't need all of it and we're always making more. Other people could really use the blood pumping through Jerry's dick way more than he does. So assuming that Jerry is a healthy but mediocre person, it would be almost nonsensical for him not to donate blood regularly. This makes it look like a basic moral obligation, and not supererogatory. It's not looking good for Jerry's dick.

But there's another kind of donation that might be a little more like the situation Jerry is in: kidney donation. More than two million people die each year, around the world, from kidney failure. These people's lives could be saved if someone else were to donate a kidney to them. Now, assumedly not all of these people are noble civil rights leaders like Shrimply Pibbles. Plenty of them are probably downright mediocre people, like Jerry, at best. But, to make the situations the same, let's say that Peter Singer, the utilitarian who thinks we should donate our money to the poor, needs the kidney. Singer is also well-known for championing the animal rights movement and improving the lives of perhaps hundreds of billions of lifeforms here on Earth.

Donating a kidney to Singer would let Singer continue his work as an ethicist, and influence the hearts of minds of people around the world, which would continue improving the lives of lifeforms on Earth. Most people have two kidneys and could function perfectly well with a single kidney. Singer, in fact, does think that we have an obligation to donate our kidney.

If Singer is right, Shrimply Pibbles has a pretty strong moral claim to Jerry's dick. There are some larger effects on a person's life though. First, the recovery time for the donor is pretty significant, four to six weeks. But on top of that, doctors recommend that the donors don't engage in activities that could injure their remaining kidney, since they don't have a spare one to pick up the slack. Contact sports like football, soccer, hockey, martial arts, aren't a good idea. So donating a kidney may change the way you live your life. Nobody ever picks Jerry for their team, so this isn't likely going to affect Jerry much. But, aside from academic philosophers like Singer, not too many people think that donating a kidney is a moral obligation. Most people think that people who donate their kidney are Good Samaritans, and so they think that donating a kidney is a supererogatory act.

A Large Tip

So what makes an act supererogatory? It isn't clear. It would be easy to say that any act that requires you to change your plan for your life in significant ways (so long as they aren't immoral plans) would be a supererogatory act. Donating a penis or a kidney could impact your life-plan in pretty significant ways. But not all supererogatory acts have to be acts on par with giving a kidney, or a penis, to a stranger.

I could give an extra-large tip to my waiter. I don't have to give an extra-large tip, but it's a nice thing to do. So this act goes above and beyond my basic obligations. I wouldn't be considered a bad person if I just gave a regular-sized tip to my waiter, but that doesn't require me to change my life-plan in any significant way (depending on the size of the tip). And remember that some people, like utilitarians, don't even believe that supererogatory acts exist. If giving an extra-large tip to my waiter makes more happiness than me keeping the money, then I should do it, for the sake of creating the best consequences possible.

Trying to define exactly what a supererogatory act is might be impossible. At its heart, supererogation might be a vague concept. Games, for example, are similarly vague. There isn't anything that all games have in common. Not all games have winners or losers. Not all games have clear defined rules or objectives. But games might help us understand what Jerry's situation a bit more too. Not all games have a score system. But if a thing has a score system, it very likely is a game. We might not be able to define what supererogation is, but we might be able to say that Jerry's case is an example of supererogation because of some features it exhibits.

One feature is that it seems to require Jerry to alter his life-plan. Jerry was planning on using his dick for the rest of his life. He's used to masturbating with his dick, and not the XP-20. It's not wrong to masturbate with his dick. When Beth asks if he prefers the XP-20 or the XP-20xs he says that he prefers his own penis. Now, however irrational it is to prefer your own penis to a better apparatus that would please your wife more, it's still your preference.

Nobody chooses the preferences that they have. Beth doesn't get to choose for Jerry. If Beth were going to have a mastectomy, it would be reasonable for *her* to decide what kind of reconstructive surgery she would have, if any, and not give the decision solely to Jerry, as it affects her life-plan more than it affects his life-plan. This respect for people's life-plans is often expressed as respecting a person's autonomy, or ability to live their own lives in accordance with their own values.

Jerry donating his dick would require him to make a pretty big (or apparently small) sacrifice, at least when viewed from the perspective of his life-plan. Since we're not saying that all supererogatory duties need to alter a person's life plan, small acts like giving a big tip to the waiter could still be supererogatory.

This life-plan factor also explains why some kinds of acts are almost always considered supererogatory. For example, if my plumbus didn't get spit on by a schlami, the chumbles might explode, getting dinglebop everywhere. So what's one to do when their plumbus's chumbles are about to explode? It might be too much to ask a Splorpian to jump on top of it, since it would probably kill them. Dying tends to interfere with most people's life plans, Meeseeks being a notable exception. But if somebody jumped onto my plumbus, I'd consider that person a hero, because I'd think their act would be supererogatory, and I wouldn't have to clean dinglebop off everything.

A second quality that should be considered is an act that is beyond necessity, morally speaking. Pibbles is a great person, because he engages in acts that are better than necessary. He didn't have to march on Flurtblurt Square; Pibbles could have simply written a strongly worded letter. But the fact that he organized this historic march and raised awareness of the atrocities in the universe indicates that he went beyond moral necessity, which reflects the supererogatory nature of his act.

Jerry's act is necessary to save Pibbles's life, but if it isn't a moral obligation to give up your genitals for a civil rights leader, then it goes beyond necessity. There's no particularly compelling moral reason, as Rick would attest, that any particular individual exist, including Pibbles. Even if Pibbles were to continue to do good things, it doesn't mean he needs to exist, since someone else could also do those good things.

Artificial Organs

Another feature that comes to light late in the episode is that there's an alternative to Jerry donating his penis. Pibbles doesn't actually need Jerry's dick. Shrimply Pibbles could have an artificial heart implanted into him, which would actually be superior to Jerry's pathetic penis. In fact, because beings across the universe have donated money, and in doing so engaged in a possible supererogatory act, there's no need for Jerry to donate his penis any longer.

Of course, Jerry is offended by this, because his life-plan, besides masturbating, involves trying to get some respect awarded to himself. But the fact that there were alternatives available makes Jerry's act of donating his penis much more of an *optional* action, which reinforces the idea that the act is supererogatory. If it weren't optional, it would be a basic moral obligation!

Utilitarianism has been the thorn in the side of supererogation so far, but with this new information the utilitarian has to have a different take on this scenario. If the doctors can give a better artificial heart to Pibbles, then this would produce the best outcome. Jerry is happy that he doesn't have to give up his penis, and Pibbles can have the best artificial heart, and not a pathetic dick. So we have the optimal situation that should be done and anything less is morally wrong. Jerry, being the dick that he is, thinks differently now. After being exposed himself as a morally shallow person and not actually wanting to give up his penis, Jerry now wants to donate his penis. After all, who wouldn't want to be considered a Good Samaritan? So if the morally optimal thing to do is give Pibbles the artificial heart, would Jerry's sacrifice of his penis still be a good thing? Is it supererogatory? Why does it matter at this point?

I think it matters to Jerry, at least, since I believe that his life-plan is about gaining respect. Jerry hopes that giving up his dick will show people he "didn't flinch" at the call of moral duty. He's concerned about his moral character, or more precisely, how others perceive his moral character. If Jerry donating his dick to Pibbles is still supererogatory, despite it being non-optimal, then he could still be considered a Good Samaritan. I think that this is plausible at the very least.

Let's think about the tipping the waiter again. We can tip our waiter the normal amount, which would make us minimally decent people, or we can tip a larger amount that might make us Good Samaritans. But let's say that the waiter needs a new expensive heart. My tip can't pay for his heart, but I could give an even larger tip to help offset the cost of the heart. If my larger than normal tip was supererogatory, does the expense for a new heart change the supererogation status of the tip? It isn't optimal, but it sure seems as if I don't need to give enough money to pay for a heart, and despite it being less than optimal, it still is a better than necessary act. It's certainly optional to give more than what I'm required as a tip.

Finally, depending on how big my tip is, it may or may not alter my life plans. So, there is at least a reasonable case that doing something less than optimal can still be supererogatory. So maybe Jerry can still donate his penis, and it be a good thing. If Pibbles doesn't use it, then maybe another, more mediocre person, could. Pibbles could be even more of a Good Samaritan by taking Jerry's dick and donating the artificial heart to someone else!

A Dick Claimed

I think it makes a lot of sense to say that if Jerry gave up his dick to Pibbles, that it would be supererogatory, which means that Pibbles has no real moral claim on Jerry's dick. If Jerry had an obligation to donate his dick, then we wouldn't say it was supererogatory. It still might be a heroic thing to do, but he shouldn't be considered a Good Samaritan for donating his dick if it's required of him, any more than I would be a moral hero for not murdering the person who sits next to me on a bus. Supererogation captures an important aspect of the moral world: some acts are just more praiseworthy than others. If we were strict utilitarians, we wouldn't be able to say something like this, but if *Rick and Morty* has taught us anything, with an infinite number of dimensions, there has to be an infinite number of ways of thinking about morality. To say that there has to be one correct way of thinking about morality is to say that there is one *real* "Morty."

So to Jerry's relief we can finally reach a couple of conclusions. He doesn't have to give up his dick, and if he did, he really would be a good person. Unfortunately, he doesn't go about doing it in the best way, and gets shot up trying to force his dick on to a civil rights icon. But it's Jerry, so we kind of expected that.

Wayne Is Wrong

WAYNE YUEN U-964

Let's talk about Jerry's penis. In "Interdimensional Cable 2 Tempting Fate," Jerry has the opportunity to save the life of Shrimply Pibbles, the galaxy's most influential civil rights leader. But Jerry doesn't want to, because it seems to be a pretty huge personal sacrifice!

Who can really blame him? The guy is constantly picked on, and getting the short end of the stick, and now he's being asked to give up his penis? Now, I know a lot of people enjoy the schadenfreude that is Jerry's character, but I think in this case, Jerry doesn't have a moral obligation to give his penis to Pibbles, but you probably have an obligation to give up your kidney.

I know, you've probably read a really compelling essay from some guy named Wayne Yuen, but I'm also Wayne Yuen. Wayne from dimension H-232 really likes to use the word dick a lot, but more importantly, doesn't seem to see the serious moral implications of his position. It's the end of morality if H-232 Wayne is right.

The obvious position to take, is that Jerry doesn't really have to give up his penis for Shrimply Pibbles. It would be a good thing, but it isn't morally required of him to give up his penis. This would make giving up his penis a supererogatory action. But why should we think that this is a superogatory act? At the heart of Jerry's situation is the choice between helping someone in need and not helping.

There are plenty of people around the world that we can help, even if they are far away from us, but we don't help them all, but does that mean we shouldn't help? Saying an action is supererogatory means that it isn't important that we help people. "Should" is a strong word because it states that there is a moral obligation, so when we say we "shouldn't" help we are saying it isn't a moral obligation to help. It's a denial of a moral obligation, which would have huge implications for our moral behavior.

Let's say that you're taking a walk, enjoying a Simple Rick Wafer Cookie, and you come across an unconscious bloodied person. They're alive, but clearly in need of assistance. Instead of calling for help and staying with this person, you continue your walk, checking up on the latest Rick and Morty memes on your phone, and happily munching on your wafer cookies.

If Jerry can choose to not assist Shrimply Pibbles, then you can choose not to assist this stranger in need, and not be in any moral fault. After all, Jerry didn't *cause* Shrimply Pibbles's heart problems, nor did you beat this stranger to unconsciousness. But both are in positions to render assistance, possibly saving a life, and most would say that not assisting is wrong. We *should* assist. It isn't supererogatory.

Now, obviously, there are situational differences, and these differences can change our moral obligations significantly. You don't have to give up your penis to save this stranger's life. You're giving up some time, and maybe the rest of your walk to help this stranger. Jerry is giving up a body part that plays a huge role in his life. Jerry shouldn't give up his penis, because his life-plan would need to be significantly altered for him to fulfill this moral obligation, and when our life-plans need to be altered, to fulfill a moral obligation, it's just too much of a sacrifice.

A Moral Life Avoided

But this life plan response has its problems. Almost any action that you don't want to engage in, is contrary to your life plan. Part of your plan for today, which is part of your life, was to take a walk. Helping this stranger is contrary to your life plan, so you don't have to help. Or, maybe your life plan is to be a healthy individual, and your plan to stay a healthy individual is to take daily walks. And, of course, we could have immoral life plans, like whatever Evil Morty's ultimate plans are.

Either way, if we take the life plan objection seriously, then we undermine all basic moral obligations. I can justify any immoral action, by appealing to a life plan. Evil Morty has plans and the Citadel of Ricks stand in his way, so it's correct for him to murder all the Ricks so his plan can begin to come to fruition. Morality sometimes makes huge demands upon us, and that includes altering our life plans. Parents of disabled children might have to make huge sacrifices to their life plans, depending on the disability. This is why some people elect to have abortions, to avoid changing their life plans. But of course children can become disabled after birth, through no fault of anyone. Would it be morally acceptable to abandon the child at this point so that the parents can continue with their life plan?

Life plans also change through time. Few people have the same life plan that they had when they were children. What we want out of life radically changes as we age: young people often proclaim that they want to die before they become "old" and of course older people wonder why they would even entertain such a silly notion. But the fact that they change through time also points to the idea that we can change them for basically any reason, and if they can undermine our moral obligations, then we might just change our life plans out of convenience to avoid moral obligations. All of Jerry's actions in "Inter-dimensional Cable 2 Tempting Fate" after he is pressured to give up his penis are to avoid his moral obligations.

Another defense for supererogation might be the idea of an act going beyond moral necessity, but it's hard to come to grips with what "beyond necessity" means, in a moral context. Wayne from H-232 thinks that Pibbles could have written a strongly worded letter, and fulfilled his moral obligations to the universe, but that's to say that a strongly worded letter would have produced the same change in the universe as the famous march on Flurtblurt Square. But the reality is that a march is probably going to be far more effective at raising awareness of an issue, than a strongly worded letter that is ignored by everyone.

It's hard to ignore a mass of people inconveniencing others for a cause, it's easy to ignore a letter when *Man vs Car* is on. So, it was necessary for Pibbles to march, and not write a letter, because the important part of the action is that change occurred. If it wasn't important that change occured, then Pibbles, as well as all the beings in the universe, could just send their thoughts and prayers to the oppressed, and have done enough.

Moral obligations are obligations, because they're necessary for us to bring about a world that is good world. A "good enough" world is a world where we ignore moral wrongs as unsolvable. But if they are truly unsolvable, then we don't have any moral obligation to do anything about it, since we can't have moral obligations for impossible acts, we only have moral obligations for things that can actually be done. If they aren't unsolvable, then we're simply shirking our moral responsibilities, for whatever reason, be it life plan, convenience, or whatever else we might use to justify immoral behavior.

Finally, Wayne H-232 points out that for an act to be supererogatory, it needs to be optional. But the very point of morality, is that morality isn't optional, in the sense that we should be allowed to choose not to act in a moral way. Saying that moral acts are optional undermines the obligatory nature of ethics. Sure it's optional to save the unconscious person, in the sense that I could do otherwise, but it isn't optional in the moral sense. When Jerry learns that there are better alternatives for saving Shrimply Pibbles, his act doesn't become optional, it becomes immoral. After all, why should we not want to save Pibbles *and* spare Jerry the trauma and humiliation of having his penis removed? This would be the better outcome, and so Jerry never really had an obligation to donate his penis.

If we take away H-232's argument for supererogatory acts, then the utilitarian argument for donating our kidneys to people who need it stands. We don't live in a world where we have perfect artificial organs that can be used in place of donated organs yet, like Jerry does. So, it might not be an obligation for Jerry to donate his penis to Pibbles, but we have an obligation to donate our blood and organs to other humans today.

13
Rick, Morty, and the Cure for Unhappiness

WILLIAM TEBOKKEL AND ADAM BARKMAN

In the world of Rick and Morty, life often seems meaningless.

As we see throughout the show, the humorous and logic-defying adventures of Rick and Morty often entail them traveling through various dimensions and realities. Rick's intellect combined with Morty's ignorance often get them into a lot of trouble. In each episode, they defy death in search of some sort of meaning in their lives. However, because of their knowledge of the existence of infinite universes, for them, this meaning is not likely to be found. This is because with infinite universes, they are deprived of any unique qualities in their lives. Any one thing they do, given an infinite number of universes, has more than likely already been achieved by another version of themselves. In "Rixty Minutes," Morty makes this clear saying, "nobody exists on purpose, nobody belongs anywhere, everybody's gonna die."

When Morty says this, he isn't only talking to Summer to calm her down; he is, more importantly, talking to himself. This is a pivotal point in the show because Morty is telling himself the greatest truth his primitive mind can comprehend: life is meaningless. This clear sense of meaninglessness in life combined with infinite universes creates a life for Rick and Morty where nothing they do has any ultimate purpose.

The belief in a futile world has left Rick an alcoholic and Morty a very confused teen. Due to the gloomy way they mutually view life, they're forced to live for something beyond "conventional" or perhaps "natural" ways of living in order for their lives to be worth carrying on with. Could Rick and Morty find any subjective meaning in life when they live in a universe where there is no objective meaning to be found in life?

One ancient philosopher, Epicurus, would suggest that subjective meaning can be found through "happiness," which, for him, is broadly understood as maximizing pleasure and avoiding suffering. For Epicurus, however, happiness is not just a feeling, but a lifestyle which involves constantly seeking pleasure while at the same time avoiding pain in all areas of life.

Epicurus was a Greek thinker who believed, amongst other things, in the *tetrapharmakos*. Now as a *Rick and Morty* fan when you hear the word *tetrapharmakos*, you may think it is an alien defeated by Rick and Morty on one of their crazy multidimensional adventures. Although this word may sound like an intergalactic space term, it's actually an idea that Epicurus coined long ago.

This fancy Greek word is commonly translated as "four part cure." This isn't a cure for meaninglessness per se, but it is a cure that Epicurus recommended to cure unhappiness, which could then give a person meaning in his or her life. The four parts of this cure are: Don't fear the gods; Don't worry about death; What is good is easy to get; and What is terrible is easy to endure. This cure may be what Rick and Morty are actually looking for.

God Is Nothing to Fear and Neither Are Aliens

"There is no god, Summer, you gotta rip that band-aid off now; you'll thank me later," says Rick. If the gods or God exist, then there would likely be some objective purpose to human life. Yet Epicurus differs here. He didn't deny the existence of the gods but he did claim that the gods took no interest in any part of human life. Part of the reason for this is the Epicurean view of the world that everything is ultimately atoms and void. All things in the world simply move around in this void and atoms bounce off of one another. Even the gods are material beings—although highly refined material beings—and, as such, they are mortal.

On the surface, Epicurus's position seems different than Rick's—Epicurus was a materialist who believed in refined material gods. Rick is a materialist who seems to deny the possibility of the existence of any immaterial gods. Yet, perhaps

Rick isn't totally against the possibility of gods after all—perhaps he is more in line with Epicurus—since we do see Rick praying to God while fearing for his life in "A Rickle in Time."

Rick may have prayed to a rationally possible being (that is, God) out of fear; but he also could have prayed because he irrationally feared God. Rick might think that God is a rationally possible being since he himself bears witness to a number of strange beings in that very episode (beings from the fourth dimension). However, it seems more likely that Rick prayed out of irrational desperation rather than out of thinking his prayer would be heard. Regardless of what Rick was thinking at the time of his great sacrifice, however, we do know that he did pray to a god. His mistake, according to Epicurus isn't believing in the divine, but rather thinking the divine would care about his human actions.

Now let's say that likely Rick doesn't actually believe in God or the gods—that his prayer was just a knee-jerk reaction. A man invested in naturalistic science as much as Rick probably wouldn't believe in anything he couldn't make or measure physically. Epicurus said that if the gods exist, then they must be completely unconcerned with human affairs. The gods live where there is no pain and just pleasure. If they stepped into human affairs, they would experience imperfect human sensations of pain and pleasure, which Epicurus does not think they would do.

Furthermore, Epicurus writes, "If god listened to the prayers of men, all men would quickly have perished: for they are forever praying for evil against one another." This shows the contrast between the corrupt nature of man and the perfect nature of the gods. Despite his incredible rationality, Rick still can't say for certain that the gods don't exist. Proving that the gods don't exist is not possible because Rick has not seen any tangible evidence for or against their existence. Even if Rick does not want to admit it, he does understand that despite his vast knowledge, there are a lot of things he does not know. Rick is a man of science, so he hasn't closed the door on the idea of the gods; he just hasn't seen enough evidence to rationally concern himself with the gods' existence.

"If god exists, it's me"—this is a bold statement issued by Toxic Rick after discovering a new element. The evil parts of Rick that came out in the detox machine say that there is no god. This is in fact the evil parts of Rick speaking, so we must take it with a grain of salt; however, what we can learn from this is that deep down Rick can't help but wonder about the existence of God. Alongside Toxic Rick, we have Purified Rick, who doesn't concern himself with science and actually seems to be happier for it. Purified Rick does not wonder about the gods because this wondering can bring the pain of not knowing; instead Purified Rick simply accepts he does not know whether the gods exist and is all the happier for it.

We can read this in light of Epicurus and say that while Toxic Rick seeks pleasure, Purified Rick seeks to avoid pain. Toxic Rick is all the bad parts of Rick, which would include his irrationality. Since he's driven by pleasure and irrationality, this may account for why he rejects the Divine. Toxic Rick's rejection of God, then, doesn't stem from a careful philosophical basis, as with Epicurus, but rather from an irrational state of mind. Epicurus said the gods are simply not interested in human affairs and this is why they do not intervene. Toxic Rick says he is god, which gives him the greatest feeling of pleasure, which feeds his toxic ego. Regular Rick, on the other hand, thinks the gods won't save him when he prays to them, but it's not because he outright says they don't exist. Perhaps he thinks they're off watching interdimensional cable or making more gooble boxes. But regardless, Regular Rick does agree that god is nothing to fear. If god is nothing to fear, then the only thing to fear is pain. This is the very pain Epicurus seeks to cure and is just one more hint that the *tetrapharmakos* is a cure that may work for Rick.

Death Is Nothing to Worry about Because Death Is Everywhere

It's no secret that Rick and Morty face death on a regular basis. Each episode records Rick and Morty's adventures, but there is evidence in the show to suggest they go on way more adventures than are actually recorded. One example is at the very start of the series, when we discover that Morty has attended a total of seven hours of school in two months. This constant exposure to death has, presumably, taken the fear of death out of Rick long ago, and as we can see throughout the series, this is also what seems to happen to Morty.

Epicurus was a lot like Rick in that he also didn't fear death. Epicurus believed that because the gods won't intervene in life, they won't punish you after you die. Death shouldn't be feared because when you're alive death isn't there and after death there is no person left to experience death. Epicurus famously wrote in a letter to his friend Menoeceus saying, "Where I am, death is not, and where death is, I am not. Death is nothing to fear because it does not concern the living or the dead."

For Epicurus, there's little reason to think that a person would suffer after death. The reason people fear death is because they don't know what happens after it or because they fear the pain that often leads up to death. To this, Epicurus said that since we don't worry about what happened before our birth, we shouldn't be concerned with what happens after our death. Rick and Morty have no need to fear death because there are infinite versions of each person and infinite realities where each person exists.

However Rick C-137 and his Morty are special to one another. They see each other as irreplaceable even though they could easily be replaced. Rick C-137 and his Morty do not fear what happens after their own death; they fear the pain that would be felt by the other person after the other's death. Rick hates the Citadel and wouldn't want to be replaced by one of those guys, so even if he has no need to fear death, he certainly doesn't welcome the idea of it. If a person were to concern themselves with these infinite universes, they would go insane. We can see this when Morty and Rick replace their dead selves with themselves. This confuses Morty and makes him start questioning life and death. In response to Morty's internal struggle Rick asks, "What about the reality where Hitler cured cancer, Morty? The answer is: Don't think about it."

Death is all around us but we cannot fear it because it is not with us while we are alive. The fear of one's own death is irrational. Fearing death takes away from the pleasure of life and can result in pain and suffering. When Epicurus tells us not to worry about death, he is also telling us to seek out an understanding of it. Death is one thing that unites all of us: we all die at some point and so instead of fearing it we should understand it as a part of human life.

The Good Things Come Easy as Long as the Liquor Is Cheap

Rick seems to have found a partial cure for his life's meaninglessness in alcohol. According to Epicurus, however, this isn't a long-lasting cure. At the end of Season Two, when Rick sacrifices himself to protect his family, he seems to have found a greater cure for his misery. Despite being in jail, he seems to be remorseful of the way he treated his family, and at the same time happy he redeemed himself. Rick doesn't just drink his pain away—he begins to take action for his life. The complete sense of happiness Rick feels is what Epicurus says will come easily once we live a more simple lifestyle.

Epicurus believed the good things in life, the more natural things, like water and friends, are very easy to get. We are generally able to make friends and we often have lots of water—these two natural things are easy to come by and are crucial for life. As delicious and as fun as alcohol can be, it is not all that easy to come by compared to the simpler things in life. Epicurus stressed that we have enough to survive and when we realize this, we reach a state of relaxation. This is a state where we live a very simple life and avoid as much pain as we can.

Rick's alcohol may bring him a lot of pleasure but it also brings a lot of pain, which can be seen through his hangovers and barf constantly present on his chin. Things like alcohol, Szechuan sauce, or mega-seeds are highly sought after by Rick but also bring a lot of pain to his life. These things aren't what Rick should put his trust in; instead, he should put it in things like his family.

Epicurus said that there is a threefold division of desires in human life. The first set of desires are natural and necessary things like air, water, and food. Rick looks right past these things in everyday life because he sees them as necessary but redundant, with no real need to be thankful for them. He doesn't see the need to be thankful for them for the same reason Epicurus sees the need to be thankful for them, namely, because they are so easy to come and cause little pain. Take Eyehole cereal for an example; it is delicious cereal that Rick loves but if you eat it you get beat silly by the Eyehole man. Maybe Rick would have a bit less pleasure but significantly less pain if he just ate normal cereal for breakfast.

The second set of desires are the natural things in life that aren't necessary; these are things like expensive foods or fancy spaceships. Rick is completely satisfied without these things in life; he eats whatever food is given to him and his spaceship looks like he built it out of garbage. Rick sees the unnecessary things in life as necessary as long as they aren't fancier than they need to be. We can see this in the Meeseeks episode where the Sanchez family asks for natural things that they want but in a way that isn't necessary. They ask for the Meeseeks to help them with things that they could improve on their own if they truly wanted to—Jerry getting a few strokes off his golf game, Summer being more popular in school and Beth becoming a more complete woman.

However, there are times where Rick does think these unnecessary things are necessary for his happiness, like mega seeds or Kalaxian crystals. He puts his Morty in danger to acquire such things, so although he sometimes sees natural things as unnecessary, this is not always the case. Rick needs to take Epicurus's second point about desire a bit more serious if he wants to avoid more pain in order to be happier.

The third set of desires are things neither natural nor necessary; these are things like the desire for fame and fortune. Rick doesn't appear to seek fame or fortune; all he cares about is impressing himself. Epicurus was a lot clearer than Rick in his distinctions of these three desires. Epicurus says we need little to be happy and nature is abundant in giving these things to us. Rick would say he needs himself to be happy—which seems to be a sort of narrow sense of selfish pleasure—and he can easily give himself this happiness. This purely selfish sense of happiness that Rick strives for doesn't fulfill him, however. Rick still has a drinking problem and on several occasions tries to kill himself. If Rick put less emphasis on himself and paid more attention to the simple things in life, he would be a lot happier, according to Epicurus. Rick's strong desire to impress himself is an unnatural and unnecessary desire which leads to some pleasure but a lot of inner pain. Unfortunately Rick can't seem to get past the idea of outdoing himself in his everyday life. He can't keep up with his desire to invent and be the best, which leads him into depression. The only time Rick seems genuinely happy is when he is with his family and looks past their differences.

Bad Things Are Easy to Endure, and, Yes, That Means Living with Jerry

Rick may never cure his unhappiness if he doesn't put down the bottle and, at the same time, learn to view his family properly. At the end of Season Two, we see that Rick feels immense sorrow that he was losing Birdperson to marriage. He resents Birdperson for a short time because Rick sees that his friend's life, as he has always known, was over. Yet, throughout the course of the wedding, Rick sees that his friendship doesn't have to end because of a marriage. After Rick acknowledges this, he seems happy for Birdperson and actually delivers a speech at his reception.

The reception goes very badly, and leads to the apparent death of Birdperson. When Rick sees that he spent Birdperson's last day being resentful, he feels great pain and suffering. This pain felt may have partially led Rick to sacrifice his own life by going to prison in order to save his family at the end of the episode. Rick didn't want to make the same mistake of pushing away those closest to him, so at the end of Season Two, he put aside his families differences and did what he thought was best for everyone. He turned himself in to the Federation out of love for his family, and perhaps as an act of redemption.

Rick felt a deep pain when he lost Birdperson as well as when he heard his family speak of turning him in to the Federation. Rick wanted to end this pain, so he decided to turn himself in. Epicurus said that intense pain is short while chronic pain is long and dull. Pain, to Epicurus, is always bearable in life; however, painful experiences like Morty breaking his legs or Mr. Poopybutthole getting shot are instances of extreme pain for a short duration. A chronic pain that is fairly dull can be seen in Rick's life as a whole. Rick seems to have an existential pain that is topped with moral guilt. Going to jail may be painful but it is a remedy to the existential pain felt, since he is starting to live for something or someone other than himself.

The catchphrase "Wubba Lubba dub-dub" that Rick often says isn't simply the words of a crazy old man. Birdperson reveals that in his language those words mean "I am in great pain, please help me." Rick's life is a cry for help; he knows that no one will understand his pain except for those closest to him, like Birdperson. The chronic pain Rick feels is a recurring theme in the series. He wants to be happy but he doesn't know how. His will to live diminishes each day as he faces a meaningless life. Epicurus can relate to such a chronic pain because he suffered both from the inability to urinate and a troubled stomach for much of his adult life. He said that these pains were so bad that nothing more could be added to make his suffering worse. This is exactly the type of chronic pain Rick feels.

The reason Epicurus said he was able to live and be happy despite the pain was because he was able to keep his mind on the simple things in life like the philosophical conversation he had with friends. He said that remembering these conversations allowed for him to live a happy life even though he felt pain on a daily basis. Philosophy is what made Epicurus live in peace during the last years of his life. Unfortunately, Rick doesn't have something like philosophy to look back on and be comforted by. He has his science but because he largely does science for himself he doesn't have the same satisfaction from it as Epicurus did from philosophy. Instead of recalling deep conversations Rick looks back at his life and sees countless painful experiences and time alone in a garage inventing things. The long list of negative experiences allow little for Rick to recall and be happy about. The things he cares about the most never seem to be what other people care about, which adds to the pain.

Another fragment found of Epicurus's says, "Unhappiness comes either through fear or unbridled desire, but if a man curbs these, he can win for himself the blessedness of understanding." Rick doesn't fear anything, but we can see that he clearly does have a lot of unrestrained desire. Rick sleeps with Unity, loves to drink and has an irrational desire for Szechuan sauce. However, as Epicurus would say, Rick will never understand himself or his life unless he puts away these desires and refocuses. Going back to the example of the detox machine; when Rick and Morty go through the relaxation spa and lose the negative parts of themselves, we're able to see the good parts of them for a few brief minutes. There is a huge change in Rick's character when this happens. This is heard and seen through his larger and smaller actions like putting his seatbelt on. It is very easy to miss but until this point, Rick never buckles his seatbelt. This shows that the negative parts of him have left and that he does in fact want to live. The *tetrapharmakos* may help Rick later on in the show to cure his unhappiness and potentially find some subjective meaning. The positive parts of Rick show that when he accepts that life is meaningless, the sad parts of him leave and with them, the desire to die. Rick can be happy with life even though it doesn't appear to have any objective meaning it.

There May Be More to Life than Meaning

The world of Rick and Morty is meaningless, yet they both still seem to have something to live for. However, whatever it is they're living for doesn't fulfill them enough. Instead of just continuing to live that same way, they should, according to Epicurus, try to apply the four-part cure to unhappiness to their lives.

According to Epicurus, Rick has some correct beliefs that help him be happy; for instance, Rick doesn't fear god and doesn't worry about death. These are the first two parts of the *tetrapharmakos*. Yet Rick needs to apply the final two parts of the cure, namely, allowing for the good things to come easy and enduring the difficult. If Rick starts to see these latter two things in a new light, we would see a happier Rick in the future.

Of course, this is just one idea. In an infinite world, perhaps Epicurus's cure is also wrong, and perhaps there is an objective happiness yet to be found.

14
Jerryboree!

DANIEL MALLOY

Jerry Smith may be the most put-upon man in the universe. In several universes, actually. He's unemployed. His teenage children don't respect him. His wife blames him for ruining her life and getting in the way of her dreams. His father-in-law, who lives with them and is the smartest person in existence, has nothing but contempt for his son-in-law, whom he considers an idiot. Worse, Jerry *is* an idiot.

It's tempting to tell Jerry to stand up for himself. In fact, a few people have told Jerry to do just that—Beth, Summer, and Morty have all encouraged Jerry to get a spine. Rick never has, because he sees preying on other people's pity as Jerry's signature move. Jerry standing up for himself not only wouldn't be good, it would be almost impossible. The sniveling spinelessness of all Jerrys seems to be one of the few constants across all universes—hence the profitability of Jerryboree! And, Rick's view of his son-in-law seems to be borne out by events in *Rick and Morty*. On the rare occasions Jerry shows some degree of self-respect, he is either slapped down immediately or something goes horribly wrong because of it.

In spite of these unfortunate consequences, I think that Jerry should stand up for himself. His lack of self-respect does a disservice not only to himself, but also to those around him, and possibly even to all rational beings everywhere. Regardless of the unpleasant consequences of doing so, Jerry owes it to himself and everyone else to insist on the respect that is due to him as a person.

A Rick and Jerry Episode

It isn't nice to say that Jerry is the cause of all his own problems. It isn't true, either. Rick is due some share of the blame. But it's undeniable that Jerry causes some of his own problems. Mainly because he lacks self-respect. In fairness to him though, no one in the *Rick and Morty* universe has any self-respect.

Jerry's opposite number here seems to be Rick, but even Rick lacks self-respect. This can seem surprising, given Rick's general attitude toward himself. He even proclaims "God damn it, I love myself" ("Pickle Rick"). And there's little reason to doubt that Rick does, indeed, love himself—or at least, this version of himself. But there's also reason to believe Morty's pronouncement that "Ricks hate themselves the most. And our Rick is the most himself" ("The Rickshank Rickdemption"). All of these attitudes are compatible with one another. Rick loves himself because he's the smartest man in the universe and he values intelligence. He hates himself for a variety of good reasons, including his habit of letting down the people he loves. But none of this amounts to self-respect, at least in the sense that I mean.

The key here is provided by philosopher Stephen Darwall's analysis of respect. Darwall argues that there are two kinds of respect: recognition respect and appraisal respect. Recognition respect is the kind that any rational, autonomous being is entitled to by virtue of being in control of their own actions. Appraisal respect is the kind that we pay to particular individuals for their unique attributes. So, for example, were you to meet Jerry or Rick, you would owe them both recognition respect. They are both rational, autonomous beings capable of making their own choices. Whether you granted either your appraisal respect would depend on whether you value the attributes they seem to possess. If you value intelligence, then it would make sense to respect Rick since he is very intelligent. If, on the other hand, you value simplicity in people, it would make sense to respect Jerry.

This distinction between recognition respect and appraisal respect gets more complicated when we start talking about respecting ourselves. I maintain that Jerry lacks both kinds of respect for himself. In lacking recognition respect for himself, he is far from exceptional in the *Rick and Morty* universe—his lack of self-respect is just a bit more pronounced than others'. In part, that's because unlike many others, particularly Rick, Jerry also lacks appraisal respect for himself.

When Rick declares that he loves himself, he's proclaiming his appraisal respect for himself. Rick's appraisal respect for himself is plain. Rick values intelligence, and he happens to be the smartest person in existence.

Less obvious is my claim that Rick, like Jerry, lacks recognition respect for himself. But it's the lack of recognition respect for himself that lends truth to Morty's claim that all Ricks hate themselves. Oddly, the source of Rick's appraisal respect for himself, his intelligence, has robbed him of one of the essential components of recognition respect for himself. Having recognition self-respect means accepting responsibility for your actions. You can't acknowledge your own control over your own actions, without also recognizing the consequences that your actions cause. But Rick's portal gun is little more than a get out of jail free card that means never having to be responsible at all. Every time he messes something up, be it Beth's childhood or the entire world, he can just open a portal and hop to another world, rather than deal with the fallout.

My Sixth Promotion This Week

Lacking both kinds of respect for himself, Jerry goes looking for it from other sources. This perpetual search for approval may seem to be a simple function of Jerry's neediness, and in some ways it is, but it's also a function of Jerry's lack of self-respect. Since Jerry refuses to acknowledge that he's an autonomous, rational being capable of making his own choices, he winds up living a life of what philosopher Jean-Paul Sartre called "bad faith."

We live in bad faith whenever we deny that we are free beings who make choices. We do this in all sorts of ways every day. The most prominent, at least in Sartre's analysis, is when we over-identify with the roles we play in society. If I were to say, for example, that I wear shoes to class rather than sandals because I'm a professor and professors wear shoes, I would be surrendering responsibility for the choice I made. I am effectively pretending that my role made me act in a certain way.

The fact of the matter, though, is that I choose to wear shoes in class. I could just as easily choose not to.

Jerry doesn't have pronounced roles he can hide behind, apart from husband and father, and he doesn't seem to identify strongly enough with them to shield himself from making choices. Nonetheless, Jerry is desperate to live a life of bad faith. His desire to deny his free choice in anything leads him to celebrate the Galactic Federation's conquest of Earth. When the Smith family returns home after Rick's capture, Jerry is "assigned a function," and immediately proclaims "Honey! I got a job!" He didn't earn it; he doesn't even know what he does, but that doesn't matter. Jerry has so little to hang his hat on that being "assigned a function" counts as an accomplishment in his mind ("The Wedding Squanchers"). Similarly, once he's settled into his function, Jerry "achieves" promotion after promotion (six in one week, according to him), in spite of not knowing what his function is ("The Rickshank Rickdemption"). That doesn't matter; what matters is that someone, anyone, is showing him some approval.

A Predator Acting Like Prey

We may well ask what the problem with bad faith is. So what if Jerry doesn't want to make any of his own choices? Isn't that all to the good? Jerry's an idiot, after all. Doesn't it actually show a degree of responsibility for him to avoid making decisions? Being an idiot, he's unlikely to make good decisions, so maybe it's for the best that he renounces responsibility.

There's a very basic metaphysical problem with bad faith that underlies the more pressing problems. What makes bad faith bad is that what it attempts is impossible. When Jerry leaves a decision in Beth's hands, he's actually making a decision. Deciding not to decide is still deciding, which means that bad faith doesn't alleviate responsibility.

Start with Beth. Now, Beth is an intelligent woman—she's Rick's daughter, after all. But as both Beth and Rick prove thoroughly, smart people can be wrong too. Rick refuses to acknowledge that because there's no one who can stand up to him. Beth, on the other hand, has Jerry. For their marriage to work, they have to be equal partners, which means having equal say in things. In this, Jerry doesn't hold up his part of the bargain. Jerry's bad faith leads him to just go along with what-ever Beth says, including standing in the corner and speaking to no one at Birdperson's wedding. That's unfair to Beth in two ways.

First, it means that no one keeps Beth honest by challeng-ing her when she's wrong. Philosopher William Clifford (1845–1879) argued that this is one of our duties to those around us. In his essay "The Ethics of Belief," Clifford argued that we have a duty not to become gullible because it presents a temptation for others. It's easy not to lie when you know you'll be called out; it's harder when you know you won't. Although Jerry is certainly gullible, his general spinelessness presents the far more pressing problem. Jerry does Beth a dis-service by simply giving in to her, even when she's wrong. His bad faith encourages her to keep being wrong and not to cor-rect herself.

Second, by trying to live in bad faith, Jerry foists his respon-sibilities onto Beth. It means that Beth is pretty much solely responsible for the welfare of the entire family. Instead of a husband and two kids, Beth effectively has three kids. She has to make the right choices not only for herself, but also for Morty and Summer without any input from Jerry. On top of all that, she has to make decisions for Jerry because he won't make them for himself.

So, Jerry's bad faith isn't just his problem. It makes those around him over-confident and more likely to engage in ueth-ical manipulation, and it can be easily manipulated to feed and reinforce false beliefs and sheer stupidity. Rick may have over-stated the case when he said Jerry was a predator disguised as prey, but Jerry is definitely a danger.

How Do I Know I'm Real?

As problematic as Jerry's bad faith is, though, it's not the root of his problems. Bad faith is a symptom of Jerry's overall lack of self-respect. People live in bad faith for all sorts of reasons; some do it because it's easy; others because responsibility is frightening; others because it never occurs to them to be any other way. In Jerry's case, all of these may play a role, but there's a deeper cause: Jerry lives in bad faith because he does-n't respect himself. His lack of respect for himself leads him to not only renounce responsibility for his choices, but also to set a low value on himself overall. As such Jerry's lack of self-respect leads to various kinds of self-destructive behavior.

Jerry places so little value on himself that he won't even stand up for his own existence. Classically, your own existence is the only thing you can take for granted. Whether you're awake or asleep, whether you're reading this book or remembering reading it or imagining that you're reading it, you must exist. This is the insight encapsulated in the famous phrase from philosopher René Descartes (1596—1650), "I think therefore I am".

But when the Smith household is invaded by memory-altering parasites ("Total Rickall"), Jerry accepts the existence of all of them, from his nonexistent brother Steve to cousin Nicky to Reverse Giraffe without any problems. He even accepts that Sleepy Gary is Beth's real husband and the kids' real father. All of that poses no problem at all for Jerry. The problem he winds up having, when everyone is doubting everyone else, is that he doubts himself. In the midst of all the confusion, Jerry's inability to value himself leads him to entertain the notion that he himself is a memory-altering parasite and therefore not real. He needs the reassurance of memory-altering parasite Sleepy Gary to feel secure even in his own existence.

Stand and Face the Corner! Talk to Nobody!

For all that the world, his employers, his father-in-law, his wife, and even his children tell him otherwise, Jerry is a rational, autonomous being. He's capable of making his own choices, and responsible for the choices he makes. As such, it is Jerry's moral duty to value himself and to respect himself, at least in the recognition form of respect. His sniveling servility and spinelessness is beneath the dignity of a rational being.

No one has brought out the moral problems in a character like Jerry as clearly as philosopher Thomas Hill. In his essays "Servility and Self-Respect" and "Servility Reconsidered," Hill, building on the moral philosophy of Immanuel Kant, argues that servility and spinelessness like Jerry's is the result of a lack of self-respect. But self-respect is more than simply a feeling or attitude. Self-respect is a recognition of yourself as the subject of moral law and as the bearer of rights. So, in failing to respect himself, Jerry does a disservice not only to himself, but to morality. This lack of respect for morality itself makes it easier to disrespect others.

The clearest example of this is Jerry's failed relationship with Keara the Krootabulan Warrior Priestess ("The ABCs of Beth"). When Jerry finally accepts that the relationship was a mistake, he has a choice: he could be honest with Keara, or he could lie. His spinelessness leads him to lie. In doing so, he disrespects both himself, by failing to acknowledge that he has legitimate reasons to end the relationship, and Keara, by trying to manipulate her out of blaming him for the breakup. He also disrespects his children by lying about them to Keara and insisting that they are the ones who have a problem with her.

The Eighth to the Last Straw

In fairness to Jerry, we have to admit that he does occasionally show some backbone. Very, very rarely, Jerry shows glimpses of self-respect. It seems it's possible to push the little man too far. On some level, Jerry knows that he's a person and as such is worthy of a certain kind of treatment. It just takes a lot to get him to the point where he'll actually demand that treatment. And that's unfortunate, because on those few occasions when Jerry does stand up for himself, it usually goes badly for him.

The most prominent such case was when Jerry finally put his foot down about Rick ("The Rickshank Rickdemption"). After his father-in-law made it necessary for the family to flee Earth, got arrested, escaped, and brought down both the Council of Ricks and the Galactic Federation, Jerry had had enough. Pushed to his limit by Rick's antics and general disruptiveness, Jerry issued an ultimatum, insisting "It's him or me." Beth, of course, chose Rick. And Jerry, it seems, sticks to his guns. Refusing to compromise, demanding his due rights as both a husband and a father, Jerry leaves. He could have caved. He could have just accepted his continued humiliation. Beth knows that's a real possibility, which is why she says "I better tend to Jerry before he changes his mind and doesn't move out." Whether because of her intervention or not, Jerry doesn't change his mind. Standing up for himself costs Jerry everything—his wife, his kids, his home.

The ultimatum over Rick is an extreme case because of the stakes, but it's also typical in its results. Jerry draws a line in the sand, and someone else promptly erases it. This doesn't say much for the people Jerry usually associates with, who have a habit of disrespecting him, but it also doesn't say much for Jerry, who has a habit of going along with his own degradation. The reason Jerry's few attempts at standing up for himself go poorly isn't because Jerry is somehow intrinsically unworthy of respect—again, he's a rational, autonomous being.

The reason things go badly for Jerry when he stands up for himself is because he does it so rarely. Since he doesn't get a lot of practice standing up for himself, Jerry does it badly. Instead of demanding the respect he deserves, he acts out of wounded pride, or frustration, or petulance. In turn, the people around him are so accustomed to Jerry backing down that that's just what they expect him to do. When he does, it isn't perceived as Jerry finally standing up for himself, but as Jerry throwing a tantrum. For that, Jerry has only himself to blame. As Immanuel Kant said, "One who makes himself a worm cannot complain afterwards if people step on him."

I Can't Leave Now! Everyone Hates Me!

For all their differences, Rick and Jerry have some things in common. Neither has enough respect for himself to accept responsibility for his choices. The difference is only in how they flee from the consequences of their choices. Rick acts, sees the blame or misfortune coming, and just steps through a portal. Jerry tries to avoid responsibility by not making choices at all. He lets other people make all the decisions and take all the risks. Jerry's spinelessness, his subservience, and his cowardice all come down to the fact that he doesn't value himself as a person.

It's not that Jerry's worried he'll make the wrong choice. He's worried that in making any choice at all, he's taken on the responsibility for that choice. But that, in itself, displays a misunderstanding. Whether Jerry accepts responsibility or not, he is making choices, because he is a person. Acknowledging that wouldn't solve all of his problems, but it would solve his greatest problem. Jerry wouldn't be a problem for himself anymore.

15
Loving Your Pet Is Better than Utilitarianism

Rob Luzecky

In "Lawnmower Dog," Rick solves everyone's problems by giving Snuggles a helmet that raises his IQ. But is it the right thing to do? Maybe we should just keep our pets dumb. Or maybe we should try to make our pets super-duper-smart. Is a smart pet better than a dumb pet? Or is it the other way around?

While it may be that we all want smart pets, I think the morally right thing is that we love our pets. Utilitarian philosophers try to go about telling us all that something is morally right if it increases the pleasure of beings who can think. In Rick and Morty's world this tends to lead to some disastrous consequences. On the other side of things, David Hume says that it is morally right to love our pets.

Do you think Snuffles has the same moral worth as you, your family, your friends, and all the other people that you care about? If you don't know the answer to this question, that's cool. Let's try with asking another question; do you have a problem with Snuffles suffering? If you don't like the idea of Snuffles in some sort of pain or emotional distress, then this indicates that you think that Snuffles is a moral being. (Good job, give yourself a pat on the back.)

If we think that Snuffles is a moral being, then we might think that making Snuffles smarter would work to reduce his suffering. This is the case in "Lawnmower Dog," when we find Emperor Snowball (the name a super-smart Snuffles prefers—because, well, it sounds more distinguished and noble) living in a palace, not suffering any misery. But we can only reduce the suffering of a being who is *already* conceived as moral being. Any argument that hopes to reduce the misery experienced by an oppressed group must first establish that the oppressed are beings to which morality can apply—that imposing a morality would alleviate their suffering. Before we can alleviate the torment of Snuffles, we have to recognize that Snuffles should be treated like a being that has some sort of moral rights.

In *A Treatise of Human Nature,* Hume says some pretty cool stuff about animals. Hume was on board with the claim that some animals just are smarter than other animals, but he also recognized that intelligence isn't the correct way to think about things when trying to figure out if we should give an animal moral rights. Hume didn't think that intelligence was really that important in trying to figure out whether we should think of animals as having any moral worth. Hume recognized that being smart would not prevent you from becoming a tyrant, and Hume didn't have much use for tyrants.

Instead of using intelligence as a benchmark to determine whether a being should be considered to be moral, Hume thought that there must be another good reason to know that it's morally wrong to harm Snuffles. There he is, standing there, wagging his tail with that stupid look on his face; he isn't so bright, but he loves you; why on earth would you make him suffer by denying him anything that his little doggie heart desired? As Hume sees it, you'd have to be a pretty heartless, unloving, ignorant jerk if you didn't pet Snuffles on the head and give him a doggie treat.

Snowball Would Have Had Some Issues with Peter Singer

Have you ever had your face rubbed into a pool of your own urine just so some stupid jerk could try to teach you a lesson? If so, then you should be able to empathize with Snuffles. Once you wiped the urine off your face, you might think to yourself that you had been the subject of abuse.

If you happened to relate the story of your abuse to a philosopher, they would most certainly say that you have been morally wronged. If this wronging wasn't an isolated incident, but an event in a much more comprehensive system of abuse and degradation, the philosopher would probably encourage you to take up arms and start a revolution that aims at over-throwing your oppressors. Yeah, philosophers tend to be like that; they tend to get very punchy when they hear of cases of oppression. If you're oppressed, be angry, be rebellious, and be assured that there are philosophers out there who have your back. A lot of philosophers tend to be against animal abuse.

Peter Singer is one philosopher who would have taken issue with Jerry's actions. If you were alive in 1975, one of the must-read texts of that year was Peter Singer's *Animal Liberation*. The late twentieth century was a pretty awesome time for environmentalists and those who wanted to support the well-being of our furry little friends. After decades of lobbying, the Environmental Protection Agency was founded in 1970. While not exactly a clear supporter of the moral worth of animals, the Agency did have as its mandate the protection of the natural environment—the forests, streams, lakes, and meadows—that might be considered to be the home of many animals that have not been domesticated. (If you want to read some really compelling philosophical arguments—that laid the conceptual groundwork for the creation of the Environmental Protection Agency—you'd love Aldo Leopold's *A Sand County Almanac* or Rachel Carson's *Silent Spring*). While there have always been philosophers who liked animals, Singer really made a career of developing arguments for why we should be nice to animals—and even grant them legal rights. Singer, being a utilitarian, thinks that if we don't hurt animals, then there will be more happiness in the world—the net happiness of beings who can feel happiness will increase—and therefore we should not hurt animals.

Singer didn't really care too much whether an animal was smart or dumb; he thought all animals should be treated as being of the same moral worth as any given human. This isn't to say that that we should treat animals the same way that we treat humans. Singer thinks that animals and humans are equal in the same way that men and women are equal. Men, women, and animals all deserve equal attention and value, despite their differences. Singer recognized that some animals—like pigeons, who strut around and peck and shit anywhere they want, thinking they own the city, all the while blithely ignorant of the fact that corporations own most of everything—are just not bright. But Peter Singer also recognized that there are some human—

like Jerry strutting around after selling his apple campaign—
who are also not that bright. Singer thought that we could not
use intelligence as a clear determiner for which sorts of thing
we could morally justify harming, because the criterion of intelligence could also be used to justify the harming of really stupid humans. Hell, if we are morally justified in harming things
that are not as bright as we are, then why not hurt the dumb
people as well? That doesn't sound good.

Singer proposed that we don't harm things that can feel
pain. If an animal can feel pain, then we should, usually, spare
it the misery and degradation involved in animal experimen-
tation or being raised to be some other being's dinner. This
sounds pretty great for Snuffles, who—quite frankly—thinks
that his collar a bit too tight.

Unfortunately, Singer, being a utilitarian, makes the mistake of thinking that happiness is something that can be quan-
tified. You can count material things—physical things that
have a location in space-time. You can't count immaterial
things. If you were as smart as Emperor Snowball, you'd
instantly recognize that immaterial things are unquantifiable.
Happiness may variously be considered to be an emotional
response, a feeling, a concept, or a sensation that informs the
lives of those who watch *Rick and Morty*. Happiness is absolutely not a material thing, which means that happiness is
unquantifiable. Utilitarianism—even though it might suggest
some good outcomes for animals—is fucked up, in the sense
that it misidentifies the nature of happiness. By assigning an
attribute of material things to non-material things Singer and
all utilitarians get it wrong, which is really too bad, since we all
want a moral theory that says it is morally wrong to rub
Snuffles's face in his own urine.

Snuffles Would Have Loved David Hume

One of the coolest things about Hume was that he was Scottish.
Anyone who tries to tell you that Scottish people are fools is
probably a bit of a fool themselves. The people of Scotland
invented bagpipes and haggis. The Scottish figured out that
you could both blow into a sheep's gut as you march off to war,
and then stuff the sheep's gut with delicious spices and eat it
when the war was done. That is some next-level thinking.

David Hume's next-level thinking—which very well might have been inspired by the melodious tunes of bagpipes—was the observation that statements about morality are different from statements that describe the nature of things—like the weight of a freshly cooked haggis. In Hume view, it's just stupid to think that you can talk about the way people should act and think that you're doing the same thing as telling people about the nature of the world.

Hume, who was a very astute dude was kicking about Europe during the eighteenth century, observed that there was a hell of a lot of blood flowing in the streets. There was cannonfire everywhere. (Over the course of Hume's lifetime—from 1711 to 1776—there were a total of twenty-two separate wars fought on the European continent). Hume observed that most of these wars were justified by moral absolutists; you know, all those people eagerly stand their soapbox to preach that some actions are absolutely right or wrong.

Hume's aim was to specify a distinction between absolute truths and moral claims. Moral claims, for Hume, just aren't like descriptive claims, in the sense that they can't be proven absolutely true or false. For Hume, any time we make moral claims about what people should or shouldn't do, we risk people getting too excited to make good choices. Claims about the nature of reality are much less exciting. Do you know what the fifty-seventh decimal place of pi is? Do not fret if this information escapes you—no one really gives a shit. The question isn't as important as whether we should cut the testicles off of all male humans ("Lawnmower Dog"). Hume suggests that thinking moral and descriptive claims can imply one another is a horrible logical error that has been used to explain away all sorts of hardships and suffering. To rid the world of these entirely inadequate explanations for genuine miseries, we should let Hume's guillotine blade fall and cut the claims apart.

Fans of empiricism will probably know of "Hume's guillotine." For Hume, if I'm making a statement about the nature of reality, I'm making a statement that can either be proven to be true or false, in an absolute or objective sense. Metaphysics, for Hume, didn't allow for much wiggle room. Things like what we can know, and what we value as good or bad, allow for a great deal of wiggle room, in the sense that the validity of the standards we use to make any value judgments is partially dependent on our situation, and our point of view. Hume's guillotine was to draw a distinction between metaphysical and moral claims.

Perhaps the most important outcome of separating absolutism from morality is that it allows us to consider non-human animals, like Snuffles, as beings who should have moral significance. The story before Hume was that humans—and even then not *all* humans—were the types of beings that could be given moral rights. All types of animals, and other non-human things—like that forlorn looking tree in your yard that has been taken away and transplanted into a foreign environment that is so very far away from all its family and friends—were not the subject of morality. The implication of separating claims about the nature of reality from moral claims is that metaphysics no longer determines what can count as a moral object.

Hume's basic argument for why we should give some moral consideration to dogs is that they—though clearly not as smart as humans—have some modicum of intelligence. One clear difference between Singer and Hume is that while Singer is willing to grant moral status to pretty much any animal that could possibly feel pain, Hume was a lot more discerning about which animals he liked. In a pretty remarkable section of *Animal Liberation,* Singer makes the argument that we shouldn't hurt chickens (because they could feel pain). Hume didn't give a shit about chickens.

Hume observed that chickens were about as dumb as animals can get, and yet still be considered alive. The chicken's stupidity is one of the reasons that Hume would have no problem with putting it on the supper table. But dogs, that's a different story. Dogs, according to Hume, were fine and wonderful animals who were worthy of some moral consideration. Perhaps we should care about how we treat dogs because they're smart—perhaps not as smart as a nose-picker like Jerry, but smart nonetheless.

But to make the determination that something is smart is really a tricky thing. For instance, in America, we have idiots who can't spell the words "unprecedented", "council", or "tap" correctly during their early-morning Twitter rants, but who also proclaim that they are smart and stable geniuses who always use "the best words." Just saying that you are smart, doesn't make you smart. In order for the claim to higher intelligence to mean anything, there must be a set of agreed upon criteria that measure intelligence. Hume thinks that the baseline measure of intelligence is a being's ability to use reason. As you might guess, a being's ability to use reason is sort of complex and not every being has it. (This is evidenced by the observation that some beings who think that they're rational are—in fact—fools).

In *A Treatise of Human Nature*, Hume elaborates on why we should recognize Emperor Snowball's intelligence. Hume makes the observation that smart beings use reason correctly. Emperor Snowball is a smarty-pants because he uses reason correctly. The correct use of reason comes down to two things: a being must be able to make correct inferences (that is, inferences that adequately assess the meaning of a situation), and in order to make correct inferences a being requires some memory of previous experiences. The second condition—of having a memory of past experiences—helps us make correct inferences in the sense that memory allows us to recall the previous things that happened to us and use these as justifications for our judgments about whatever present situation we are in.

As Hume sees it, dogs have both of these capacities—of making inferences and remembering the past—and this is what makes them intelligent. Just look at a dog who seeks the pettings of its master when its master is happy, and which cowers under the bed when its master is angry; the fact that it performs these actions, indicates that it is making correct judgments about what its master is feeling. Who's a smart doggie? For Hume, a smart doggie is every one who recalls past instances of the master's anger or joy and then uses these recollections to infer whether they should seek to be petted or run away, tail tucked between their hind legs.

But wait a minute. It seems that giving something moral consideration just because it is smart seems a bit dodgy, in the sense that intelligence and moral worth seem to be different types of things. In his elaboration of the intelligence of animals, Hume seems to suggest that we should treat animals as though they were moral beings because their intelligence is similar to that of humans, and all things with intelligence have some moral worth. This claim rests on an assumption that intelligence is either identical to or a cause of moral worth.

We can't say that intelligence leads to moral worth. We also can't say that there is anything that causes smart things to be morally good things. Smart people can be total assholes. Rick is an asshole who is smart enough to build a contraption that can make dogs into super-geniuses and an "inceptor" which allows him to enter into people's dreams ("Lawnmower Dog"). Were it the case that intelligence and moral worth were the same sort of thing, then we should give Rick more moral consideration than a great kid like Morty (who never committed an evil deed, or harmed anyone, or said a mean thing in his entire life). That just doesn't seem right.

The absurdity is even more obvious when we try to claim that being smart makes you morally better. The suggestion that a being's level of intelligence somehow causes them to be morally valuable implies that we should treat really smart beings as our moral superiors. The chain of inferences is straightforward: first, we assume that level of intelligence seems to cause a being to be moral; next, we acknowledge that a being who is smart enough to blow up planets with a Neutrino Bomb ("Pilot") is smarter than all the rest of us who lack the mental wherewithal to make the Earth go boom; finally, since we assumed that higher intelligence causes a being to be morally better, we should treat a planet destroying scientist as our moral superior. Were it the case that a being's level of intelligence was an indicator of their moral worth, then we would have to treat beings (like Rick) who create entire microverses constituted of fully rational slave populations to serve as batteries for us as our moral superiors—they are smarter than us, so they must be morally better than us. Any set of considerations that leads to the conclusion that Rick is morally superior to the tiny population he's enslaved is clearly fucked up.

But, if we can't fall back on the criterion of intelligence as a justification to granting entities moral status, what else do we have? Hume thought that all we need is love (yep, love is all we need) to recognize that animals should be treated as our moral equals. Hume observes that the sentiment of love may extend across various types of species:

> Love in animals, has not for its only object animals of the same species, but extends itself farther, and comprehends almost every

sensible and thinking being. A dog naturally loves a man above his own species, and very commonly meets with a return of affection. (*A Treatise of Human Nature*, II, 2, 12)

When a dog wags its tail, it is showing that it loves you. For Hume, if you think otherwise, you just have mis-identified the nature of love. Love is a trait that does extend beyond the narrow confines of what passes for human. Animals can love. Humans can love. Animals can love other animals—just ask any lovebird, who mates for life. And animals can love other types of animals. Animals can love humans, and humans can love animals. So maybe Hume shouldn't be so quick to cook up that chicken after all. If something can love you and you can love it back, this implies that the being should be considered as a moral entity. If your dog loves you, and you love your dog, you really shouldn't try to harm him or make him smart. Hell, maybe if you make him smart, he'll get revenge on you for all the misery your human-kind has inflicted on him (by denying him doggie treats and pets on the head, not to mention having his testicles removed).

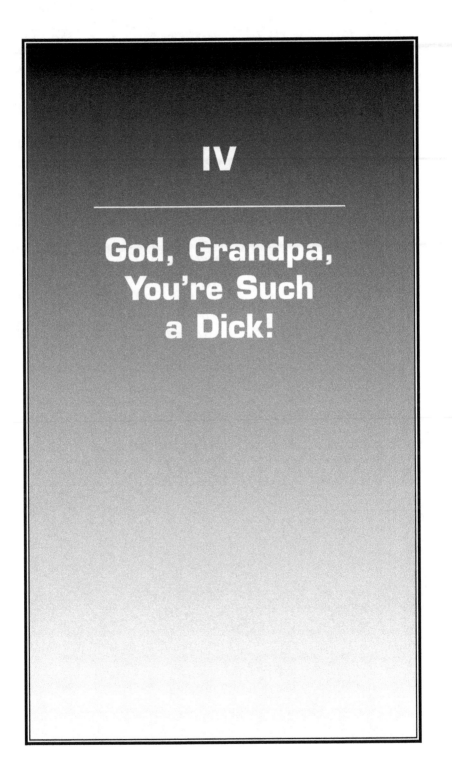

IV

God, Grandpa, You're Such a Dick!

16
He's Ethickle Rick!!!

MATTHEW HUMMEL

Except not really. At least not in the way we're used to thinking about ethical people—the Mortys of the world, if you will.
They do their best to do the right thing only to be hindered by
adolescent lust and Cronenberging the world.

That's not our Rick Sanchez, or well, not the Rick Sanchez
of Dimension C-137. He's a complete egotistical maniac. He's
self-centered, frustratingly overconfident, and a genius. He's a
standout, lonely loner, a lover (of Szechuan sauce among other
things), and a user (mostly of Morty . . . to get Szechuan sauce).

Looking at Rick from the lens of this (our) Earth, we love to
hate him. If *Rick and Morty* wasn't such an eye-catching and
hilariously quotable show, we'd be angry that Rick is so cruel.
From the perspective of ethical people, it's almost infuriating
that Rick's seemingly mean-spirited behavior so often saves
the day while Morty's attempts to be good nearly kill them.

It's not simply that Rick is self-centered, but being self-centered seems to be preferred in *Rick and Morty*. And that's usually because it is. The best way to be in a never-ending
multiverse that is "so big, nothing in it matters" is to be an egoist. As Summer would say to an angsty Tiny Riiiiick, "those
facts are who you are."

But this isn't a freaking character study. Leave that to the
nerds who graduate from places that aren't for smart people.
We're talking about something much bigger, and something much
older. So clear the ants in your eyes, Johnson. Because like a
Cthulhu creature that has yet to actually appear in any episode
except right before the title screen, here comes *The Leviathan*!

Gaggablaghblagh[1]

Leviathan was written by philosopher Thomas Hobbes. The name is derived from the biblical creature of the sea and conjures an image of some vast beast, like gonorrhea swimming around the bowels of Rick's hobo friend Reuben. Hobbes used the term "Leviathan" to refer to what he called a Commonwealth or more simply the Sovereign. The Sovereign is essentially a government authority, and it stands as a check against a person's natural tendencies to be "a selfish irresponsible ass," like, say, a genius who abandons his wife and child.

The Sovereign comes about when people freely give up authority to govern themselves in order to gain security, peace, and justice in an otherwise chaotic world. Hobbes says the Sovereign uses its "essential and inseparable rights" like the power to be a judge in all cases, the power to make war, the power to establish laws and an economy, and most importantly the power to be immune from any claims of tyranny or injustice. Hobbes's vision of the Sovereign supports his overall belief that a civil society can only endure under an absolute authority as the alternative is living in a constant state of war among individuals.

Already this Sovereign sounds like a bureaucratic control freak, and if I'm thinking like Rick Sanchez, "They're bureaucrats. I don't respect them." And we shouldn't want to respect the Sovereign. The threat to individuality, to personal advancement, to genius itself is too great under the rule of some controlling body accountable to no one. So if you're "the smartest thing in every conceivable universe—the Infinite Rick" able to hop in and out of realities at will, then the Sovereign is your single greatest threat. If, say, you're more of a Jerry, a spineless wormuloid mythologue who thrives on codependence and just wants to go home, then living under the Sovereign becomes a good thing. And let's face it, we're all a little bit of a Jerry sometimes—willing to compromise our convictions for a safe and contented life. That's what the Sovereign offers in exchange for some things . . .

---

[1] "Gaggablaghblagh" is Garblovian for "Philosophy section incoming: pay attention!"

Standing Scrung in Scrung with the Galactic Sovereign

If we're thinking dominating, oppressive government, then the Galactic Federation has to rank near the top of the list of Sovereigns present in the multiverse. It's the epitome of order with 6,047 planets under its rule. Once Earth joins the Federation, we get a look at what life is like under Galactic control.

For starters, there's a *joining* process. As with Hobbes's Sovereign, the Galactic Federation exists because planets consent to its rule. Hobbes calls this joining process "making a covenant," which just can't help but sound sinister. Although we don't see any sort of treaty-signing, we can assume Earth agrees to be inducted into the Federation and therefore agrees to any actions it takes in exchange for security and self-preservation from an otherwise chaotic and lawless galaxy. Earth then joins what Hobbes refers to as a "Commonwealth."

A Commonwealth is the state under rule by the Sovereign. Humanity surrenders its livelihood to the monopoly the Federation has on political power. For instance, there is a Ministry of Tourism. Earth is no longer a haven of the species native to the world but rather a stop-off for any planetary being within the Commonwealth of planets to "visit" or perhaps call home. Earth itself loses its individuality and instead becomes a market for "Earthling culture."

Existence with the Federation is strictly controlled within the Federation's "essential right" to execute civil laws, like where a person can be, what they can own, and to make their business known while on Federation property. When the Smith family arrive back on Earth after Rick surrenders himself to the Federation in exchange for their safe return, they're greeted at an interplanetary TSA where their DNA is scanned ("The Wedding Squanchers"). They're promptly ushered outside where a droid analyzes Jerry and prescribes him some antidepressants "compliments of the Galactic Federation," which, again, just can't help but sound sinister.

The Federation's control of its subjects is as much carrot as it is plumbus. In fact, the Federation confusingly uses pills as currency, even though the pills Jerry receives incur a debt of seven thousand fed credits. It would be useless for Jerry to argue the confusion (not that he would) because the Federation

controls the economy. Paying people in pills while simultaneously tracking debts in a separate currency ensures the
Federation will always hold economic power over its subjects.

The reward system for performing your "function" is even
more arbitrary, as Jerry brings in a "six chewable figure
income" after six promotions at a job where he doesn't know
what he does. Keeping people in a state of stress-free function
seems to be the Federation's way of ensuring no one thinks too
hard about how little freedom they have under its rule. If
you're having a Jerry day, then that might not seem so bad. But
if you're feeling Rickish, then you're existence is on par with a
Meeseeks who can't get Jerry to be on par.

Freethinkers are dealt with differently than subservient
subjects of the Federation. Along with pills and meaningless
achievement, the Federation monitors its subjects to judge
"what opinions and doctrines are averse" (Chapter 18). The
Smiths' new robotic butler Conroy serves this purpose. He is
eyes and ears for the Federation, able to become a legal authority at any overt sign of dissent. For example, Conroy catches
Summer and Morty digging up the portal gun off of dead Rick
in the back yard ("The Rickshank Rickdemption").

At first sight of the portal gun, an illegal technology, he
immediately transforms into a terrifying enforcement robot
complete with taser claws and grappling robotic tentacles,
because simply sounding sinister is played out by now. Had he
successfully captured the children instead of meeting the business end of Jerry's machete on the Cronenberged Earth, he
would have either terminated them on the spot or remanded
them to a Federation prison. Just like Rick, they would have
been housed in cube-like cells with restraints on all mobile
appendages and left to the horrible mistreatment of the
Gromflomite prison guards.

A CoMortywealth

While we get a brief glimpse of the Galactic Federation's inner
political structure just before Rick brings it crumbling down, there
isn't much to dissect how it all works. On the other hand, the
Citadel of Ricks exemplifies Hobbes's three different types of
Commonwealths. Hobbes says "the difference of Common-wealths
consisteth in the difference of the sovereign" (Chapter 19).

The Council of Ricks ran the Citadel before Rick nearly destroyed it during his prison escape. As only a small portion of the millions of Ricks and Mortys residing at the citadel, the Council as sovereign would be considered an aristocratic type of Commonwealth. Post-Rick-destruction, however, the citadel would appear to be more a democratic type of Commonwealth. An election is held among various Ricks and one charismatic Morty. But the democracy appears to be a new type of control over the residents of the Citadel ("The Ricklantis Mixup"). Even after the Morty candidate's landslide win (those on "joke security" would tell you it was close enough to trigger a recount), a group of Rick oligarchs forming a secret Council of Ricks teased the newly elected "president," telling him they really ran things on the Citadel even when the old Council was in charge. In a final regime shift, President Morty then reveals himself as Evil Morty and dispatches nearly all of the secret council. Evil Morty's first acts show him establishing himself as a dictator over the Citadel, which happens to fit in perfectly with the third version of Hobbes's Commonwealth, a monarchy.

We don't get to see (yet) what becomes of the Citadel of Ricks past Evil Morty's rise to power. The jarring reveal that the new president is Evil Morty, through floating photographs near the frozen corpse of his former campaign manager drifting in space, is a chilling one. The Citadel may yet become a floating fortress of evil. But if Evil Morty is truly a sovereign in Hobbesian terms, then his actions will be above any consideration of justice or injustice. As the one with power, the Sovereign, Evil Morty's rules become whatever he so chooses. His decisions become the law. No one could claim to have suffered an unjust fate under Sovereign Morty, and neither would any Rick or Morty dwelling within the Citadel be able to rightly accuse him of injustice. The Sovereign is justice.

This all of course simply follows the *logic* of the idea of the Sovereign. If Evil Morty makes life utterly miserable in the Citadel, *practically* speaking he would need to toss something extremely important into the wishing portal to save him from the Citadelians tossing him into . . . well . . . the "wishing" portal. He's under no obligation to be completely just according to whatever idea of justice his subjects subscribe to, but he would do well to keep some Simple Ricks on hand to calm the masses and avoid at least blatant corruption within his new seat of authority. In Rick's eyes though, that's not possible, nor should it be. But we're getting ahead of ourselves. Let's head over to Shoney's and use a brainalyzer to see what it takes to ~~manifest butts~~ be the smartest man in the universe and the Sovereign's worst nightmare.

EgoRickstical

Rick seems like everything Hobbes's political philosophy is trying to avoid or rise above. But actually Rick is the principal building block to Hobbes's whole case for the Sovereign. His central thesis is that nobody does anything unless it's for their own benefit—"the object to every man is his own pleasure" (Chapter 15). And aaawwwww yeah, son, does Rick love his own pleasure. We're talking about a guy who sells weapons to killers so he can spend an entire afternoon at, admittedly, the coolest arcade in the galaxy.

Rick displays a strong form of psychological egoism. He always acts in his own self-interest up to and including deviously hiding his motivations to look like he cares about others, in order to further a greater goal for himself. Rick hops from mind to mind to not only escape Galactic prison but also to bring down the Council of Ricks in glorious fashion ("The Rickshank Rickdemption").

In a particular exchange with Riq IV, one of the Rick Councilmembers who takes Summer hostage, Rick plays a mind game. He suggests he has no problem with Summer dying if it means he could get a cleaner shot at Riq IV. He has to reveal his true intention when Morty blows up his spot by threatening to shoot Rick to save his sister. Rick claims he was never going to let Summer die, but the idea was for Riq IV to think he would in order to gain the upper hand. He then "lets" Morty shoot him with a fake gun, giving him the element of surprise to take out Riq IV. The fact that Rick hides his motivations from everybody in the room (unintentionally so from Morty who fails to read clear directions on fake guns . . . dumb as a bag of sand) shows the depth of psychological egoism that is rampant in Rick. But we're not even done here! At the end of that same episode, Rick descends into a drooling tirade, telling Morty he had to save him and Summer before he could return home to become "the de facto patriarch" of the family and the universe (and to get that

Szechuan McNugget sauce, even if it takes nine seasons!). He's hidden his motivations within the revealed motivations from before during the hostage exchange, like some legally safe knock-off of everyone's favorite confusing and stupid movie.

Hiding motivations is a good calling card of psychological egoism, but not every instance of faking it should be considered a sign of egoism. It could just as easily be a sign of shame. The difference is clear if we think of shame as someone who's dissatisfied with his selfishness—a Morty! Morty's hidden motivations when asking Rick to purchase a Gazorpian sex robot for him is a perfect example ("Raising Gazorpazorp").

Morty strives to be wholesome, so it's very improper for him to be getting a sex robot. But he's a stereotypical teenager who has admitted to having masturbated everywhere in the house, much to Summer's dismay when she catches him in the kitchen. In order to get that sex robot and save face, Morty tells Rick he wants it for a souvenir, a lie Rick clearly does not buy—though he still buys the robot. While Morty's poorly-thought-out lie does serve a selfish purpose, the reason behind the lie belies its true intention which is to hide Morty's shame for making such an improper request.

He's not trying to actually fool Rick because he doesn't need to. Rick is as shameless a pervert as any. He even congratulates Morty when he "got some of that mermaid puss" during their adventure to Atlantis. He could have just asked Rick to get the robot for its intended purpose. There would have been some slight ribbing on Rick's part, but ultimately Rick may have respected Morty for committing to, and being satisfied with, such an egoistical impulse. So we can tell the difference between shameful hidden motivations and psychological egoism with the reason the motivations are hidden.

Whereas Morty is unnerved at not wanting to seem improper to someone who wouldn't really care, Rick's strong egoism spits on the idea that anyone else's opinion matters. The only one that does matter is Rick's own opinion of himself. As Rick says, "Grandpa goes around, and he does his business in public because Grandpa isn't shady" ("Mortynight Run"). He hides his motivations tactfully and without regard to the perception of others because they don't matter unless, as was the case with the prison escape, he needs to manipulate those perceptions to serve his own ends.

Big Ethics in Immoral Sanchez

Now, it's one thing to say Rick is a psychological egoist and another thing entirely to suggest that his egoism is the best way to be, the preferred behavioral path. It's the difference between saying "I'm a pickle, Morty!" and "You should always be a pickle, Morty!" The former is an example of descriptive ethics—just telling it like it is, like if we were to call a guy who sells cursed items "the literal Devil." No judgments, just science.

Prescriptive or normative ethics takes things a little further by mixing in judgments, such as "selling cursed artifacts to people is an evil enterprise that ought to be put down through genius science that can counteract the negative effects." We can see Rick getting his kicks trouncing the devil Mr. Needful, but for his egoism to be prescriptive, we would want to say that his insistence on pursuing his own self-interest is something everyone should do in all cases. And that's a little hard to do when we see Rick give up hammering on Needful's business once he gets bored.

If egoism means letting "the literal devil" curse people with impotence-inducing aftershave because we're bored, then morality, specifically the struggle to determine good and bad behavior, is lost. That is, assuming we ignore when the uncursed people "haven't learned a thiiiiiing" after their curses are lifted and subsequently return to their vices ("Something Ricked This Way Comes"). That seems to be Rick's upshot for egoism. On the one hand, upholding good over evil is the long-held "ethical" thing to do. It limits immoral behavior with the unending struggle against vice. But, as Rick would tell us about that traditional take on ethics, "scientifically, traditions are an idiot thing."

Good and evil isn't something that an egoist necessarily needs to struggle with. For Hobbes, the real struggle is simply competing to make a life in a world full of people trying to do the same. He determined two truths to living in a competing world: that resources will always be scarce and that no one person would be able to dominate all other people at a single time to gain mastery over the resources (Chapter 13). Rick can get Morty to put rare megaseeds *way* up his butt, but he couldn't get everyone to do so anytime he wanted.

As an egoist, Rick doesn't need to care about doing the right thing, he just needs to maximize his own self-interest. He needs to outcompete anyone who stands to take or would prevent him from taking any resource that he wants, be it the ingredients to concentrated dark matter or uninterrupted time with his grandson so he can use him on his crazy sci-fi adventures. Hobbes believed that, in a state of competitive chaos in which the life of any person could be "solitary, poor, nasty, brutish, and short," people would naturally surrender their freedoms to the Sovereign to guard against that.

It's like the Council of Ricks banding together to ensure enough resources to combat the many enemies Ricks make across all timelines and dimensions. The genius of "our" Rick, however, and why his particular brand of egoism could be considered ethical lies in understanding exactly why a Council of Ricks or a Galactic Federation is a bad thing. Lost individuality means lost opportunity.

Rick knows "the point of being a Rick is being A Rick," an entity unto himself with his own pick of the resources spanning the vast multiverse. Hobbes's theory of surrendering rights to a Sovereign makes sense when indeed there are scarce resources. But Rick gets the bigger picture. Infinite realities means infinite resources if you know how to get them (and being a genius doesn't hurt). The goal for Rick then is to be so self-interested as to let the multiverse be his oyster.

If he wants to create a theme park inside a human that glorifies his reverence for pirates, then he can scour the multiverse for people who won't build "a monument to compromise" on that dream. If he wants to get "wriggedy wriggedy wrecked," then he can utterly destroy his daughter's house and stop time to avoid the possibility of Beth keeping Morty from him on future adventures. If he wants to escape a Cronenberged world without skipping a beat in his life, then he can just take the place of a Rick with a little more "success" at not Cronenberging things. Mastery over traversing the multiverse is the key to surviving it, and Rick's egoism lets him maneuver through that state of infinity seamlessly. Relentlessly pursuing his own self-interests is not simply the way he is, it's the right thing to do. To not do so would be to live a life of regret-filled mediocrity under some uncontrollable power (see: a Beth and Jerry marriage).

AltruRicktic?

Let's put Rick's egoism to the test because that's the scientific thing to do. If Rick truly cares only about his own self-interest, then what about the times when he behaves altruistically? That's a blurry line to walk because Rick's seemingly altruistic actions could so often hide a selfish motivation. When he gives the Meeseeks box to Beth, Jerry, and Summer, he's not really interested in solving any of their problems, only providing a quick, comprehensive fix so he can get on with winning his bet that Morty's selected adventure will suck ("Meeseeks and Destroy"). Likewise, buying Morty the Gazorpian sex robot certainly seems caring, but it could easily be argued that Rick had some personal interest in irritating Jerry for buying something Morty thought was cool.

Those instances don't really compare with a more serious one, like Rick sacrificing himself by placing his time-fusing collar on Morty, leaving him moments from time-fractured inexistence ("A Rickle in Time"). It's hard to square away Rick's egoism when he says, "I'm okay with this. Be good Morty. Be better than me." "Be better than me" could imply a lot of things, including that Rick hopes Morty will find a way to exist in the multiverse without being an egoistical jerk.

The sweet moment turns out to simply be a moment of weakness, though, and a convenient point for Rick's argument in favor of egoism. When Rick suddenly finds Morty's collar and is able to activate it on himself in time, he reasserts there is no God, implying he alone is the master of his destiny. He also shuts down Morty's one sixty-fourth of a memory that Rick was altruistic by reminding Morty (and himself) that Morty's non-egoistical ways are what lead them so often to peril in the first place.

Rick's brush with prison is another instance of supposed altruism. On the dwarf Earth-resembling planet, Rick overhears the family—well, Jerry—arguing to turn Rick in to the Galactic government so that they can return home to their actual-Earth ("The Wedding Squanchers"). Rick slumps within the dwarf-planet's core, and then we see him take off, setting in motion a plan to ensure the family's safe return to Earth at the cost of his own freedom. As far as egoistic choices go, that one wasn't. And if we didn't get the first episode of Season Three to show us how Rick subverted the government and brought it to its knees, we would be left wondering if Rick finally came around to caring about something besides his own interests.

Perhaps Rick's egoism does have a limit, the limit to how far ahead he can see that pursuing his own interests actually pays off. He could have continued to keep the family exiled on the dwarf planet until he figured out a way to bring the Galactic Federation down without turning himself in. Then again, Season Three did happen, and Rick's egoistical genius proved itself once again.

Rick didn't really care about providing a better life for the family than the less crappy choice among a tiny Earth, an Earth on the cob, and an Earth with a sun that screams endlessly. He cared about claiming his seat as the most powerful person in the universe. Because as long as Rick's in control (meaning out of control), then we don't have to worry about a "de facto" Sovereign.

And that's something worth not thinking about.

17
Who Is "Rick" Anyway?

Ethan Landes

We all know Rick is the Rickest Rick who ever Ricked. This is beyond dispute. But take a moment to think about that first sentence. It's a mess.

Rick's name appears in the sentence in some form four times. Four! The first time, the name is referring to the main character of the show. Then both Rickest and Ricked refer to a state of mind embodied by Rick. But what about the second use of Rick? Does it refer to the main character of the show again? That doesn't make sense. There must be something else going on. How exactly do names work across the multiverse?

How Names Work in the Single-verse

Normally, we use names without issue. When I say "Justin Roiland" in the sentence "Justin Roiland was born in California," both you and I know who I'm talking about—the voice actor behind both Rick and Morty. This can go wrong. You might have a friend who's also named Justin Roiland who wasn't born in California. You might then wonder how I know your friend and wonder why I think he was born in California. But this can be cleared up easily. Even though many people are named "Justin Roiland," we can always clear up which person I am talking about.

We've come across the first distinction we need to draw to figure out who or what exactly "Rick" refers to. Names are not the same thing as objects. Names are bits of language, but objects are things out there in the world. Names are words we use to talk about objects. Distinguishing names and objects can be confusing because to talk about an object, it's easiest for me to use its name. It's much easier to talk about Justin by calling him "Justin" rather than always saying "the voice of Rick and Morty" So we can use quotation marks to talk about a name without talking about the object. "Justin" is a name consisting of six letters that comes to us from Latin. Justin is a person. "Justin" has two vowels in it. Justin has two arms.

Fortunately (or unfortunately) *we* do not have to worry about the multiverse. The multiverse significantly complicates matters. There is only one Justin Roiland, but there are way more Rick and Mortys. As far as we know there are a few thousand or even million in the Council of Ricks, but outside of the Central Finite Curve, there may be an infinite number of Rick and Mortys. So when Morty uses the name "Rick" who exactly is he talking about? One Rick in particular? Every Rick? Only the Ricks that don't have a schtick? (Sorry, Simple Rick . . .). Luckily, philosophers of language have already helped lay the groundwork to answer the question. To determine what "Rick" refers to in the multiverse, we find help in David Lewis's and Saul Kripke's competing theories of how names work when we talk about what could have been or what could be.

Possibilities and You

Understanding Lewis's and Kripke's competing theories of names requires stepping back and thinking about what happens when we consider what could have been. Called *counterfactuals*, these are events that might have happened, but for whatever reason haven't.

We think about counterfactuals all the time. I sometimes think about what a Noob-Noob and Mr. Poopybutthole crossover episode would have been like. Obviously it would have been a buddy-cop detective story (Justin and Dan, please write this episode), but I am not thinking about something that actually happened. Instead, when I think about the *clearly* missed opportunity of two of the show's most loveable characters striking out together to hunt down a murderer, I am thinking *counterfactually* what would have happened had the writers' room been different. A counterfactual where there's an episode where the two hapless optimists must face the grim truth of a dark world.

Counterfactuals work a lot like the multiverse does, but one belongs to the realm of physics and the other belongs to the realm of what is possible. A world where *Rick and Morty* has twelve seasons and a movie? Where gravity does not exist? Where I win a Nobel Peace Prize for writing this chapter? If we are in one universe in an infinite multiverse, there is a universe where each of these happens. But they also describe counterfactual claims about what could have been in *this* universe. The multiverse is, within the fiction of *Rick and Morty* (and if it turns out to be true in our reality), a physical fact. The multiverse is the way in which reality is made up. In contrast, counterfactuals are claims about possible situations. There are ways in which things could be, but aren't.

I sometimes wonder what it would have been like if I had been born in Europe instead of America. When considering this I might say "If I had been born in Scotland, I would have eaten more haggis as a child". In this sentence, "Scotland" refers to Scotland itself—a very real place that I can visit—and "haggis" refers to an actual food that actual people eat. What about "I"? I can't be talking about myself in quite the same way as I do when I say "I am losing my hair" because I wasn't actually born in Scotland.

The same puzzle arises in the multiverse. Trying to cheer Summer up, Morty says in "Rixty Minutes," "I eat breakfast twenty yards away from my own rotting corpse." Does "my" here mean the same thing Morty means when he calls Summer "my sister"? Taken literally Morty is saying he is both alive *and* buried in the backyard. Morty is both alive enjoying pancakes and was blown to pieces in the garage.

There are two possible ways we should understand how Morty talks about himself. First, "my" in "my own rotting corpse" doesn't mean the same object that Morty means by "I" at the start of the sentence. "I" is about someone who is alive and enjoys pancakes. "My" is about someone who was scraped off the wall of the garage. But normally "my" and "I" mean the same thing. Maybe then this situation is no different, and "my" and "I" mean the same thing in the sentence. Both refer to Morty himself.

Given the similarities between counterfactuals and multiple dimensions, let's look at how philosophers have explained "If I had been born in Scotland, I would have eaten more haggis as a child" to see if it helps us understand "I eat breakfast twenty yards away from my own rotting corpse."

One Rick to Be Them All

Saul Kripke argues that when I talk about what could have been, I'm imagining myself in that situation. Any time I wonder what Mr. Poopybutthole/Noob-Noob cross-over episode Dan Harmon and Justin Roiland might have written, I am thinking about Dan and Justin, just in an imagined scenario. When I talk about what would have happened if they had written the episode, I'm talking about the Dan and Justin. *Dan* and *Justin* would have written a different episode, and *they* would have spent time storyboarding and editing the script. While this all should seem so obvious to be hardly worth stating, the cracks start showing when we think about what this means Dan and Justin are. Since it's them that would have written the cross-over episode, Kripke thinks there's a sense in which they extend out into different possibilities. They exist in the real world, but they also exist in possible situations too.

Let's swap out possibilities for different dimensions of the multiverse and see how this works. Applying Kripke's theory to the multiverse, when characters in the show use names like "Rick" and "Summer" or pronouns like "I" or "you", they are referring to every version of the object across dimensions. "Rick" doesn't just refer to the Rick from dimension C-137, it refers to all of the Ricks across the Central Finite Curve.

Summer, Jerry, and Beth talk this way when looking at their alternate lives through VR goggles in "Rixty Minutes." When looking into another dimension, Beth says "I'm winning a Nobel Prize" and Jerry says "I'm a lion tamer." Here they are talking about themselves as not only existing in one universe, but also existing in another. Indeed, we see seconds later how similar the multiverse is to counterfactuals. As the fight between Beth and Jerry escalates they switch from talking about themselves across the multiverse to what could have been. Jerry says that if he hadn't married Beth, "I'd be on DiCaprio's yacht banging Kristen Stewart." Jerry is talking as if he isn't just in this universe. He is also in other universes and across different possibilities.

Maybe it makes sense to talk about the characters or ourselves existing in possible situations, but it's crazy to think we exist in the same way across the multiverse. If characters exist as one object in different universes, then there is only one Rick, one Morty, one Summer, and one Jerry. This means the Council of Ricks only has one member—Rick. The Morty torture device hiding Evil Rick's lair was only torturing one person—Morty. The different bodies being tortured were just different parts of the same person, and the different bodies composing the Council of Ricks are just different parts of the same person.

Perhaps there really is only one Rick across the multiverse and we should adjust how we think. But since when should we use what Jerry, Beth, and Summer say as guides to the truth? Luckily, we do not have to accept this absurd conclusion. There's an important difference between the sorts of counterfactual statements Kripke considers and different people across the multiverse. According to Kripke, the counterfactual situations are in my head. It's true that I could have been born in Scotland, but this doesn't mean there's part of me that was actually born in Scotland. I'm just considering a non-real possibility. In the multiverse everything is real. As impossible as it may seem, there's really someone out there banging Kristen Stewart.

One Rick Among Many

David Lewis argues that possible situations are not merely imagined—they really exist. Just like you and I exist, there are people who really wrote and produced a real cross-over episode. For every possible way things could be, there is a corresponding reality where that possibility happens.

Remember that counterfactuals are not the same as the multiverse. For us, the multiverse is a theory of physics. Lewis's theory is a theory of what it means for something to be possible (that is, a counterfactual). Even if it turns out that there isn't a multiverse and there is the only universe, because the cross-over episode was written, Lewis argues that there really is a cross-over episode in some unreachable place.

When I say "Dan and Justin could have written the episode", according to David Lewis, I'm talking about two real people who live in a real apartments who eat their real breakfast every morning. But these are distinct from the Dan and

Justin in our world. Every possible situation really exists. There is really someone who won the Nobel Peace Prize for writing a chapter on names in *Rick and Morty and Philosophy*. We reach the craziness of Lewis's argument much sooner than we reached the craziness in Kripke's. There cannot possibly be a real person corresponding to every way I could have been *independently of whether or not there is a multiverse*!

Let's set this aside for a moment and explore what Lewis's view says about me. Remember Kripke says possible situations are imagined and so when I imagine what my life could have been like, I am thinking about myself. This means I exist across different possibilities. Lewis instead thinks of possibilities like the multiverse. Lewis argues that because each possible situation involves real living people, it's a mistake for me to think of them as literally myself. You and I are different people who live separate lives and deserve separate names, and so do I and possible beings just like me. When I say "I could have been born in Scotland," I'm not talking about myself. Rather, I'm talking about someone just like me who was born in Scotland (or more accurately, a place just like Scotland). So "I could have been born in Scotland" really means "Someone just like me was born in Scotland."

Applied to the multiverse, Lewis's arguments make better sense of things than Kripke's. Objects only exist in one universe, rather than existing across all universes. Each use of "Rick" by a particular Morty refers to his particular Rick. That is, Morty is referring to the Rick from the same universe as himself. All other Ricks to that Morty are counterparts—people like Rick who are not literally Rick.

Unlike before, when Beth and Jerry talked about themselves stretching across the multiverse, we are in good company. The Council of Ricks talks the way Lewis's theory say they should. According to the Council of Ricks, Rick is not called "Rick"; he's called "Rick C-137." Sure, at the breakfast table, "Rick" is enough, but it isn't when on trial in front of the council.

This is way less crazy than there only being one Rick across the whole multiverse that exists in multiple universes at once. In fact, we talk this way normally. If I talk about Justin and you aren't sure which Justin I'm talking about, I can say "Justin *Roiland*". Normally a first name is enough, but occasionally just a first name does more harm than good. "C-137" works just like a last name. Just like we sometimes need to use Justin Roiland's last name to distinguish him from other Justins, Rick sometimes needs to add "C-137" to clear up which Rick among many he is.

Even better, while neither Kripke nor Lewis were considering the multiverse, we can see the arguments defending Lewis's use of names applies easily to the multiverse. The multiverse is full of real universes that are themselves full of real people, and some of those real people in one universe resemble real people in a different universe. Lewis thought we needed to talk about possibilities as being about people just like us because he thought every possible scenario really exists and has real people in them. Well, in the world of Rick and Morty (and maybe ours, too), the multiverse really exists and each universe is full of real people.

Names Across the Multiverse

When Morty said "I eat breakfast twenty yards away from my own rotting corpse," or when Beth said "I won the Nobel Prize" were they wrong? It isn't Morty's corpse; it's the corpse of someone just like him. And Beth didn't win the Nobel Prize, someone just like her did. It was the corpse of someone who looked just like Morty, spoke just like Morty, and even had the name "Morty." But in the same way your friend named "Justin Roiland" isn't the person I talk about when I say "Justin Roiland co-created *Rick and Morty*," Morty saying "myself" isn't talking about the person who ended up splattered all over the garage and buried in the backyard. Instead "my corpse" is just a way of saying "the corpse of the guy just like me."

Similarly according to David Lewis, I can say "I could have been born in Scotland" and say something true—even though I'm talking about someone else who was born in Scotland. "I" just means something other than what it might first seem. It looks as if I'm talking about myself, but I'm talking about someone else.

But, you might think, "I could have been born in Scotland" is different than "Someone just like me could have been born in Scotland". Beth obviously thinks "I could have won the Nobel Prize" says more about being married to Jerry than "Someone like me could have won the Nobel Prize." Plenty of people like me were born in Scotland. Scotland has its fair share of balding, bearded, and freckled red-headed men, but when I think about how I could have eaten loads of haggis growing up, I'm not thinking about them.

Why Rick Truly Is a Pickle

While this looks like a problem for Lewis, it isn't curtains for him. He can explain why Beth should care about people just like her and why I should care about people just like me. But for that, we need one final (I promise!) detour to talk about what makes sentences true.

When Rick exclaims "I'm a pickle!", what makes it true? Let's not overthink this. Rick saying "I'm a pickle" is true if he is indeed a pickle. The same thing goes for when Morty says "Nobody is born on purpose, nobody belongs anywhere, everybody's gonna die. Come watch TV." The sentence is true because nobody is born on purpose, nobody belongs anywhere, and everyone is going to die. The sentence corresponds to reality. Similarly, "I'm a pickle!" is true because Rick is indeed a pickle, at least when he said it.

It's easy to talk about the truth of simple statements "I'm a pickle" because it's pretty easy to figure out what makes it true or false. But what about these counterfactual claims about possibility? What makes it true that I could have been born in Scotland or that Beth could have won the Nobel Prize? Kripke and Lewis have slightly different things to say here. Kripke thinks, remember, *I* am what makes things possible about myself. "I could have been born in Scotland" is right if it is true *of me* that I could have been born in Scotland.

Lewis instead thinks possibility works a lot like the multiverse. "I could have been born in Scotland" is not true because of anything *I* could have done. We have to look further afield to other people in other possibilities. What makes "I could have been born in Scotland" true is whether or not beings just like me were born in Scotland. And we mean beings *just* like me— at the very minimum they have the same DNA.

We are now in position to answer the question at the start of the section. Why should Beth care about people just like her when she says she could have won the Nobel Prize? According to Lewis the facts that make "I could have won the Nobel Prize" true are exactly the same facts that make "Someone just like me could have won the Nobel Prize". In both cases other possible beings make each statement true.

But we're interested in the multiverse and the question of how "Rick" and "Morty" work with an infinite number of dimensions. And again we see points in Lewis's favor. Why is Morty right when he says "I eat breakfast twenty yards away from my own rotting corpse"? It's not that *his* corpse is moldering in the backyard. Otherwise Morty would not be eating breakfast. Instead, what Morty says is true because some other Morty's corpse is keeping the grass green.

C-137 and Beyond

David Lewis does not give us a complete guide to talking about the multiverse, however. Lewis never considered travel across realities. Lewis thought names used to describe things that actually happened refer to the objects in our reality. "Justin" in "Justin Roiland was born in California" refers to an object in our world and nothing else. Since he thought we couldn't travel between possible worlds, then there's only one person the name could refer to—the real Justin.

But when Rick and Morty travel through realities, do names refer to the people in the reality they are from or the reality they are in? When Morty C-137 abandons his universe when it is Cronenberged and talks about "Summer," who exactly does he refer to? The Summer left fighting Cronenbergs in universe C-137 or the Summer in his new universe? It seems we still have work to do.

18
What Makes Rick Tick?

JOHN V. KARAVITIS

Many people have weighed in on the philosophy that is the foundation of *Rick and Morty*. The proposals have spanned from absurdism to existentialism to nihilism and back.

I think it's a good thing that more people have come to embrace the idea that philosophy has a lot to tell us about Life, and that so many people are willing to come out and tell it like they think it is.

Too bad in this case they're all wrong.

First off, it's not about Rick AND anyone else. Oh, sure, don't get me wrong. Morty plays an important part in Rick's life. And, as of the end of Season Three, with Evil Morty running the Citadel of Ricks, we'll see even more versions of that obnoxious, jittery, whiny, pubescent doorstop. (No, no, this is nothing personal, Evil Morty! I just call it like I see it. That's all. It's how I Rick-roll.)

You see, this animated television series is NOT about Rick AND anyone else. *It's ALL about Rick. Our* Rick. Always has been. Always will be. Get used to it!

That's some serious game to throw down, word up. Well, you'll just have to get over the idea that you had it "all figured out" by crowing about absurdism (an *absurd* idea all its own, don't you agree?); existentialism (Rick does NOT give a damn whether *you* exist, son! Accept it!); or nihilism (which is itself a big fat *nothing*, if you really think about it). All of your YouTube video "theories" were a complete waste of ego-stroking and Internet real estate!

So, what's *Rick and Morty* all about then, you ask?

Well, if you'd been paying any attention: *It's all about Rick.* But more so, it's all about what Rick *is.* His being; his existence; his ego; his *raison d'être*, if you'll pardon my French (although I really don't care if you do or not). This chapter WILL explain Rick, and it will do so in an orderly, rational manner. As for the rest of this trainwreck that you're holding in your hands, I'll let my fellow contributors to this *magnum opus* on *Rick and Morty*—a regular Trans-Dimensional Council of (rhymes with) Ricks—go after the low-hanging philosophical fruit.

I'll rely on the first three seasons to prove my point. We'll look at Rick's habits, what he likes to do (and not do), all of his "crazy" behavior, and then wrap everything up in a nice, neat, little package. I won't get to the philosophical punchline right up front. I refuse to! Rather, I want you to earn the answer, to savor the exquisite deliciousness of all your hard, virtuous reading. This knowledge—the truth about Rick, and what he really is—has to be earned through your own honest scholarship. But if you happen to have a violent, visceral, negative reaction to this revelation, well... as Birdperson would have said, "Gubba nub nub doo rah kah!"

Rick Sanchez, Philosopher King!

To understand someone, you have to know what he does, and how he behaves. Doing so will clue you in to how he views the world. How someone views the world influences how he behaves, don't you agree? And if you're trying to dissect someone—the way Rick was dissecting a rat while trapped within the Zygerion simulation, which proved to him that he was in fact trapped within a simulation ("M. Night Shaym-Aliens!")—you'll want to do so in an orderly, rational manner. Rick's views within the major areas of philosophy—metaphysics, epistemology, ethics, politics, and aesthetics—are our immediate focus.

Metaphysics is the branch of philosophy that looks at the nature of reality. We know that Rick's universe is parallel to an infinite number of alternate universes, so Rick must subscribe to the "many worlds" interpretation of quantum mechanics. This means that, for every event that has more than one possible outcome, a separate universe exists wherein each outcome occurs. Hence, the "Multiverse." If Rick's interdimensional hopping didn't convince you, then surely interdimensional cable

TV—"infinite TV, from infinite universes"—would have proven the existence of the Multiverse. Rick fixes the family cable TV box to get "programming from every conceivable reality" ("Rixty Minutes").

Whenever anyone refers to a higher power, Rick always dismisses this. "There is no God, Summer. Gotta rip that band-aid off now, you'll thank me later" ("Pilot"). Some fans may challenge Rick's atheism. Summer's first job is working in a shop owned by Mr. Lucius Needful (the Devil!) ("Something Ricked This Way Comes"). Flying through the interdimensional void to grab a time-stabilizing collar, Rick exclaims "Oh, sweet Jesus, please let me live! . . . Please, God in Heaven! Please God, oh Lord, hear my prayer!" But after all of the timelines are fused together, Rick's true feelings emerge. "Yes, I did it! There is no God! In your face!" ("A Rickle in Time").

Epistemology deals with how we know things about the world. Here, we care about Reality (with a capital "R"), and not just opinion (with a lowercase, and humble, "o"). What's Rick's view on how we know things? Rick is first and foremost a scientist. (He must be. He wears a lab coat all the time!) We see Rick constantly tinkering with inventions. For example, to persuade Jerry to let him take Morty on an adventure, Rick quickly creates a cognition-amplifying helmet for Snuffles, the family dog ("Lawnmower Dog"). Rick certainly loses no opportunity to revel in his ability to "invent, transform, create and destroy . . . when I don't like something about the world, I change it" ("Pickle Rick"). Rick's view is that we come to understand the world by taking things apart and seeing how they work. It's a view so deeply ingrained in Rick that we might even accuse him of "scientism," which is the belief in the power of science to solve all of our problems.

Ethics deals with moral principles. How does Rick behave toward other people? Unsurprisingly, both Rick and Morty share the same opinion here. Right before he's arrested in the family dining room to be taken before the Council of Ricks, Rick is very clear that he understands what's happening. "Everybody relax! If I know these a-holes, and I *am* these a-holes . . ." ("Close Rick-counters of the Rick Kind"). Morty concurs with this assessment. "Come on, Birdperson. Rick's not that complicated. He's just a . . . huge a**hole" ("Ricksy Business"). Also, "All of Rick's moves are 'dick' moves . . . He doesn't care about anyone but himself. He doesn't think about the consequences of anything he does" ("Get Schwifty"). Rick's ethical system seems as if it's based on equal parts egotism, narcissism, and selfishness! Rick's in the game—any game—only for himself.

Politics deals with the creation and characteristics of various forms of government, and related ideas such as justice, rights, and the rule of law. Rick hates the idea of government, regardless of who runs it. After Rick is arrested, but before both he and Morty stand before the Council of Ricks, he explains his situation. "As you know, Morty, I've got a lot of enemies in the universe that consider my genius a threat . . . Galactic terrorists, a few sub-galactic dictators, most of the entire intergalactic government . . ." ("Close Rick-counters of the Rick Kind").

At Tammy and Birdperson's wedding, we learn that he and Rick have fought against the Galactic Federation in the past, and that they are both now outlaws in hiding. During pre-ceremony cocktails, Birdperson tells Beth, "The road your father and I walked together is soaked deeply with the blood of both friends and enemies . . . The galactic government considers us terrorists . . . We have committed numerous atrocities in the name of freedom" ("The Wedding Squanchers"). When Rick is finally captured and placed in maximum security prison by the Galactic Federation, he's asked by a fellow prisoner, "Hey, what are you in for?" Rick replies, "Everything" ("The Wedding Squanchers").

Aesthetics is concerned with art and what's beautiful. Something is aesthetic if it is inherently pleasing. For Rick, it's hip-hop and rap music. This music is the soundtrack of his soul! It represents everything we've known and come to love about Rick: his striking out against oppression, against the elements, against anything that stands in his way! You may not be aware that rap is our time's version of Romanticism, an art movement that celebrates the individual as central to the world. And I'm sure you'll agree that, with his thirst for adventure and his fierce individualism, this is one hundred percent Rick. It's Rick *to the MAX*!

After Beth and Jerry leave on a trip to a historical re-enactment of the movie *Titanic*, Rick throws a party at their home, where he leads party-goers in the hip-hop Rick Dance ("Ricksy Business"). When a Cromulon arrives and demands "Show me what you got!", Rick performs a rap song that gives the Earth a temporary reprieve, along with entry into "Planet Music," an intergalactic reality television show where only the planet that wins the musical competition survives ("Get Schwifty"). After surviving the deathtraps that he had set to test the Vindicators, Rick, along with Morty, ends up at the after-party he planned, featuring rap star Sir Robert Bryson Hall II, a.k.a. "Logic" ("Vindicators 3: The Return of Worldender").

Will the Real—OUR—Rick Please Stand Up!

Let's summarize what we've discovered so far. Rick is a scientist who believes that the world can be understood by taking things apart and analyzing them. For him, reality is objective; and science is the answer to any and all problems. Rick is extremely rational and independent; and he puts himself and his self-interests first. Rick despises any form of government (even one made up of Ricks!); and he prefers a musical art form that celebrates the individual standing his ground and striking out against oppression. Rick's stance—his fierce individualistic streak—is as "Me against the world" as it could possibly be.

Some people have proposed that Rick's an anarchist. To support their claim, they point to the flag that Rick planted at the south pole of the small world that he and his family escaped to after the abrupt and calamitous conclusion of Birdperson's wedding. Rick's flag has a circle with a capital "R" in the center. This looks surprisingly similar to what is currently considered the anarchist flag, the "Circle-A": a capital "A" set within a capital "O" ("The Wedding Squanchers").

The center of the symbol of the Citadel of Ricks is similar. We see it on, among other things, the back wall of the stage at the election debate ("The Ricklantis Mixup"). I don't subscribe to the theory that Rick is an anarchist; although the closest version would be "individualist anarchism," or "egoism," proposed by German philosopher Max Stirner. Stirner believed that your only limitation in getting what you want out of life is your ability to do so. You should act according to the dictates of your self-interest; and neither religion, nor the state, nor any moral code is allowed to stand in your way. But curiously, Stirner also held that such "egoists" could band together in a loose association held together by their mutual needs and concerns. This doesn't describe Rick at all. *Our* Rick is a loner. *Rather, anarchism, in the form that Stirner proposed, describes the Citadel of Ricks!*

When I Don't Like Something about the World, I Change It

Everyone has values that set the standards by which they live their life. These values are defended and promoted by their actions. We know what Rick's philosophical values are, but how do they affect his behavior in specific areas of his daily life? To enjoy life and to flourish, people need such things as meaningful work, close relationships, recreation, access to cultural experiences, sex, and the freedom to choose their own path in life. Does Rick sustain his values here?

Rick doesn't have a job; we only see him tinkering with his inventions in the garage. But although Rick may not need a full-time job, we know that he does engage in the occasional business deal—on his terms. He thinks nothing of selling yet another gun to hitman Krombopulos Michael in exchange for 3,000 flurbos ("Mortynight Run").

It may seem as though Rick is so self-centered that he has no close relationships with anyone. But he clearly does. He's known and been friends with Birdperson and Squanchy for a very long time. He spends time with his immediate family, especially at breakfast. And, contrary to any scenes which might imply otherwise, he does love them. (Can't say the same for Jerry, though!) Rick has relationships; but they are with people whom he values, and on his terms.

Rick's adventures with Morty in alternate universes are his recreation, and these are also on his terms. Well, nine out of every ten are. Morty has a card stamped for each adventure, and he gets to choose every tenth ("Vindicators 3: The Return of Worldender"). Rick's preferred art form is hip-hop and rap music, and he certainly knows how to throw a party ("Ricksy Business").

Rick does have sex; and it's with people—or entities—that share his values. A part of Rick's amorous past was revealed when he and Morty landed on a planet whose inhabitants had been assimilated by the hive mind Unity. Rick had once been in a relationship with this hive mind; and, when he runs across her (it?) again, he very quickly picks up where he left off. In fact, everything that he and Unity do is driven by what *he* wants to do, when *he* wants to do it. It's as though *he* assimilated *her*! ("Auto Erotic Assimilation"). As for choosing his own path in life, Rick is as Rick does. As always.

It all makes sense, no? Rick's fierce individualism, which flows from his values, and his rationality, are the tools which he uses to solve problems and overcome challenges. He views the Multiverse as malleable to his will and full of opportunities, even if it means having to start over in another universe. He defends his values and his self-interests by doing things his way, on his terms. *Rick is running Rick's show.* What philosophical system explains Rick? It's not absurdism, existentialism, nihilism, or anarchism. What makes Rick tick?

Objectivism.

Don't Hate the Player; Hate the Game, Son

Rick Sanchez lives his life as an Objectivist. Objectivism, also known as "rational egoism," is a philosophical system created by Ayn Rand. Objectivism explains *our* Rick *perfectly*. Rick looks like Rand's "ideal man." He's a scientist, which Rand saw as the most useful occupation. He's independent. No one can claim his time or his efforts without his consent. *So he rejects altruism.* He despises and has fought against any form of government or association that could oppress him. *So he rejects collectivism.* And Rick uses his rational mind to solve whatever problem he may be facing. *So he rejects any form of mysticism.*

Objectivism is a form of egoism, not *egotism*. It's the difference between self-interest and selfishness. Rick isn't selfish. He seems to be because he vigorously defends his self-interests. Objectivism also explains why Rick despises Jerry so much. Jerry is unemployed, has no direction in his life, and is living off of the earnings of his wife. He's a parasite that destroyed his daughter Beth's chance for true happiness. While Jerry's being devoured by a gibble snake, Rick vents his anger. "You act like prey, but you're a predator! You use pity to lure in your victims. It's how you survive. I survive because I know everything . . . you survive because people think, 'Oh, this poor piece of shit, he never gets a break . . . I guess I'll hire him, or marry him . . .'"

("The Whirly Dirly Conspiracy"). *Jerry is the exact opposite of Rand's ideal man!*

In the Multiverse, everything that can happen does happen. So, when Rick makes a catastrophic mistake, *it doesn't matter*. He can always move on to an alternate universe and start over. After Rick "Cronenberged" the world, he simply located a universe where humanity hadn't been transformed into hideous monsters, and where that Rick and Morty had died ("Rick Potion #9"). This may also explain why *our* Rick had been gone for twenty years (according to the show's Facebook page), and has only just recently returned.

After our Rick is captured by Evil Rick, we see that he has memories of Morty *as a young child!* ("Close Rick-counters of the Rick Kind"). But both scenarios can't be true in the same universe. So, if we've been following *our* Rick through each and every episode (and this has to be, or this animated series really makes no sense!), then the Multiverse, with its infinite possibilities, is a metaphor for Rick daring to seize the freedom to make choices. As Rick tells Beth, "When you know nothing matters, the universe is yours" ("The ABCs of Beth").

You may not be pleased with where we've ended up in *our* adventure to find out what makes *our* Rick tick. You may very well be having that violent, visceral, negative reaction to this revelation which I feared might happen. But if you still don't want to accept where we've ended up, then listen to co-creator Dan Harmon during the *Rick and Morty Live* event that announced the release of Season Three:

> Season Four might not happen, it depends on how much of the "hot topic slipper money" we get. You can't keep making hot topic slippers and pretending the show's not turning a profit. We're onto you! Gimme my slipper money!

Harmon apparently wanted to see a monetary return from his earlier work before he continued to provide Cartoon Network with more episodes! Does this sound like someone who really cares about *his fans? Harmon is steadfastly protecting his self-interests—his work product!* He's being *Objectivist* in his business dealings, just as Rick would be! Where *did* you think that Rick got his philosophy of Life from?

But, as nothing in Life, or in an animated series, is ever really perfect, there's one fly in this philosophical ointment. Rick's certainly firing on all cylinders as he runs rampant through the Multiverse. And that's the problem. Ironically, Rick's access to the Multiverse makes him vulnerable. In every episode, we see that Rick lives a life of adventure. But after a while, this constant chase after the next high will surely begin to lose its attraction. At some point, Rick may come to feel that his life has no meaning; and he will fall into despair. By having an infinite number of choices, each choice becomes no better than any other. Boredom sets in. Yet by trying to counteract this by constantly chasing after the next adventure, Rick risks falling into the paradox of hedonism. His attempts at finding happiness only end up making him miserable!

This may have happened already. After having broken up with the hive mind Unity, we saw him set up a device in the garage that can vaporize living beings; and then he put *his* head in it! But he falls asleep, and his head drops down to the tabletop, right before the machine turns on ("Auto Erotic Assimilation"). This may indeed have been a half-hearted attempt at suicide; it's never made clear. However, Rick can escape this despair if he decides to give his life meaning by pursuing constructive goals.

Rick would also have to start being more attentive to the possible consequences of his actions. He'd have to become a kinder, gentler, more thoughtful Rick. He could still hew to the Objectivist course, as long as he can honestly conclude that it is indeed to his benefit to be more aware of the effect that his behavior has on other people. Especially on those closest to him. Like Morty, Summer, and Beth. And yes. Even Jerry.

But seriously. What am I saying? Why should *our* Rick—the *Rickest* Rick—bother?

Some *other* universe already has *that* Rick!

19
The Citadel of Ricks
Is Untruth

MATTHEW BRAKE

"Close Rick-counters of the Rick Kind" introduces the Citadel of Ricks which consists of Rick Sanchezes from across the multiverse.

These Ricks, along with their Mortys, live in a society governed by the Trans-Dimensional Council of Ricks, who oversee all of the Rick-related business throughout the multiverse. There is, however, one Rick who opposes the very idea of the Council of Ricks—Rick C-137, the main protagonist of the show.

When he's falsely accused of murdering other Ricks, C-137 expresses his disdain to the guards who arrest him by stating, "The whole point of being a Rick is to be 'a' Rick." Later, in the Season Three premiere episode, Summer and Morty are captured by the Citadel of Ricks, and when Summer asks Morty why the Citadel hates their Rick so much, Morty replies, "Because Ricks hate themselves the most, and our Rick is the most . . . himself."

A person's self cannot be defined by large numbers or by the crowd, or at least it shouldn't be. In many ways, Rick's disdain for the Council of Ricks, and by extension the Citadel, is akin to Søren Kierkegaard's own view that in order to attain authentic selfhood, you must remain an individual. In *Philosophical Fragments*, Kierkegaard says that the only thing humans can do for each other is to help each one become themselves, but afterward, they must push each other away.

In many ways, this is reminiscent of Rick's advice to his daughter in "The ABC's of Beth." In that episode, Rick advises

Beth to leave her world and explore the vast multiverse, only participating in a life that she herself has chosen, apart from the input or baggage (*cough*, Jerry, *cough*) of others. Ultimately, the journey to authentic selfhood is one that can only be achieved by the individual, because the crowd is untruth.

The Council Knows (Belch) Best

In "Close Rick-counters of the Rick Kind," the Citadel arrests Rick. As they're leading him away through a portal, they decide to bring Morty along. As Rick protests, one of the Citadel Ricks tells him, "You lost the right to have a say in these things when you refused to join the Council." When Rick and Morty are brought to the Citadel, Rick explains to Morty:

> As you know, Morty, I've got a lotta enemies in the universe that consider my genius a threat. Galactic terrorists, a few sub-galactic dictators, most of the entire intergalactic government: wherever you find people with heads up their asses someone wants a piece of your grandpa. And a lot of versions of me on different timelines had the same problem. So a few thousand versions of me had the ingenious idea of banding together like a herd of cattle or a school of fish or those people who answer questions on Yahoo answers.

Rick's disdain for the council is apparent. The Council of Ricks represents every attempt to determine someone's worth via mass consensus.

Kierkegaard is equally a hard-ass in his approach to the public, or the "herd" as Rick calls them. For him, the public is an abstract entity and the product of a crude, passionless age in which the masses are no longer individuals with their own opinions and thoughts, but instead, people who just follow the crowd. You don't have to have an individual opinion because public opinion is guaranteed by the large numbers of people who all believe the same thing. Kierkegaard refers to this process as "leveling."

In his journals, Kierkegaard writes about how the public jealously prevents individuals from having a life that is "all their own" apart from the approval of the public. The crowd finds such individuality to be in "bad taste." Rick is the target of such accusations of having bad taste as he is accused of terroristic "anti-Rick speech" and is considered the prime suspect in the murder of other Ricks. Rick asks, "You think I did this? Why am I the first Rick you pull in every time a Rick stubs his toe?" The reply from the Council is:

> You have a history of non-co-operation with the council . . . Who else would you have us question? You fit the profile. Of all the Ricks in the central finite curve, you're the malcontent. The rogue.

An individual who stands apart from the crowd or the public will always be looked upon with suspicion for not adhering to the majority consensus, but Kierkegaard, like Rick, would argue that determining your life by the public lessens your self, as Rick exclaims, "I'm the Rick. And so were the rest of you before you formed this stupid alliance. You wanted to be safe from the government so you became a stupid government. That makes every Rick here less Rick than me."

Passionlessness on the (Belch) Citadel

And Rick C-137 does prove himself to be "the Rickiest Rick." Whereas all of the other Ricks live in fear of the Galactic Federation, it is Rick C-137 whose actions ultimately lead to the Federation's destruction. Why was our Rick able to accomplish what thousands of Ricks were unable to do? Because our Rick is able to most be himself and allow his passions and actions to be unencumbered by the mediocrity of other people.

Kierkegaard would say that this lack of action on the part of the Citadel is due to a lack of passion, which is the result of the masses joining together as a public in enthusiasm but then "wisely" avoiding all meaningful action. Passion requires a person to throw their entire being into their activity and to risk being wrong or failing. It's easy to look at the objective facts of a situation, but that doesn't mean you're willing to throw yourself into a risky action with your whole being.

This is why the crowd is deceitful. It encourages people to accept the objective "facts," but it won't encourage them to passionately risk upsetting the status quo by acting in response to those facts. As Kierkegaard would say, "action and decision are just as scarce these days as is the fun of swimming dangerously for those who swim in shallow water." Instead of action, Kierkegaard states that the following is more likely:

> If someone went around listening to what others said ought to be done and then with a sense of irony . . . did something about it, everybody would be taken aback, would find it rash. And as soon as they started thinking and conversing about it, they would realize that it was just what should have been done.

The public, like the Council of Ricks, cuts itself off from the passion that could lead to action through endless talking and gossip. This would certainly have been the case if Rick had told the Council about his plans to overthrow the Galactic Federation. In fact, the Council, in their fear of Rick disclosing Citadel secrets, almost fucked up his whole plan when Sealed Team Ricks broke into the Federation prison he was being held in and tried to assassinate him in "The Rickshank Rickdemption." As Rick C-137 might say to such a "gallery-public" (as Kierkegaard would call it), "Yeah, murmur it up, d-bags" (and keep doing nothing about what makes you afraid).

Envy and Leveling on the (Belch) Citadel

Kierkegaard notes that envy has become "the *negatively unifying principle* in this passionless and very reflective age." People carefully watch each other, becoming the subject of each other's gossip, and becoming trapped by their envy of other people. The public's envy causes a leveling that "stifles and impedes" anything that might alter or agitate the status quo.

When Rick is captured by the Galactic Federation, Summer (with a reluctant Morty) obtains a portal gun and attempts to rescue him in "The Rickshank Rickdemption." Intercepted by a paramilitary group of Ricks for operating an unregistered portal gun, who also inform Summer and Morty that they will assassinate Rick C-137 to keep Citadel secrets from falling into enemy hands, they are taken to the Citadel to stand trial before the Council of Ricks:

> RIQ IV: Operating an unregistered portal gun, radicalizing a Summer, conspiring with a traitorous Rick. How do you plead?

MORTY: How is this a fair trial? Our lawyer is a Morty.

RIQ IV: It's not fair, you have no rights, and he's not a lawyer. We just keep him here because he's fun. Look at him go.

"LAWYER" MORTY: Ha ha, yeah!

RIQ IV: We'll be lenient if you renounce your Rick. What say you, Summer?

SUMMER: I say fuck you! My grandpa was my hero. You killed him because you were jealous of him. That's pretty obvious from the haircuts.

In the previous case of the murdered Ricks, the Council was forced to apologize and release Rick, but here again, they seize upon another opportunity to accuse Rick of being a traitor and a rogue. Summer, however, sees through the ruse (perhaps because she is a high schooler who recognizes a clique when she sees one) and calls the Council out of their real problem with Rick C-137—they're jealous of him. He's everything they refuse to be: a decisive, passionate individual. Riq IV admits as much when he tells Rick, "You're a rogue Rick—irrational, passionate"—passionate enough to take decisive action that the Council wouldn't dream of because they merely seek to protect themselves and the status quo. Yet, they are envious of the one Rick who refuses to join their crowd. This is the type of thing that leads to leveling (d-bags!).

This issue of envy and leveling is best illustrated in the Citadel-centric episode, "The Ricklantis Mixup," which features a number of tales from the Citadel from various Ricks and Mortys. In a very real sense, as Rick C-137 states, the Citadel is full of "the unfortunate millions held hostage by their terrible ideas." From the newscast that introduces us to everyday life on the Citadel, we see the mix of envy and leveling that defines life on the Citadel:

Rick D-716: Good morning.

Rick D-716B: I'm Rick D-716B.

Rick D-716: And I'm Rick D-716.

Rick D-716B: Must be nice.

Already, despite all of the Ricks being the same, there are jealousies that lead to a mediocre leveling where all Ricks fail to live up to their potential. "Candidate" Morty addresses this problem in his own campaign speech for Citadel president: "I see it in our schools where they teach Mortys we're all the same, because they're threatened by what makes us unique; I see it in our factories where Ricks work for a fraction of their boss's salary even though they're identical and have the same IQ."

One of the stories follows Rick J-22, a factory employee who helps to operate the facility where Simple Rick's wafers are made, which are produced from the brain secretions of a happy, fulfilled Rick reliving the memories of being present on his daughter Beth's birthday—an example of the crowd "luxuriating in a daydream" if there ever was one. This faithful worker is passed over for a promotion in favor of Rick K-83, or "Cool Rick." In response to this professional slight, Rick J-22 snaps, kills his former boss, and takes Simple Rick hostage. As the police lay siege to him, he shouts, "All your lives are lies! Don't you get it? They told us we were special because we were Ricks, but they stripped us of everything that made us unique!"

This is how leveling works. No one can be unique because the mediocre status quo must be maintained. It isn't that it would be different with the passage of new laws or a newly elected candidate (we're looking at YOU Evil . . . I mean "Candidate" . . . Morty) because as this episode revealed, the crowd is always subject to being duped, and any appeal to the crowd to legitimize yourself may just land you in a chair with your brain secretions making a new brand of Simple Ricks wafers.

A Rick can't be "a" Rick in a crowd of other Ricks. Joining together with others dilutes Rick's own potential and mental prowess. The only way Rick can remain himself is to push others away, a strategy which Kierkegaard himself would very well endorse.

Beth, Soc-Rick-tes, and (Belch) Developing as an Individual

Rick's ability to remain himself and explore his own uniqueness has come at a cost—not only has he rejected the Citadel, but he has abandoned his family multiple times (also, multiple *versions* of his family in the vast multiverse). This has particularly affected Beth, who accepts Rick back into her life and home, much to the chagrin of her husband Jerry, despite Rick having abandoned her as a child.

The underlying conflict resulting from Rick's abandonment of Beth comes to the forefront in "The ABCs of Beth." Beth comes to the realization, thanks to Rick, that she was a scary child, asking Rick to make a number of "toys" that could be harmful to any unsuspecting child who crossed her "sociopath." In order to keep her from harming other children (for practical purposes, not moral concern), Rick created Froopyland, a simulated world where Beth could play without risking any harm coming to other children; however, Beth and Rick discover that she took a playmate of hers, Tommy, into Froopyland and trapped him there, resulting in Tommy's father being accused of cannibalizing his own son.

After attempting to rescue Tommy, but instead killing him, Beth comes to a realization about herself and about Rick.

BETH: Dad? I feel like I've spent my life pretending you're a great guy and trying to be like you. And the ugly truth has always been . . .

RICK: That I'm not that great a guy and you're exactly like me.

BETH: Am I evil?

RICK: Worse. You're smart. When you know nothing matters, the universe is yours. And I've never met a universe that was into it. The universe is basically an animal. It grazes on the ordinary . . . You know, smart people get a chance to climb on top, take reality for a ride, but it'll never stop trying to throw you. And, eventually, it will. There's no other way off.

BETH: Dad, I'm out of excuses to not be who I am. So who am I? What do I do?

RICK: My advice—take off. Put a saddle on your universe. Let it kick itself out.

BETH: I can't do that. The kids, Jerry, my job, and, as much as I hate to admit it, ABC's *The Bachelor.*

RICK: I can make a clone of you, a perfect instance of you, with all your memories. An exact copy in every way. It'll love and provide for the kids, do your job, and consume broadcast-network reality TV on the same allegedly ironic level as you. You could be gone a day, a week, or the rest of your life with zero consequences.

BETH: If nothing matters, why would you do that for me?

RICK: I don't know, maybe you matter so little that I like you. Or maybe it makes you matter. Maybe I love you. Maybe something about your mother. Don't jump a gift shark in the mouth.

One of the important things to note about this conversation is that even though Beth and Rick reconcile, Rick doesn't give up on his insistence on being alone and unencumbered by others. In fact, he encourages Beth to do the exact same thing as him. Rick knows that there's nothing about his acceptance of Beth or spending time with her that will make her whole or complete. In other words, Rick can do nothing to make Beth become truly herself, only Beth can choose who Beth is.

Rick, like Kierkegaard, doesn't believe that joining together with other people in a permanent bond is what will make each of us individuals in the best sense. On this front, Kierkegaard holds up the example of Socrates, whose goal wasn't to teach anyone new knowledge, but to help them remember what they already knew because they had forgotten (mainly because of some stuff about the pre-existence of the soul. Or something. Don't jump a gift shark in the mouth!). He helped them do this through his maieutic method or philosophical midwifery.

In other words, he asked people questions until they arrived at knowledge of the truth instead of telling them what the truth was (like a midwife who isn't giving birth herself, but simply helps another person along while they're delivering the baby). Socrates's goal wasn't to teach people his system of knowledge or to get people to become just like him, but to discover self-knowledge, like a midwife would help deliver a baby.

Socrates was only an "occasion" for a person to find themselves. Like Rick, he believed that each person was ultimately alone and self-sufficient (well, maybe without Rick's nihilism), and like Rick, he would push others away when they learned this lesson. This is the most any human being can do for another, be an occasion for them to arrive at self-knowledge, and then push them off to be themselves—an individual task.

Socrates, like Rick, was willing to do this "even for the most stupid person" (cough, Jerry, cough).

Let's Not Suck the Ghost of His Dick Too Hard

Rick is certainly an ambivalent figure. That's something Morty points out to Summer: "Everything real turns fake. Everything right is wrong. All you know is that you know nothing and he knows everything. And, well—well, he's not a villain, Summer, but he shouldn't be your hero. He's more like a demon or a super fucked up god" ("The Rickshank Redemption"). Yet it can't be denied that of all the Ricks on the Citadel he's able to come out on top consistently and outsmart them all again and again. What liberates Rick is his ability to recognize his own individual uniqueness and to act upon it despite the scorn he receives from the crowd, whether that be Morty, his family, or the Citadel of Ricks. There's no other way to become an individual, for the crowd will only hold you back . . . because the crowd is untruth.

20
Getting Your Shit Together Stoic Style

Travis Taft

It's hard to fit Rick C-137 into any single philosophical box.

He's a man who will build an entire fantasy universe just for his daughter to play in, but mostly to keep her troublesome tendencies safely locked away somewhere they won't be a problem.

He enjoys taking his grandson out for a day at the arcade, and has no problem selling weapons to assassins to fund the trip.

And if we can take him at his word—which we very possibly can't—he's prepared to build a decade-long arc around getting some dipping sauce for his chicken.

But while Rick might not unfalteringly adhere to any specific school of thought besides his own, he does generally show some patterns of behavior that would earn a nod of approval from one noteworthy classical thinker—Epictetus, the Rickiest Stoic.

You've probably heard the term 'Stoic' before. You probably have a sense of what the word means—or at least of what you *think* it means. Chances are you're imagining something along the lines of being cold and emotionless, like the literally cold Ice-T, who was exiled from his home planet Alphabetrium for not caring about anything.

But using that definition for the word is actually a gross misrepresentation of the truth. Stoicism doesn't discourage putting value in people and relationships, though Epictetus does have some rather Rick-y definitions as to what makes for a healthy connection, as we'll see. Really, if there's one thing

Stoicism is focused on, it's not cutting off emotions—it's making the right choices.

Maintaining the Single Dot

According to Epictetus, "choice alone is vice, choice alone is virtue." So, if we want to make sure we make the right choices in life, we should examine our decision making process from the ground up. As Epictetus says, "the beginning of philosophy is this: the realization that there is a conflict between the opinions of men . . . and the discovery of a certain standard of judgment, comparable to the balance we have discovered for determining weights, or the ruler, for things straight and crooked." In other words, our goal should be to find some objective standard, so that whenever we need to make a decision or we find people in conflict we can definitively determine which opinion is the correct one. Like Rick, Epictetus has a pretty unsympathetic view of ethical decision making.

But whatever we intend to base our code on, we must first make sure we have a steady foundation. Our code is meaningless if we aren't strict about sticking to it even if it becomes inconvenient. Once we have come up with our standard of judgment, we must be ready to "make use of it without fail ever after, so that we do not even stretch out a finger without it". And before we even get into the specifics of how and why Rick and Epictetus make the decisions they do, it's promising to note that, whatever Rick's code happens to be, we know that he doesn't seem to flinch a muscle unless he's positive that it's the correct action.

We know this thanks to the Season Two premiere episode, "A Rickle in Time." In the episode, time is a bit fragile after being frozen since the end of the previous season. As a result, any uncertainty from the main characters can and does result in time splitting into different streams, where the characters respectively did and didn't do the thing they were considering. As the story unfolds, we see Morty and Summer each cause quantum confusion as they both do and don't do things they are indecisive about. Rick, however, shows no such variation. His words and actions are perfectly synced up across both timelines until one version of Rick stops to respond to a comment his Morty makes. But the other Rick's Morty stays quiet so there is no delay.

If it hadn't been for this outside influence of Morty's indecision, Rick would have stayed on beat without variation. That's because for as twisted as Rick's code is, he sticks to it no matter what, which isn't always as easy as it sounds as Morty and Summer show. And Epictetus would certainly praise Rick for the fact that he's *so* strict in his code that he *literally* does "not even stretch out a finger"—or burp for that matter—unless he is *certain* it's what he should do in that moment, just like Epictetus says any proper Stoic should.

So why is it so hard for us to stick to our standards? Epictetus would say that it's because most of us suck at using reason. And that is a problem since he also thinks reason is the most important thing we have. His reasoning is that the rational faculty is the only faculty we have that can analyze and refine the other faculties like sight, speech, and even the rational faculty itself. Or, in his more flowery words:

> How, then, can any other faculty be superior to this, which both uses all the rest as servants, and tests each of them and pronounces judgement upon it? . . . For that alone of the faculties that we have received comprehends both itself—what it is, what it is capable of, and with what valuable powers it has come to us—and all the other faculties likewise.

Rick consistently demonstrates that he shares this preference for rationality above all. Like Epictetus, Rick thinks that most people don't make proper use of their capacities as rational creatures, and this prevents them from having any chance of living the way he thinks they should.

Loving Logically

This the part where Stoicism tends to get its reputation as a cold and emotionless mindset. Putting so much emphasis on logic doesn't sound like it leaves a lot of room for love and happiness. But truth is that Epictetus puts a *lot* of stake in emotions. In fact, in his eyes, this process of self-examination is the best way to be *capable* of true love:

> Do men set their hearts on evils? —By no means . . . good things alone are what they set their heart on . . . Whoever, therefore, has

> knowledge of good things would also know how to love them; and he
> who cannot distinguish good things from evil . . . how could he still
> have the power to love? It follows that the wise man alone has the
> power to love.

So, why do people have this idea that Stoicism is about cutting
off emotion when Epictetus says that strict rationality *enables*
love? It's because Stoics say we should treat love very differently
than we generally do. Love is an important part of this
code we are building, yes, but while there is a trend in our culture
to excuse irrational behavior in the name of passion,
Epictetus says that this behavior is one of the primary reasons
we struggle with happiness in the long run.

Love for a spouse or child, desire for wealth and comfort,
and even fear of death are all examples of what Epictetus
refers to as *impressions*. Impressions are anything that we
might be tempted by or adverse to but are ultimately outside
our sphere of control. Our refusal to critically analyze our
impressions leaves us choosing things that are not as good for
us. We are persuaded by fear, greed, and even love, to throw
away our consistent moral standard. And whether it's creating
a Gazorpazorpian hybrid or infecting an entire version of Earth
with a love potion, Morty offers plenty of examples of how
things can go wrong when we let our passions guide our decisions.

We know Rick understands this, because when he purges
everything he believes to be toxic in himself in "Rick and
Relaxation," he shows no issue with being loving and considerate
to Morty, yet his "irrational attachments" end up in his
Toxic version. The attachment is not a problem in of itself, as
long as we don't do anything irrational on its behalf. But even
if it may seem cold, we have to be strict about doing the right
thing, even if it means bad things for people close to us—
including our own family.

For instance, Rick injects 'Healthy' Morty with his Toxic side
again, even though Rick knows it'll make Morty lose the money,
women, and status he has amassed since being split. But it's
the right thing to do. If the person holds a grudge for it, well,
that's their decision which is outside your control and therefore
not worth your concern. But if the person hurt by the choice is
wise, they'll understand that you did what you had to do, and

you both grow as a result. Either way, we either cut out negative influences or nurture positive ones, so it's a win-win. In other words:

> The good is thus preferred over every form or relationship. My father is nothing to me, only the good . . . But, if we place the good in right choice, then the preservation of such relationships does in itself become a good.

Developing a proper relationship with our impressions isn't easy. But it's a key step in developing a proper rational faculty. Epictetus says that

> in a word, neither death nor exile, nor pain, nor anything of that kind is the cause of us doing or not doing anything, but rather, our suppositions and judgments . . . From this day forward, then, whenever we do anything wrong we will ascribe blame only to the judgment from which we act.

To put that another way, we're inevitably going to run into a LOT of outside influences, "impressions," like threats of pain or exile. But since those threats are outside our control we should not let them factor into our judgment when trying to decide what the right thing to do is.

Rick tends to be a bit more blunt, but a lot of the underlying ideas are the same. For example, compare the quote above to a line from the episode "Rick Potion #9": "What people call 'love' is a chemical reaction that compels animals to breed. It hits hard, Morty, then it slowly fades . . . Break the cycle, Morty. Rise above. Focus on science."

Hormones aren't as *visible* an influence as a gun to your head, but a wise Stoic would recognize them as an impression just the same. In these quotes, Epictetus and Rick are both saying that too many people let their emotional reactions and impressions get the best of their decision-making processes, but true wisdom comes from being consistent and not making exceptions for your feelings.

But how *do* we rise above our impressions? For starters, it's important to remember that despite their influence on our desires, impressions are things we do not have control over. If we are banished, or robbed, or fall ill, we can't simply choose not to be. But remember: choice alone is vice and choice alone is virtue. We're not responsible for anything outside our sphere of choice, so it's impossible for us to do the wrong thing when we *have* no choice. As such, a good Stoic might actually take comfort in the face of an unpleasant fate, if they know that there's nothing they can do to change it, because if they can't do *anything* that means they have not and cannot do the *wrong* thing.

In fact, Epictetus would go beyond calling this lack of choice a comfort and would call it an outright *strength*. Because impressions are not just outside of our control—unless we let them, they also can't do anything to influence the one thing that *is* in our control. Our reason. It might seem almost silly to most people, but Epictetus believed that if a person became truly devoted to the Stoic mindset then they could be free anywhere they were—even in prison.

> "I will fetter you." —What are you saying, man? Fetter *me*? You will fetter my leg; but not even Zeus himself can get the better of my choice. "I will cast you into prison." My wretched body, rather.

Pain, banishment, slavery, and death are all externals. They are all outside our control. But what *is* in our control is how we *react* to these fates. "It is not death or pain that is to be feared, but the fear of pain or death. That is why we commend the man who says: 'Death is no ill, but to die shamefully'. Our confidence, then, ought to be turned towards death, and our caution towards the fear of death."

We should face death, says Epictetus, like a Floopfloopian warrior, calmly and without fear. So calmly, in fact, that we can casually accept an offer to go get lunch first. Or, to cite a line from Epictetus which mirrors that scene to an uncanny degree: "I must die. If instantly, I will die instantly; if in a short time, I will dine first, since the hour for dining is here, and when the time comes, then I will die."

When forming our ethical standard which we will abide by, "secure and unshaken, not only while we are awake, but even when asleep, and drunk, and depressed," we must remember that all we have, all we *are*, is our rational faculty, the decisions we make. The universe (or rather, multiverse) is a crazy place. We can't possibly control all or even most of it. So when we run into something we can't fix, if we find ourselves getting hung up over ways reality could be different, we should remember Rick's voice asking us "What about the reality where Hitler cured cancer, Morty? The answer is don't think about it."

Rough Timelines and Natural Law

So according to Epictetus and Rick, we have to develop a moral code strict enough to account for every flexed muscle, and that code should only be concerned with things we have direct power of choice over.

But with those parameters established, now we reach the big question: If choice alone is vice and choice alone is virtue, then how do we know *which* choice is the virtuous one? Well, as Epictetus said, we are naturally inclined to want that which is good, and the thing that makes our rational faculty so powerful is its ability to analyze itself. So, by combining those two facts we can say that continually refining our logical abilities is itself a great virtue. For, "unless we have come to know thoroughly and examined accurately the standard of judgment for all other things, which we use to gain a thorough knowledge of those things, how shall we ever be able to examine everything else accurately and gain a thorough knowledge of it?"

Or to put it in more Jerry-friendly terms: we can't make good judgment calls or learn from situations if we don't make sure our standards are properly refined first. This feels like a bit of a copout, but it's an important point to drive home. The theme of constantly re-examining your assumptions is a cornerstone throughout philosophy, as Epictetus reminds us when he quotes one of *his* favorite philosophers: "Socrates used to say that an unexamined life is not worth living."

But what are we refining our will *towards*? Epictetus would call it "Natural Law," and coming into alignment with it is the ultimate goal of the Stoic path. "What, then, is it to be properly educated? To learn how to apply natural preconceptions to particular cases, in accordance with nature." In other words, we need to learn how to figure out how our universal code applies in specific cases without contradicting ourselves. If we can do that consistently, we will be acting properly within the laws of nature. If we're successful, and we learn to accept the things outside of our control while being rational about the things within our control, then we will be able to face whatever the world throws at us.

But why face these challenges at all? If we're all doomed to die eventually and suffer until then, shouldn't we just give up? Certainly not. As Epictetus reminds us, the decision to give up is still a decision, and—in most cases—the decision to let your life end is not what Epictetus would ever call the "rational" option. I will exist "as long as reason requires I should continue in this paltry body . . . Only, let me not abandon it without due reason, or from mere feebleness, or on some casual pretext; for that, again, would be contrary to the will of God."

If your fate is sealed, face it without fear, as Rick does in "A Rickle in Time" when he thinks he has to die to save Morty. But as long as we still have the ability to choose, we should react like Rick spotting the collar which could save his life, and go from open acceptance of the inevitable to doing everything within our power to carry on, so that we can continue making proper choices for another day.

Why? Because as long as we are rational in regards to what we have control over, and we are confident in the face of what we don't, we have nothing to fear. Instead, as long as we approach our challenges properly, and we accept any outcome like good Stoics, we will be guaranteed to grow as people. "What, then, should each of us say as each hardship befalls us? 'It was for this that I was exercising, it was for this that I was training.'" And like any training, the end result isn't just deterring weakness—it's gaining strength. "'Then is there any advantage to be gained from these things?' Yes, from all of them . . . What advantage does a wrestler gain from his training-partner? The greatest."

Rick has already been through a lifetime of crazy adventures by the opening of the series, so he's already pretty hardened after countless tests and trials. But we *do* get to see a rather interesting transformation from Jerry, of all people. Most of the time, Jerry is the epitome of everything Epictetus says we should avoid. He doesn't think things through, he lets fear and desire rule his decision-making process, and he gets hung up over things outside his control.

But Jerry's also a product of his environment. He has been able to build a life and family off the pity of others, and without anything to challenge him he never got to train his willpower. That all changes after the events of "Rick Potion #9," when Jerry is finally given something important to fight for. And we see in "The Rickshank Rickdemption" that, for as grungy and rough their lives are in the Cronenberged universe, this version of Jerry seems to have maintained his dream of being the respected head of the household better than any other version in any other universe. It's evidence of Epictetus's belief that struggles aren't just a healthy part of life—they're the key to unlocking our greatness. "Pray, what figure do you think Heracles would have made if there had not been a lion like the one they tell of, and a hydra, and a stag, and unjust and brutal men . . . What would have been the use of those arms of his, and his strength overall; of his endurance, and greatness of mind, if such circumstances and opportunities had not stirred him to action and exercised him?"

Never Say Wubbalubbadubdub

So, what can we learn about ethics from a guy like Rick? More than one it might seem at first. At least going by certain schools of thought. Living life the way Rick does, or as a Stoic might, doesn't promise riches, or fame, or even basic physical comforts. Rick is the smartest entity in the multiverse and he's crashing at his daughter and son-in-law's house working out of their garage. And it's true that he is far from the *ideal* role model, Stoic or otherwise, given his multiple moments of drunkenness and despair.

But even if he's not always super upbeat and chipper, he seems to be leading the life he has chosen for himself. His life might not always be one of *pleasure*, but it is one of *contentment*. Because whether or not Rick has ever formally studied Stoicism, when he's at his best and doesn't need his signature catchphrase, he shows us hints of what Epictetus promised a Stoic life offers:

> Desire that never fails in its achievement; aversion that never meets with what it would avoid; appropriate impulse; carefully considered purpose; and assent that is never precipitate.

Bibliography

Abbott, Edwin A. 1992 [1884]. *Flatland: A Romance of Many Dimensions*. Dover.

Aquinas, Thomas. 2018. *Summa Theologica: Unabridged Edition in a Single Volume*. Coyote Canyon.

Aristotle. 1999. *Nicomachean Ethics*. Hackett.

Barrett, William. 1962 [1958]. *Irrational Man: A Study in Existential Philosophy*. Anchor.

Bostrom, Nick. 2003. Are You Living in a Computer Simulation? *Philosophical Quarterly* 53: 211 (April).

———. 2008. Where Are They? Why I Hope the Search for Extraterrestrial Intelligence Finds Nothing. *Technology Review* (May–June).

———. 2014. *Superintelligence: Paths, Dangers, Strategies*. Oxford University Press.

Bruner, Jerome. 2009. *Actual Minds, Possible Worlds*. Harvard University Press.

Camus, Albert. 2018 [1942]. *The Myth of Sisyphus and Other Essays*. Vintage.

Carson, Rachel. 2002 [1962]. *Silent Spring*. Houghton Mifflin.

Darwall, Stephen. 2009. *The Second-Person Standpoint: Morality, Respect, and Accountability*. Harvard University Press.

Dawkins, Richard. 2006. *The God Delusion*. Houghton Mifflin.

Descartes, René. 1993. *Meditations on First Philosophy*. Hackett.

———. 2008. *A Discourse on the Method*. Oxford University Press.

Deutsch, David. 1997. *The Fabric of Reality: The Science of Parallel Universes—and Its Implications*. Penguin.

———. 2011. *The Beginning of Infinity: Explanations that Transform the World*. Viking.

Dewitt, Bryce Seligman, and Neil Graham, eds. 2015 [1973]. *The Many Worlds Interpretation of Quantum Mechanics*. Princeton University Press.

Epictetus. 1983. *The Handbook (The Encheiridion)*. Hackett.

Epicurus. 1994. *The Epicurus Reader: Selected Writings and Testimonia*. Hackett.

———. 2012. *The Art of Happiness*. Penguin.

Hartshorne, Charles. 1991 [1962]. *The Logic of Perfection and Other Essays in Neoclassical Metaphysics*. Open Court.

———. 1991 [1965]. *Anselm's Discovery: A Re-examination of the Ontological Proof of God's Existence*. Open Court.

Hill, Thomas E. 1973. Servility and Self-Respect. *The Monist* 57.

———. 1991. *Autonomy and Self-Respect*. Cambridge University Press.

Hobbes, Thomas. 1968 [1651]. *Leviathan*. Penguin.

Hume, David. 2000 [1739]. *A Treatise of Human Nature*. Oxford University Press.

Hurley, S.L. 1989. *Natural Reasons: Personality and Polity*. Oxford University Press.

Kahneman, Daniel. 2011. *Thinking, Fast and Slow*. Farrar, Straus.

Kant, Immanuel. 1993 [1785]. *Grounding for the Metaphysics of Morals*. Hackett.

Kierkegaard, Søren. 1967. *Philosophical Fragments or a Fragment of Philosophy by Johannes Climacus*. Princeton University Press.

Krauss, Lawrence M. 2005. *Hiding in the Mirror: The Mysterious Allure of Extra Dimensions, from Plato to String Theory and Beyond*. Viking.

———. 2012. *A Universe from Nothing: Why There Is Something Rather than Nothing*. Simon and Schuster.

Leibniz, Gottfried Wilhelm. 1991 [1686]. *Discourse on Metaphysics and Other Essays*. Hackett.

Leopold, Aldo. 1986 [1949]. *A Sand County Almanac: With Essays on Conservation from Round River*. Ballantine.

Lewis, David K. 1973. *Counterfactuals*. Blackwell.

———. 2001. *On the Plurality of Worlds*. Wiley-Blackwell.

Mackie, J.L. 1982. *The Miracle of Theism: Arguments for and Against the Existence of God*. Oxford University Press.

New Scientist. 2017. *The Universe Next Door: A Journey through 55 Alternative Realities, Parallel Worlds, and Possible Futures*. Nicholas Brealey.

Nietzsche, Friedrich. 1961. *Thus Spoke Zarathustra: A Book for Everyone and No One*. Penguin

———. 1972. *The Gay Science: With a Prelude in Rhymes and an Appendix of Songs*. Vintage.

———. 2010. *Beyond Good and Evil: Prelude to a Philosophy of the Future*. Vintage.

———. 2017. *The Will to Power*. Penguin.

Paley, William. 2008 [1802]. *Natural Theology*. Oxford University Press.

Parfit, Derek. 1984. *Reasons and Persons*. Oxford University Press.

Plato. 1997. *Complete Works*. Hackett.

Popper, Karl R. 1992 [1982]. *The Open Universe: An Argument for Indeterminism*. Routledge.

Rand, Ayn. 1963. *The Virtue of Selfishness*. Signet.

———. 1986 [1967]. *Capitalism: The Unknown Ideal*. Signet.

Rucker, Rudolf v. B. 1977. *Geometry, Relativity, and the Fourth Dimension*. Dover.

Sartre, Jean-Paul. 1993 [1943]. *Being and Nothingness: A Phenomenological Essay on Ontology*. Washington Square.

———. 2007 [1967]. *Existentialism Is a Humanism*. Yale University Press.

———. 2013 [1938]. *Nausea*. New Directions.

Saunders, Simon, Jonathan Barratt, Adrian Kent, and David Wallace, eds. 2012 [2010]. *Many Worlds? Everett, Quantum Theory, and Reality*. Oxford University Press.

Schaler, Jeffrey A. 2009. *Peter Singer Under Fire: The Moral Iconoclast Faces His Critics*. Open Court.

Singer, Peter. 1975. *Animal Liberation: A New Ethics for Our Treatment of Animals*. Random House.

Steele, David Ramsay. 2008. *Atheism Explained: From Folly to Philosophy*. Open Court.

Stirner, Max. 2005 [1844]. *The Ego and His Own: The Case of the Individual against Authority*. Dover.

Suppes, Patrick. 1984. *Probabilistic Metaphysics*. Blackwell.

Tartaglia, James. 2016. *Philosophy in a Meaningless Life: A System of Nihilism, Consciousness, and Reality*. Bloomsbury.

Tegmark, Max. 2017. *Life 3.0: Being Human in the Age of Artificial Intelligence*. Vintage.

Wason, Peter Cathcart. 1968. Reasoning about a Rule. *Quarterly Journal of Experimental Psychology* 20:3.

Citadel of Authors

LESTER C. ABESAMIS

Lester C. Abesamis is an adjunct Philosophy instructor at Ohlone College and Chabot College. He received his BA from UC Berkeley and his MA from San Francisco State University. His interests include Ancient Philosophy (whether old ideas have any modern relevance), ethics (whether we make it up or discover it), and existentialism (whether his life means anything at all). These days, he spends way too much time trying to overcome his own awesome Tiny Rick.

JOHN ALTMANN

John Altmann is an independent scholar in Philosophy who works primarily in Philosophy of Disability, and has membership with both the European Network of Japanese Philosophy and the *Public Philosophy Journal*. Unfortunately, Rick perceives John as another Jerry, and dropped him off at the nearest Jerry Jamboree, where he is still waiting to be picked up.

I'm John Altmann from Universe C-457, a Universe where people's orifices have been all switched around and it's one hundred percent as unseemly as you'd imagine. I live in this universe teaching Philosophy to the Ricks of this universe who, unsurprisingly, are as narrow-minded about Philosophy as Neil Degrasse Tyson and Bill Nye are. Which, incidentally, makes the switching around of their orifices seem appropriate.

ADAM BARKMAN

Adam Barkman (PhD, Free University of Amsterdam) is Professor of Philosophy and the Chair of the Philosophy Department at Redeemer University College. He is the author or editor of a dozen books, most recently *A Critical Companion to James Cameron* (2018). He has been invited to speak on the philosophy of film and popular culture in universities across North America, Europe, and Asia. Adam1099 is an angry nihilist who became that way because he had no patience for deep reading or thought.

COURTNEY BERESHEIM

Courtney Beresheim is an educator and graduate of DePaul University; her interests are in narrative study and why we tell stories, and why we do other stupid things as well. She spends most of her free time watching TV with her husband and not thinking about how no one's here for a reason.

WILLIAM TEBOKKEL

William teBokkel is an independent scholar interested in philosophy of religion. William 3411 was college roommates with Mr. Poopybutthole until the two had a falling out over a mutual crush. A proud accomplishment of his is that he is a three-time world hot dog eating champion. However the real glory he seeks is to one day hold the high score in Roy at Blitz and Chitz.

MATTHEW BRAKE

Matthew Brake is an adjunct lecturer in Religion and Philosophy at Virginia International University and George Mason University, where he teaches a course on Religion and graphic novels. He runs the blog Pop Culture and Theology at
www.popularcultureandtheology.com
and is the series editor of Theology and Pop Culture. He wonders if there's a version of himself that chose a more lucrative career.

Matthew Brake C-235 is from a reality where a career in philosophy and the humanities is not a bad idea. He is immensely successful (as all philosophy professors are) and bathes each day in a gold-plated tub. He only got into philosophy for the money, but the fame and power is a side benefit.

CONNOR CHANNER

Connor Channer is a student at Christopher Newport University's Luter School of Business. He has won multiple awards at International Science and Engineering fairs. His favorite pastimes are rock climbing and watching inter-dimensional cable. He holds this dimension's high score for Roy 2: Dave. Bird Person has always served as his moral exemplar.

Connor Channer 304-X is an intergalactic trader who made his fortune arbitraging flurbos and schmeckles. He spends most of his time trying to get the high score on the original Roy. All the surfaces in his house are perfectly level. Like Krombopulos Michael, he has no code of ethics. If he can make a dollar he will.

CHARLENE ELSBY

Charlene Elsby, PhD, is an Assistant Professor of Philosophy and the Philosophy Program Director in the Department of English and Linguistics at Purdue University Fort Wayne. She is currently teaching "Rick and Morty and Philosophy" and spends her research hours cobbling theories together from bits of lost texts (like Aristotle's *Eudemus*). If this is a simulation, the limits on our technology that we think would limit the quality of that simulation are also simulated.

Charlene Elsby is the plucky young philosophy doctor who travels around with Rick Sanchez in the hit show, *Rick and Elsby*. Her catchphrase, "What's that now, Sir Ricks-a-lot?" captures the skeptical nature of her character, which is balanced only by Rick's unfailing optimism. The real hero of the show, Elsby's wits and know-how never fail to save the dynamic duo from the consequences of Rick's misadventures.

MATTHEW HUMMEL

Matthew Hummel works as a Meeseeks for the Public Defender Agency in Evansville, Indiana, and teaches Legal Studies as an adjunct for Ivy Tech. He earned his Master's in Ethics and Values from Valparaiso University Graduate School and has chapters in other Popular Culture and Philosophy titles. Beyond work and writing, Matt is a performer in local theater and lives that sweet suburban life the Smiths wish they had. He was into human music before it became popular in simulations.

Matt Hummel can prove people are pieces of sh*t mathematically, but instead he passes butter . . . Oh my God. He just wants to go back to Hell where everyone thinks he's smart and funny. If you need him, he'll be cleaning up after his daughter who "got schwifty" all over the floor. He'll be buying her a backpack so she can get it together.

John V. Karavitis

John V. Karavitis is an independent philosophical warfare consultant for hire. His chapter, "What Makes Rick Tick?" looks like an innocent entry in the popular culture and philosophy genre. It's really an in-depth broad spectrum analysis of the Galactic Federation's greatest threat, Rick Sanchez! (For the record, John's crush on former Federation deep-cover agent Tammy Gueterman had nothing to do with his accepting this consulting engagement.) As for his fellow contributors, John's never met them, nor does he care to. But when he thinks about what they might be like, for some strange reason he imagines a gaggle of Mr. Meeseeks, each one running around hysterically and waving its arms and screeching to have its chapter be the center of attention.

Charles Klayman

Charles Klayman received his doctorate in philosophy from Southern Illinois University and has taught for several colleges in the southern Illinois area. His primary academic interests are art and aesthetics, history of philosophy, and classical American philosophy. Aside from contributing to the Popular Culture and Philosophy series and conducting independent philosophical research, it's believed that he is off exploring the multiverse while he left behind his clone to work as an Immigration Analyst for the United States Citizenship and Immigration Services.

Elliot Knuths

Elliot Knuths is a Juris Doctor candidate at Northwestern University. Although he spends his days studying law, he writes mostly about philosophy, especially metaphysics and philosophy of religion. His scholarly work has appeared in the *European Journal for Philosophy of Religion* and *Open Theology*. Elliot also works with two very different academic journals: *Religious Studies Review* and the *Journal of Criminal Law and Criminology*. In his free time, Elliot enjoys trying new beers, exploring Chicago, and running from Scary Terry (because he can't hide, bitch).

ETHAN LANDES

Ethan Landes is a PhD candidate in bonnie eastern Scotland at the University of St Andrews. Originally from America (or as they say everywhere that isn't America, "the States"), he has adjusted well to the change, eating haggis and black pudding like the best of them. This is not to say he does not miss his old home. Sometimes on cold rainy nights he sits quietly in front of a window sipping scotch and tries to remember the last time he ate a good taco.

Known for his practical, down-to-earth thinking, Ethan's research runs the broad range from the philosophy of philosophy to the philosophy of philosophy of philosophy. If not thinking hard about such real-world problems, you can find Ethan rock climbing, cycling, repairing his bike, or playing goal keeper.

CHRIS LAY

Chris Lay is an instructor at the University of Georgia with interests in philosophy of mind and metaphysics. He has contributed to a number of other pop culture anthologies, including *Alien and Philosophy*, *The Twilight Zone and Philosophy,* and *Westworld and Philosophy*. He's also fairly certain that he lives in the darkest of all possible multiverse dimensions. Chris's main evidence is that *Two Brothers, Man vs. Car*, and whatever show Baby Legs was on don't actually exist here.

Alternate Dimension Chris Lay (a.k.a. Doofus Chris) teaches at the University of Georgia and is especially keen on examining the ways in which philosophical notions like persistence, personhood, and metaphysical composition intersect with popular culture. He has two dogs whom he loves dearly—hopefully this will spare him Snuffles's wrath in the inevitable canid revolution to come.

DANIEL MALLOY

Daniel Malloy teaches philosophy at Aims Community College in Greeley, Colorado. He's currently on his fifth universe. Or was it sixth? No, definitely fifth. The one with all the squirrels doesn't count. He had nothing to do with what happened to those dirty little tree rats.

Daniel P. Malloy teaches philosophy at Aims Community College in Greeley, Colorado. He's currently on his sixth universe. Or was it only five? No, definitely sixth. We'd forgotten about the one with all the squirrels. Damn shame what he did to them.

ELIZABETH RARD

Elizabeth Rard is a Philosophy instructor at Reedley College. She looks like a normal human now but she's actually originally from one of the many, many Cronenberg worlds. She was at a dance when she was exposed to mutated serum that was designed to make a particular Cronenberg Jessica fall in love with a particular Cronenberg Morty. In her reality the spread was halted, but not before Elizabeth (and only Elizabeth) was transformed from Cronenberg Elizabeth to a normal, boring, human-looking Elizabeth. Horribly ashamed she fled to this reality where, fortunately the local Elizabeth had just disappeared in a poof of logic after trying for too long to imagine a square circle.

ERIC SILVERMAN

Eric Silverman is Associate Professor of Philosophy at Christopher Newport University in Virginia. He has twenty publications on topics in ethics, philosophy of religion, and medieval philosophy. His publications include a monograph: *The Prudence of Love: How Possessing the Virtue of Love Benefits the Lover* (2010) and a co-edited collection *Paradise Understood: New Philosophical Essays about Heaven* (2017). He holds an unusual view of ethics referred to as "reverse Rickism." Its central guiding moral claim is that you should watch the actions and attitudes of Rick Sanchez closely, and then live in an opposite way.

Cowboy Eric J. Silverman is Associate Professor of Philosophy at Christopher Newport University in Virginia. He has twenty publications on topics in ethics, philosophy of religion, and cattle rustling. His publications include a monograph: *The Prudence of Love: How*

Possessing the Virtue of Love Benefits the Lover (2010) and a co-edited collection *Paradise Understood: New Philosophical Essays about Heaven* (Oxford University Press: 2017). He seldom has heard a discouraging word, except when reading Ayn Rand.

TRAVIS TAFT

Travis C-137 is teaching origami lessons and is co-authoring a book on origami culture while working his way through grad school. By stoically facing a spinal cord injury during a surfing accident at age eighteen, he got a BLA from St. John's College, and is working on his MFA from Antioch University, Los Angeles. Warning: Don't ask him about Don Quixote unless you thought Gearhead's obsession with the Gear Wars wasn't obsess-y enough for you.

Travis ETM-42 lives off the success of his single accomplishment as a half-decent gene-coder. Despite dropping out of high school, he developed a gene app that lets the user give their pet the voice of any celebrity. The fad came and went, but enough people still use it to bring in some decent royalty checks. At least enough to fund food, shelter, and a room full of small customized critters each telling him he is cool and smart in a different celebrity's voice.

WAYNE YUEN / Φ-173 RICK SANCHEZ

Φ-173 RICK SANCHEZ is a philosophy professor and mad scientist in dimension Φ-173, largely populated by philosophy professors. In this dimension, philosophy professors teach philosophy students who then go on to be philosophy professors. After being overrun with philosophy professors, Φ-173 was deemed too useless and dangerous to be explored, and the dimension was quarantined. However, this Rick cleverly utilized an interdimensional cable box to bypass the quarantine, to contribute a chapter to this book.

Wayne Yuen teaches philosophy at Ohlone College, in Fremont, California. He has edited *The Walking Dead and Philosophy: Zombie Apocalypse Now* and *The Ultimate Walking Dead and Philosophy: Hungry for More*, co-edited *Neil Gaiman and Philosophy: Gods Gone Wild!*, and contributed chapters to several other books in the Popular Culture and Philosophy series. He's comforted in knowing that in some alternate dimension, there is a version of him who is actually cooler than Jerry.

Wayne Yuen H-964 teaches philosophy at Ohlone College in Fremont, California. He has edited *The Walking Dead and Philosophy: Zombie Apocalypse Now* and *The Ultimate Walking Dead and Philosophy: Hungry for More*, and co-edited *Neil Gaiman and Philosophy: Gods Gone Wild!*, and contributed chapters to several other books in the Popular Culture and Philosophy series. He's a better philosopher than that other Wayne Yuen. Really, just ignore that guy. He's a plumbus.

Index

NEIL GAIMAN

AND

PHILOSOPHY
GODS GONE WILD!

EDITED BY TRACY L. BEALER, RACHEL LURIA, AND WAYNE YUEN

Printed in the USA
CPSIA information can be obtained
at www.ICGtesting.com
JSHW012025140824
68134JS00033B/2878

9 780812 694642